THE FULL MONTY

THE FULL MONTY

The Autobiography of
JIM DAVIDSON

LITTLE, BROWN AND COMPANY

A *Little, Brown* Book

First published in Great Britain in 1993
by Little, Brown and Company
Reprinted 1993

Copyright © Jim Davidson 1993

The moral right of the author has been asserted.

A CIP catalogue record for this book
is available from the British Library.

ISBN 0 316 90777 4

Printed and bound in Great Britain by
BPCC Hazell Books Ltd
Member of BPCC Ltd

Little, Brown and Company (UK) Limited
165 Great Dover Street
London SE1 4YA

*To my kids, may they
live long and prosper*

Contents

Picture Credits

In addition to photographs from his own collection, the author gratefully acknowledges the kind assistance of the following for additional pictures: Hulton/McKenzie, the *News of the World*, the *Sun* and *SW News*/Shepherd.

Foreword

I first met Jim Davidson at a stag show at Woking Football Club and, in those unpromising circumstances, realised with an absolute certainty that he was a future star.

What I did not realise at that first meeting, but came to learn over the ensuing years, was that Jim really was two people. One, the very public performer who was, and remains, a workaholic; the other, a very private man who has undoubtedly raised more money, donated more time and given himself to more forms of charitable causes than most. Perhaps more importantly, he has never looked for recognition.

Jim is the most genuine of men and if he is your friend, he is your friend for life – through good times and bad, no matter what others may say or do.

Over the years Jim and I have developed a relationship that far exceeds that of just manager and client. We have become good friends. Just how good a friend he was I realised in the summer of 1989, when I was attempting to become a West End producer for the first time. I was involved in bringing the musical *Buddy* to London, a lifelong dream for me. Outside of the enthusiasm and commitment of my two fellow producers, I was finding it very difficult to raise the necessary finance to make the show happen.

I explained this to Jim over a drink and almost immediately – against the advice of many, including his accountant! – he wrote me a cheque for a considerable amount of money to give me a cornerstone from which the show was launched.

Buddy, of course, proved to be a big hit and Jim's faith was duly rewarded – but he had no way of knowing it that summer when he and his cheque-book went out on a limb, a gesture I will never forget, which was typical of the man. Whilst he won't thank me for letting people know how he helped me, if this book is really to be 'The Full Monty' then it is important to all of us who know Jim that the unrivalled private side of his nature be acknowledged.

Laurie Mansfield

1

Mum's Mistake

Probably the first major downfall to beset the Davidson clan happened long before I was even born. In fact, it happened when my dad was being born in Scotland.

In the bedroom of a tenement building in Glasgow a bottle of whisky crashed on to a bed next to an exhausted young mother and her new-born baby. In a broad Glaswegian accent a man's voice boomed: 'Give it a fucking drink from me!'

And so my father, John, came into the world. Dad's dad liked whisky very much. So much, in fact, that he should have changed his name to Johnnie Walker early on and had done with it.

Dad grew up in Duke Street, Glasgow and signed up early for the Army. He was a very hard man and, like his father before him, he became a very hard drinker. He was tough and wiry, and despite his deceptive looks could lift an entire engine out of a car single-handed – and did so once. He was posted to Woolwich, south-east London, and that's where he quickly found romance.

My mum, Emily, lived in Woolwich. Her mum, a strict Catholic, had arrived from Ireland hoping for a half-decent life. She didn't get it because she and her daughter, like millions of others, were poor in hard times. Their larder rarely had any food in it, and in winter the fire rarely had decent fuel. Davidson legend has it that when Dad first met

Mum, shortly after arriving in London, he was so taken with her that he pawned his suit and few belongings to buy her and her mum food and coal.

Soon John and Em were married and had a fairly hit-and-miss kind of life. They argued a fair amount, but probably no more at first than the average working-class couple making the best of a bad job before the war. They also had a family over the next eight years. Eileen, Jean, Billy and John, in that order. In 1948 they moved into a new rented council house in Kidbrooke, 118 Holburne Road, which had been built by German and Italian prisoners of war.

Two other people soon moved in with them – Dad's two brothers. Uncle Jim was a very quiet man and Uncle Bill wasn't. With five languages under his belt, he'd served as an intelligence officer in the Cameron Highlanders regiment and was fairly eccentric. Around Kidbrooke he would invariably wear his funny old kilt and big tartan scarf when he went out.

Dad, who everyone called Jock, and Jim were real grafters but Bill, the only brother with any artistic flair, worked as a graphic designer and enjoyed a slightly better lifestyle. Dad went through an endless succession of labouring jobs, all with long hours. He was rarely at home. Weekdays and weekends were the same to him – he worked as long as possible and then, if there were any hours left in the day, fell into the pub until it closed then fell back out again and home to bed.

Uncle Bill, in Dad's absence, took an active role with Mum and the young family. He even took my brothers off camping in Kent for long weekends, which they thought were brilliant.

On December 13 1953, in Mum's bed at 118 Holburne Road, I was born, apparently to the strains of Uncle Bill downstairs playing Claude Debussy's 'Clair de Lune' on the piano. Mum always referred to me affectionately as 'my mistake'. She was thirty-four when she had me and must have thought she'd seen the last of nappies until I came along. Certainly, because my brothers and sisters were so much older than me, in many ways I was brought up as an only child, with two working parents happy to leave me to my own devices.

Mum wanted to name me Cameron James Davidson, probably after Uncle Bill, but Dad got drunk on the way to register the birth and came back with a certificate bearing the name James Cameron Davidson. Despite this Mum insisted on always calling me Cameron, throughout my life, even though I always hated it. As a kid everyone called me Cameron but when years later I started out in comedy I quickly changed it to Jim.

Uncle Bill was a terrific artist and for my first birthday he painted me a small watercolour of a fully-rigged sailing ship at sunset. He devoted it 'To James Cameron Davidson, on his very first birthday' and signed it, 'From his "A-bu".' Beneath was a four-line poem which read:

'Nothing like this you've had before,
All I can wish is many more.
As you sail life's sea with a merry heart,
and be welcome on any far-off shore.'

I still have the picture, framed and taking pride of place at home. It's probably the oldest thing I have from my childhood and, as you'll discover, rightly one of the most cherished.

I don't remember Uncle Bill. By the time my next few birthdays had come around he'd left Holburne Road – and Britain – for good. He moved to Thailand, where he opened a bar, married, raised a family and died. He never kept in touch with the family, although Mum did hear a few years ago that he'd drunk himself to death, leaving just a few paintings and for some inexplicable reason roll after roll of tartan.

When I was a young kid, Christmas in the Davidson household was an overcrowded affair. Everyone we knew seemed to cram into our terraced council house for the holiday. As well as Mum, Dad and my four sisters and brothers, there'd be various uncles, aunties and family friends. For me, Christmas always meant having to sleep on a camp-bed, my own bed having been commandeered for one of the grown-ups.

Mum made all the preparations. I'm sure she bought all the presents on her own, too. I don't think Dad ever went out of his way to do anything to help, except collect the booze already paid for by Mum with the Christmas Savings Club money. Sometimes Dad spent it, without her knowing, long before Christmas.

Dad was a quiet, dour Scotsman who didn't change much on occasions like Christmas. He was a good father to us all and he wasn't really grumpy; he just never talked much unless he had a drink in his hand.

My Christmas morning started when I excitedly emptied my stocking. As well as toys and fillers I always got an orange and a bag of new, shiny threepenny bits. Mum would get up early and spend all morning preparing and cooking the Christmas feast. She took great delight in making everything as perfect as possible. We'd lay two tables in the cramped dining-room, the smaller one for us children. Then, at about two o'clock, Mum would announce proudly that the full festive Monty was ready, adding that Christmas dinner was served 'with table wine'.

'Don't give me that, it's a woman's drink!' Dad would say, full of the festive spirit. No one ever drank wine in those days; it was considered 'posh'. Dad was a funny old stick about things like wine and what he considered 'fancy' living. I never knew him to eat out anywhere, apart from greasy spoon cafés. He never went out for dinner, never. It wasn't something people in Blackheath did in those days. On the very rare occasions a family would splash out, the best they could look forward to was a Berni Inn for prawn cocktail, steak, chips and pints of bitter. If they really wanted to show off, the beer was swapped for a bottle of Blue Nun, ideally served at room temperature as Château Cats' Piss.

At Christmas Dad washed his turkey down with neither wine nor bitter but his usual: whisky and dry ginger ale. The other adults drank the wine, and we kids had orangeade.

When lunch was finally over we'd all sit down loyally

to watch the Queen's Christmas message at three o'clock. Afterwards, it was time for parlour games, bingo first. Before the first game had been won Dad would be fast asleep in his chair, nodding and jerking. Every so often, he'd twitch a leg. Mum never missed any of his funny twitching and loved pointing it out to us all, sending him up when he was past caring.

After bingo we went in for fancy dress and everyone found something to wear. I remember my brother John dressing up as Frankenstein once sending me into hysterics by putting his socks over his big moccasin slippers. John is naturally funny and reminds me enormously of the late Eric Morecambe. He's got a really weird sense of humour and was just great to be around. My other brother, Billy, who was more dominant and bossy, was hardly ever with us for family Christmases. He was in the Navy and invariably away on duty.

After a bit of telly I'd be sent off to bed and remember thinking, as I lay there trying to sleep with all the rumpus coming from downstairs, just what a great, spirited bunch all these grown-ups were. Of course, I didn't realise just how spirited. Little did I know that they were all completely pissed out of their heads.

I remember one year trying to sleep on the trick camp-bed and hearing that drunken laughter turn into a bitter argument. Dad was shouting and then followed the unmistakable sound of Mum crying. That started me off in turn, sobbing into my pillow. I heard Uncle Jim stop the arguing and once he'd calmed everyone down I drifted off to sleep, only to be woken again a few minutes later when all the adults started bloody singing again.

As a small boy I was always over-active and by four I could read and write pretty well. I was just four when I had to go in to hospital for what, at the time, seemed an eternity. The other children in the ward cuddled teddy bears and soft toys for comfort. I embraced something much better: a toy 'Tommy Steele' guitar. I loved it and played it all the time for the other children in the ward, although of course, I couldn't really play at all.

When I got out of hospital, I continued to cherish that little guitar. I'd look out for children and grown-ups passing our garden gate and rush up, singing and strumming Tommy Steele and Lonnie Donegan hits. The passing audiences were never especially receptive, and if they dared to actually laugh out loud at me I'd storm back into the house. 'That's it, Mum! I'm never singing again!' I'd wail, announcing my retirement from show-business long before I'd even started. Some might say I haven't sung since that day, but I'd rather not go into that!

Another gift, for a birthday, was a set of coloured pencils and a small paint-box. I can still recall the smell of that paint-box as if it was yesterday.

In 1959, when I was five, I had to go to school. Kidbrooke Park Junior Mixed was about 500 yards from home and was to be my second home for the best part of six years. The day I made that epic 500-yard journey up to and actually through the school gates for the very first time, I was holding Mum's hand very tight. We walked the route in silence and I was trying desperately hard to wear a brave face. I looked the part, dressed in regulation corduroy trousers which chafed my spindly legs so badly that they looked like strips of corned beef.

Within seconds of being left alone by Mum my worst fear was confirmed. School was horrible! I quite liked crying and that day I bawled my eyes out. I screamed hysterically for Mum to collect me. She didn't.

After the first few days the crying outbursts stopped and after a few weeks I even began to enjoy school life. The daily routine of endless stories and painting classes was painless. So too, looking back, were the daily cod liver oil tablets washed down with a compulsory third of a pint of lukewarm milk. If I could ever dodge either, I did.

Mrs Kenny ran the infants' school and she was a very nice, fat woman. With a beard. Another teacher, Mrs Gower, could also have done with losing a few pounds. Mrs Gower had legs which reminded you of the legs on a Steinway grand piano. She always wore comfortable shoes, just like Ma Bear's in 'The Three Bears' comic strip in the *Beano*.

Mrs Gower was exactly the same shape as her Morris 1000 car.

It was Mrs Gower who tried teaching us all to sing sweetly, making us sit in a semi-circle around the piano in the school gymnasium. And it is Mrs Gower I think of, to this day, if ever I want to make myself upset or even cry. She taught us a song called 'Bessie Was a Black Cat' which still gets me every time. The lyrics are:

> 'Bessie was a black cat, as old as a house,
> But she never scratched a dog, and she never
>   caught a mouse.
> She sat beside the fireside, from morning 'til eve,
> And this warm spot, she never would leave.'
>
> She never would leave,
> She never would leave,
> And this warm spot, she never would leave.'

In the song, poor little Bessie dies and the final few lines are:

> 'But wherever she is now,
> I bet she's sitting by the fireside, from morning
>   'til eve,
> And this warm spot, she never will leave.
>
> Never will leave,
> Never will leave,
> And this warm spot, she never will leave.'

Well, after Mrs Gower sang the song through once I was so emotionally swept up by the little cat's tale that I burst into floods of tears. To make matters worse, the entire class just turned and stared at me.

'What's the matter, Cameron?' asked Mrs Gower.

I had to think quickly. I was meant to be a tough little boy and there I was blubbing away like a right sissy. Then the tongue went into overdrive and out spurted my first ad lib: 'My cat died today . . .'

Even I was surprised by what came out. I did have a cat, a black cat with a white bib called Tibby Tibbs, but he was as fit as a fiddle.

'Dead!' I said, warming to my theme and surprising myself further by reaffirming the tragedy. 'Died! Run over by the coalman!'

Tibby Tibbs' fictitious fate came back to haunt me many times from that moment on. I lived in fear of being caught out as a fibber and, whenever I spotted kids from my class near my house, I'd frantically run after Tibby Tibbs and shut him indoors.

Bursting into tears wasn't the only thing to embarrass me around Mrs Gower's piano. It also marked the spot where I first wet myself in public. One afternoon we were all sitting around singing and I asked if I could go to the loo. Mrs Gower wouldn't let me, probably because she thought I was messing about, which probably I was. I tried to control my tiny bladder but simply couldn't and in the end I peed myself. I turned on the other waterworks, was hastily mopped up all round by Mrs Gower and then sat glumly in class until the school bell clattered. I scarpered home as quickly as I could that day, my little chapped legs running as fast as they could, to hide with Tibby Tibbs.

Progressing through Kidbrooke Park's ranks, I moved from the infants' class to the junior school, run by the headmaster, Mr Offord. He was a big man with a quick temper, which he normally tested out on me.

I was quite a confident lad and particularly came into my own playing football. I loved it and was good enough in my first year as a junior to find myself playing in the school team, albeit the third team, which was made up mostly of third- and fourth-formers. The more I played and did well for the school, the more cocky I became, and the more cocky I became, the more fights I got myself into. My finely honed skills were football and fighting and before long I was probably the best in the school at both.

I got myself into various inevitable scrapes at Kidbrooke Park. My friend Roger and I were the first two kids in memory to ever get the cane, for skipping school at lunchtime and spending our dinner money on cap-bombs. Mr Offord was waiting for us when we got back to school that afternoon. 'What did you spend your dinner money on, boys?' he asked us.

Roger and I glanced at each other and I answered: 'Beans on toast, sir.'

He knew we were lying and made us empty our pockets and hand over our cap-bombs. Out came the cane and he whacked us three times each on the hands. As he lashed into us he said, and it always struck me as such a dumb thing to have said: 'A bean for a bean and a toast for a toast!'

The whacks really hurt but neither Roger nor I cried. As Offord dished out his punishment it came home to me for the first time just how vicious and cruel caning was. Yet, looking back, two good things came of that beating. The first was fame; the second was that it got me out of violin lessons.

Mum made me take lessons for a while, and I can still scratch out the scales. But I hated the instrument and after getting the cane I insisted for weeks that my fingers hurt so much I couldn't possibly play properly again. The dodge worked and I got myself out of the lessons.

Kidbrooke Park will always hold a very special place in my heart because it is where I met Susan Sergeant, my very first girlfriend. Susan had beautiful long, ginger hair and striking looks, and lived with her parents in a house right opposite the school. She was something of a celebrity in our school, the first one I had met. She was so pretty that all the boys in our prepubescent playground fancied her and all of us shared the view that her stunning beauty made her 'the great un-haveable'.

I really didn't think I stood a chance with Susan but one day she smiled at me and that was it – I was 'in love', a condition that would haunt me for the rest of my life.

I could just see the back of Susan's house, about half a mile away across the allotments, from Dad's bedroom window. If Susan stood in her parent's bedroom we could flash the lights on and off to communicate with one another. We spent hours at night just standing and staring into the darkness for a flicker of hope from the other. Every flick of the switch sent out a message saying 'I love you.' It was the most wonderful thing.

When I wasn't with Susan, after school or at weekends, I was more often than not playing with my friend Tommy Elliott, who was well known locally as 'The Professor' because he was always making bombs and blowing things up by mistake. Together we'd taunt the neighbours. One of our tricks was when we went around kidnapping goldfish and hiding them in buckets for days on end. Tommy's family was both eccentric and ingenious and I also played with his older brother, Stephen, who had the strangest-looking bike made entirely from salvaged spare parts from other bikes. Admittedly, it didn't look much but it could really go. Stephen and I would meet to play and he'd cycle slowly, with me walking alongside, until we were both out of sight of our homes. Then I'd clamber on the back and we'd wobble off unsteadily to Blackheath Dips, a nearby common, to find some serious mischief. The Dips were quite hilly; just the job for speeding up and down on one bike.

One Saturday we headed off to catch the morning pictures at the Roxy. My all-time favourite Saturday serial was 'Tobor the Robot', who had the witty catchphrase 'I'm Tobor – Robot spelled backwards'. The robot was the best thing to grace the Roxy's screen until I was thirteen and, five years under-age, saw my first X-certificate film called *Seventeen*. Anyway, after taking in the week's episode of 'Tobor' that Saturday, Stephen and I spent our pocket money on catapults, got on to the bike and set off unsteadily for an adventure in Blackheath Dips. After a while we moved on, to Greenwich Park, to try out our catapults. We took up positions either side of the boating pond and started firing at each other with our shiny new slings.

We energetically dodged each other's shots. Then I spotted one stone coming towards me and judged, wrongly, that it would miss me by a mile. It didn't. It hit me right in the right eye. I literally saw red, and my eye completely closed up. Then the sight in my left eye became badly blurred as well. I was blind!

Worse than that, I was writhing around on the ground in agony. Stephen rushed over to me. Somehow he got me on to his bike and managed to cycle both of us up the hill to the bus stop. It must have nearly killed him. He put me on the bus back from Lewisham to Blackheath and followed behind on his bike, pedalling furiously. By a remarkable coincidence, Mum was on the same bus. 'What's happened, Cameron?' she asked, taking hold of me.

'Some boys fired a stone at me from a catapult,' I said blindly, doing my best to protect Stephen from his part in the drama.

Mum whisked me off to the family doctor, who advised her to take me home and put me to bed, which is just what she did. When I woke up the next morning I couldn't see with either eye. The left eye had also packed up and now I was completely blind.

Mum rushed me back to the doctor, then to Lewisham Hospital. Finally, I was admitted to the Royal Eye Hospital at the Elephant and Castle and stayed there a fortnight. My right eye was covered with a dressing and vision in my left eye remained blurred. The best I could do was make out shapes in a room.

Other than that, I couldn't see anything. But that didn't stop everyone from coming to take a look at me. I remember listening to the strangest bedside conversation when Mum and Billy thought I might lose the offending right eye. The doctor was nearby and both of them offered one of their own eyes to transplant. As the conversation unfolded at least one thing became transparently clear to me: if I lived, and they had their way, I'd leave the Royal Eye Hospital with one brown eye and one hazel eye to accompany my blurred left eye.

As I was visually disadvantaged my imagination was working overtime, and I had visions of being shown off by Mum, her modelling a sinister eye-patch, saying things like: 'Oh, he's such a good Cyclops. He had all our eyes!'

It transpired that the stone Stephen had so skilfully aimed into my left eye had triggered a blood clot behind my forehead, which in turn created a pressure point. The doctors treated me with special drugs and drops and, a week or so after being released, both my eyes got better again.

As a result of the incident, for a little while afterwards I had to wear glasses. But Susan hated them so I promptly lost them 'accidentally'. Although Mum went mad when I told her, Susan was pleased and that meant everything to me.

Thankfully my eyes have always been pretty good since then. I've never been able to see in the dark very well, but I suspect that might have more to do with my inborn fear of the dark than my sight. I've always hated having to sleep in the dark. As a boy, Mum had to give me a night-light, or leave the door slightly ajar to catch the hall light.

The dark petrified me on another occasion, when I moved from the local Cub group to the Scout group, based in the local church. The first big outing I went on was a camping weekend in the country at Down in Kent. We arrived one evening after school and the older boys took me into the pitch-black woods. They gave me the end of a piece of string, told me to 'follow it' and vanished into the trees. The dark was bad enough with a night-light in the safety of my own bedroom. In the middle of a wood with nothing more comforting than a length of string it was appalling.

Gingerly, I followed the string for ages. Then, without any warning, all the other boys jumped out at me. I did the only sensible thing I could think of. I burst into tears. Tibby to the rescue again: I told them my cat had been killed following a piece of string!

That frightening initiation trick wasn't the only low point of the weekend. Boiling milk was also spilled on me by accident and badly burned my chest.

Back in the comparative safety of Kidbrooke concrete jungle, three of us formed a band after school. A kid called 'Oi, You!' – he wasn't Chinese, but I could never remember his real name – said he could play the guitar. To be more precise, he could play three notes, each of them badly. Another kid joined us and I played drums. My kit was a bizarre assortment of biscuit tins and upturned boxes. It didn't matter what it looked like just as long as it made a loud clatter.

Nothing really came of our early step into entertainment, largely because we were awful. The trio disbanded but, like Billy Liar, I daydreamed on about how one day I'd be famous and, better still, rich beyond my wildest dreams.

My wildest dream as a boy did come true when I got a bike of my own. As well as Stephen Elliott, it seemed as if every other kid in the neighbourhood had their own bike so it was only natural I'd end up longing for one. But I knew Mum and Dad just couldn't afford such things, much as they would have liked to, and I tried to hide my jealousy of the others. I made do instead with rides on Stephen's boneshaker. Then, out of the blue, I got my bike.

Mum had ordered it from the mail order catalogue and had arranged to pay for it on the 'Never-never', on dreadful credit terms. She probably had to pay for that bike about eight times over. 'Come on, Cameron, we're going to collect something,' she announced one morning. We set off for the shops, where it was awaiting collection. As soon as I saw it the penny dropped. The best day of my life had arrived, unexpectedly early.

Having got the bike, the adventures soon followed. There always seemed so many things to do then, the days were full of trouble opportunities. Stephen and I had fantastic times with our bikes. Once we even cycled from Blackheath to Peckham and I felt like Ranulph Fiennes.

Another unexpected treat was a Christmas present when I was ten – a kid's drum-kit. I set it up in the front room and played along with a record for Dad's benefit. Dad, drunk, listened to my little performance then said in his broad Scottish accent, and using a great Scottish word: 'Son, I'm going to get you all the "accoutrements".'

From that day on Mum would fall about at the mere mention of the word 'accoutrements' – and I waited for Dad to buy them for me until the day he died.

Susan Sergeant and I knocked around together most of the time I was at primary school. We had a sublimely innocent relationship, more by accident than design because we knew no other way of expressing our affection for one another. But when I was ten I had my first-ever sexual experience, looking at a copy of *Health & Efficiency*. It was a nudist magazine but, as far as I was concerned, it was the hottest thing I'd ever seen, and aroused very new, inexplicable, feelings in me.

Naughty visits to the bathroom came to play quite an important part in my week. Once Mum almost caught me red-handed with my magazine. She banged on the door and my heart leaped into my mouth. I quickly stood up, and did everything I could to make binky stand down. I hurled the magazine into the corner cupboard and timidly unlocked the door.

'I'm looking for something, Cameron,' she said.

'Oh yes? What's that?' I asked, sensing my face turn a lighter shade of bright red.

'I want the bath salts. I think they must be in that cupboard,' she said, looking straight at the cupboard hiding my illicit sex magazine.

'I'll look,' I said nervously, quickly moving in front of the cupboard. I pretended to try to open the door and made out that it was stuck. She persisted and I continued to make out the door wouldn't budge until she let the matter go.

I've often wondered if a sixth sense told her what naughty thing I'd been up to. If it didn't, she must have thought it odd that the cupboard door played up because it never stuck – if anything, it would fall open from time to time.

When I was eleven I had to change schools and didn't really see Susan Sergeant again. She and her parents moved away from the area and we never kept in touch. From time to time I did see her best friend, Lorraine Cox (Susan's looks threw poor Lorraine into the shade then but, boy, by the time she was fourteen she blossomed into a real stunner).

I remember feeling that I'd missed out by never going on the annual school trip to a big adventure centre called Sayer's Croft in Surrey. I dreamed of going but mum and dad could never afford it so I had to make do with the other boys' stories of their rambling adventures there. Instead I conjured up the most magical picture of what Sayer's Croft was like and daydreamed myself there for outings.

By a strange coincidence, Sayer's Croft came back into

my life thirty years later when I bought a house with Tracy, my fourth wife, in Ewhurst, Surrey. The day we moved in I drove down a nearby lane and there was a signpost pointing to Sayer's Croft. It's still there. The place I dreamed of so many times as a child was just 300 yards from my new home.

But I still haven't been to take a look at it. After all this time I'd rather remember it as that magical place I dreamed up, a playground even Tom Sawyer would have liked.

I was pretty much king-pin of Kidbrooke Park when I left. Having grown used to being a big fish in a small pond, I was now about to become a small fish in a new, much bigger pond.

2

Retiring from Show-Business

Unlike my brothers and sisters, who at Mum's insistence were brought up as Catholics and went to Catholic schools in Woolwich, I wasn't really an anything. We were never a particularly religious family, but Dad was a Scottish Glaswegian Protestant and Mum, due to her Irish upbringing, a determined Catholic. Mind you, she'd never have seen the inside of a church if it wasn't for weddings and funerals.

Dad vehemently opposed me being christened a Catholic, and when in 1964, it was time for me to go to secondary school and Mum wanted to send me to St Austen's Catholic School in Charlton, Dad put his foot down. In a rare stand for individual liberty, he said the choice of religion, and therefore secondary school, was mine alone. Secretly I'm sure he hoped I'd become a Protestant and score the winning goal for Glasgow Rangers against Celtic.

Not to be defeated, Mum lobbied hard for me to try Catholicism. She bought me a book all about it and countered any thoughts I had of going to other schools by telling me how dreadful the Church of England schools were, spicing her warnings with fabricated horror stories of life inside their walls.

Eventually Mum made an appointment for me to meet the headmaster at St Austen's, Mr Sankey. She already knew Mr Sankey because fifteen years earlier, before he had become headmaster at St Austen's, he had taught my two sisters at another local school, St Peter's. I remember my first and lasting impression of him: he looked just like a sombre bank manager and was very polite. He had one of those scrubbed faces, squeaky clean, which made him look like a waxwork dummy, but dumb he wasn't.

During that first meeting he recommended to Mum that I should go to see a lad who would teach me 'how to be a Catholic' in just two weeks! I think Sankey expected that the crash-course indoctrination would lead to me quickly being baptised a Catholic.

My religious tutor was a little, fat kid who looked like a train-spotter, and lived near me, in the same road where my mate Ronnie Lee lived. I didn't tell any of my friends I had to go for Catholic lessons because I found the whole thing highly embarrassing. 'Spotter' hated me at first sight, and my cheeky comments really tried his holier-than-thou-ness. He would show me books and read aloud short passages. I remember he told me about Jesus and the wise men. Then he launched into the ritual of communion. He said God came along to communion to change bread and wine into the body of Christ.

'You what?' I said, nonplussed.

'You eat some bread and this – '

'This represents the body of Christ?' I interrupted.

'No,' he said, irritated. 'It doesn't "represent" the body of Christ, it *is* Christ. A miracle occurs at the altar. Christ is with us.'

'Well,' I said, 'It can't be much of a miracle, can it? If he's Christ surely he can do better than be a bit of bread? Why can't he be a chocolate cake or something more exciting like that? If I was Christ I wouldn't want to be a bit of bread, I'd change myself into a Rolls-Royce or a copy of *Health & Efficiency*!'

I think Spotter gave up after that. Catholicism didn't agree with me and I never really got to grips with it even though I learned all the responses. I went to Catholic services a few times and used to sing the songs but it wasn't for me. If anything, I became quite agnostic after my sudden religious run-in.

I've never been to, or taken, Holy Communion. And I've still never been properly christened (apart from a very odd time many moons later when the director of my leukaemia charity, Humphry Berkeley, one night drunkenly baptised me in front of Princess Michael of Kent, with champagne from her glass!).

I do believe in a God, I suppose, but I don't know what happens when you die. I tend to hope that there's some kind of life after death. Then again, none of my mates or my uncles have come back to see me – and I've begged them to many a time. Where are you, Dad?

Anyway, at eleven Mum could sway me in any direction she wanted. To make life easy, especially after those tiresome religious lessons, I opted for St Austen's, Charlton, and the nice Mr Sankey became my new headmaster. Sankey's assistant, Mr Craddy, looked a bit like Douglas Hurd with dark hair. As I was often to learn to my cost, Craddy was the complete opposite of Mr Sankey – a tough bastard.

I thought attending a Catholic school was going to be a bit like being in a convent. Wrong! The four-storey school building housed some real hard cases. There were kids it was obvious you never fought, given a choice, like Freddie Steadman, Eugene Kirk and Danny Scott.

Freddie's real name was Ernest Steadman, but you had to be very brave to call him that. He was tiny but a complete psycho. We were all scared of him. Spotty Eugene came from Deptford and was a hard scruff. Danny Scott was a very suave tough nut who lived bang next door to Charlton's football ground in Floyd Road. Danny and I became very good friends and we'd hang around with Freddie and Eugene, which meant I came fourth in the class pecking order – until all the other boys in the class started to get taller than me.

The four of us got into scrapes all the time, and as much as I enjoyed school I never did well in class. I could never really be bothered with it all. I wasn't so bad at subjects I enjoyed, like geography, but I especially hated history, because all we seemed to learn about was mediaeval people who built fires in their houses.

Fortunately, I was good at football which helped make life easier for me. In my first year I was made captain of the school team, as I could not only kick with both feet but also boss people about, and still do.

The teachers at the school were an odd assortment of men – they wouldn't give us lady teachers because we kept breaking them. Most of the masters smelled of stale tobacco most of the time. Some we regarded as friends, others, like Craddy, as enemies. Mr Davies, or more commonly, Fred, was a bit of a favourite. He taught woodwork, which we thought most appropriate because we thought he had a wooden leg. In fact the only basis for this theory was the fact that he limped badly and walked everywhere pretty slowly. Anyway, at St Austen's, having a 'limpy leg' made you nothing short of a reincarnation of Long John Silver and automatically earned you the nickname 'Peg-Leg'.

At woodwork classes Mr Davies would come in quietly and wait for us to stop shouting at each other. He had the patience of a saint and never hit anyone. Eventually we'd quieten down. 'What shall we make today, boys?' he'd ask enthusiastically.

'Want another leg, sir?' we'd shout, chuffed to death with our witty one-liner. We thought we were so original but poor Mr Davies must have heard that line every single day of his existence at St Austen's.

Fred was a great waffler. He'd even out-chat Ken Dodd. We'd keep Fred rambling on for hours, and often, before he knew it, the class was over and we hadn't done a thing. On the few occasions when he wasn't in a talkative mood I'd try my hand at woodwork but I wasn't any good. The only two things I remember making were a model boat and a fishing box. The latter, when it was finished, was far too heavy to actually carry. For ages we used it as a wicket until, solid as it was, it broke apart.

Another favourite was 'Old Robbo', Mr Robinson. He was one of those unfortunate lefty teachers who was terribly gullible and honestly believed us ruffians to be pretty angelic at heart. Before teaching at St Austen's, Robbo was rumoured to have been a commando who'd joined a monastery in protest at all the killing in the Korean War.

In the first term upstarts Danny, Freddie and I announced to Robbo that we had decided to be his class monitors, whacking anyone who misbehaved in his presence with a slipper. 'We'll try it out on you, sir, to see if it hurts!' we told him, and he actually allowed us to go ahead and slipper his hands.

'Oh look, lobster pink!' was all the silly sod said afterwards, his red palms throbbing.

Robbo was very nice and occasionally gave me a lift home. He was an intensely religious man and, when it was his turn to read out prayers in morning assembly, was the only master I ever thought really believed the words he was reading.

The whole school attended those morning assemblies and we also got a weekly mass, conducted by a priest we called 'Father Mars Bar'. He got his nickname because, if you were really nice to him, he'd give you a Mars Bar. Mind you, if you were horrid, which we usually were, he'd hit you with a length of bendy curtain rail.

One of the lads in our class, Bobby McGlone, our foil, wound up Father Mars Bar if he could after mass. 'Father, coming to school on my bicycle this morning somebody called me a "wanker",' said Bobby. 'What is that?'

The priest looked to his feet and muttered: 'Um, self-abuse.'

Oddly, it was Father Mars Bar who gave us sex lessons. On the blackboard he'd draw a triangle to represent the vagina, and large arrows for the ovaries. I used to think to myself, 'What does a Catholic priest know about shagging?' and 'Where can I get a triangle?'

In Mr Reece's music classes we'd flick out the light, throw his cane out of the window and dive under the desks to hide from him. When we had history lessons in Mr Edwards' room we'd destroy his delicate model aeroplanes suspended from the ceiling by firing elastic bands at them. I still feel guilty about vandalising those planes.

We filled our days with mindless japes and stunts. One craze which lasted the best part of the summer term involved stag beetles. We'd all go out to find stag beetles and keep them in tobacco tins. On some we would tie cotton threads as leads and allow them to fly. We'd race others.

Stag beetles are incredibly strong, and with a clothes peg on each leg they could stilt-walk. We'd race four or five at a time, often with a small bet riding on the first beetle to pass the post. Rumour had it that Robbo was such a pacifist that if you took an earthworm to him, saying 'Give me a bob or I'll stamp on it,' he would actually cough up to save the poor creature's life. So we sent Bobby McGlone to him one day, armed with a stag beetle.

'Give us a bob, sir, or I'll stamp on this beetle,' he said. Robbo didn't bat an eyelid. As much as he may have liked earthworms, he clearly didn't give a toss for the poor beetle. By the next term, and the arrival of the next craze, neither did we.

I ended up in one or two punch-ups in my first year but, for the most part, I could always make the other kids laugh so I was fairly popular. In the second year at St Austen's I became a right scoundrel, along with my mates, and soon I was getting the cane virtually every day – in common with nearly everyone else in the notorious 2A.

Some of the masters at St Austen's would dish out the cane with energetic regularity; it was the only exercise they got. The headmaster, Mr Sankey, was such a decent bloke that when he spanked me I felt sorry I'd upset him, but it wasn't my first thought if the other masters caned me.

Bobby McGlone was hauled up before the class one afternoon to be caned. 'Bend over!' rang the familiar cry.

'I can't sir, I've got haemorrhoids!' he cried, and was let off. Needless to say, for months we all had haemorrhoids, even though we had no idea what they were. Any old excuses or dodges could keep us away from dull lessons. One assembly Craddy alerted us to a highly contagious eye infection going around, so bad you had to stay home if you caught it. He said it was called 'conjunctivitis' and barely was the word out of his mouth before Bobby was rubbing his eyes to make them red and sore.

Bobby also mastered, usually in assembly, the art of fainting and throwing bogus epileptic fits. But his finest trick was chewing up cardboard and then 'vomiting' it back as his dinner from the night before.

In my second year the school got a new football coach when our sports master, known to all as Old Kirowski, left to teach in nearby St Thomas More's. The man filling his football boots was science teacher 'Bunny' Doyle. He looked like Grampa the Vampire, in *The Munsters*, and he was loathsome. He didn't have the first idea about football or sport – all he was ever interested in was appearances, although he wore outdated baggy shorts which hung down to his knees and old-fashioned football boots to go with his antiquated ideas. He was Andy Capp without the charisma.

One afternoon under Doyle's stewardship our team was playing South East London Tech, the only team in the league we were frightened of because they could beat us. They were thrashing us, and Bunny suddenly picked on me for my sartorial state.

'Davidson, tuck in your shirt or I'll send you off,' he shouted at me.

I cursed quietly but Doyle, who must have had the hearing of a vampire bat, heard me and sent me off. Our team lost that match and I never forgave him for it.

Old Kirowski did make a brief return to St Austen's football pitch when we took on his team from St Thomas More's. Everyone at our school seemed to be hanging out of the classroom windows to watch that day, cheering us on. We lined up in four-two-four formation and absolutely thrashed Kirowski's charges 10–1. I scored two of the goals, which made me a real hero for the rest of the week.

The only school trip I ever went on had a footballing connection. We spent a day over on the Isle of Wight taking part in a five-a-side football tournament. After we'd played, we spent some time on the beach before returning to London. We ran off to catch crabs, if you'll pardon the expression. I remember one of the boys who was with us, Roy Sutton. Whenever Roy caught a crab he was thrown into a real panic and screamed. After leaving school Roy became a fireman, and I often wondered what he'd have done if a fish market caught fire.

At the end of the summer term I left with Dad for a fishing and camping holiday in Great Yarmouth. We slept in a little two-man tent and our daily routine was always the same: we'd go to a pub on the river called the Bridge Inn, and I'd set up my rod outside and start earnestly fishing. I never caught anything, but that didn't matter. Dad spent most of the time inside drinking at the bar. He came out to keep an eye on me from time to time and brought me my nightly regulation half-pint of cider, a great treat for a boy of twelve!

One evening Dad got talking to a couple of blokes holidaying from Durham. They actually had their own boat which, to Dad and me, meant they had to be millionaires. They invited us back when the pub closed and we set off, Dad armed with a half-bottle of whisky and several dry ginger ales. As soon as the three adults got merry, Dad encouraged me to show off. I told a few jokes and then did a few impressions of the day I'd picked up – Peter Cook, Dudley Moore and Kenneth Williams.

Afterwards, one of the men asked: 'Are you in the Scouts?'

'Yes,' I said. 'St Austen's.'

'Good,' he replied. 'How do you fancy an audition for the Ralph Reader Gang Show?'

'Yes please!' I said keenly. In those days the Ralph Reader Gang Show was a very big deal. It ran for a fortnight at the Golder's Green Hippodrome and one night was even shown on national television. I especially fancied that bit!

Not long after we got back to Kidbrooke I heard from the great Ralph Reader's office. A few days later, with Mum and Dad either side of me, I went off to the London Palladium for an audition. I turned up in my Scout uniform and met Mr Reader in the bar at the back of the stalls (which I've fallen out of drunk many times since).

I did a few impressions for him, he thanked me and that was it. A short while later I received a letter from the production secretary saying I'd been accepted for the 1966 Gang Show that October! And what was more, if I introduced myself to an older lad called Jerry Hart who lived near me in Kidbrooke, who had started work and had his own van, he'd give me a lift to the rehearsals at Baden-Powell House in the Cromwell Road, Kensington.

When I started back at St Austen's in the third form that September I was already in rehearsals at Baden-Powell House. We'd go through the songs and routines night after night. I got on well with all the others in the show, who included a very gifted singer called Peter Straker.

Ralph Reader gave me my own six-minute spot, doing lots of little impressions and finishing with one of Ralph himself. My costume was a white polo-neck sweater, hipster trousers and Wayfinder shoes. I think Wayfinder must have sponsored the show, because wherever you looked there were boxes of new Wayfinders, the kind with a compass in them.

The big musical number in the show was a weird one, a song called 'Freedom'. It was a sort of 'black' thing. Peter Straker took the lead and the rest of the company had to be white minstrels in straw hats, dancing around in bare feet. I'm not sure it was the done thing, even then. The best bit of the song was Peter.

When the show opened in October Mum and Dad were there, watching proudly from the circle. During 'Freedom' Dad flicked his lighter twice in front of his face, so that I could locate him from the stage. I looked out into the pitch blackness and there was Dad's disembodied head floating in front of me. It was all I could do not to burst into hysterical giggles.

I looked pretty twee and I think I went down well with all the adults, less so with Ralph's adopted son Bob Court-Reader. He was more realistic and said I wasn't funny enough! One teacher from St Austen's, Mr Trinder, even came along to watch one night and complimented me afterwards for being fairly artistic – or did he say autistic?

Another enthusiastic fan was my drama teacher, Bango Wray, who always gave me enormous encouragement in that department.

His real name was William Wray but for some inexplicable reason we nicknamed him Bango and it seemed to fit. He was very different from the other teachers because he was quite extrovert. He used to wear silk shirts and flared trousers, and consequently to most of the kids Bango was rather 'iffy' and in our imagination a drug addict. I liked him enormously.

After the Gang Show I became quite good at drama and found myself in the school plays. The highlight was playing Azdac in *The Caucasian Chalk Circle*. I remember I had to say the word 'fart', and when that particular line loomed I looked quickly at the front row. There, sitting next to a po-faced Mr Sankey, was the bishop, canon and various vicars. The audience was all dog-collared up and I just couldn't bring myself to say the magic word. Instead I said 'burp'. I actually censored myself, which is something I've yet to do a second time, and, to this day, the front row in an audience puts me off. And I've never liked to say the word 'fart' on stage. I always find ways around it, like calling them 'apple tarts' or 'blow-offs'. If I say 'fart' I feel the whole Catholic hierarchy staring down and cursing from up above!

I had a letter a few years ago from an old school chum called John Smythe. In it he wrote: 'It was all right for you in those days. You got the star part but I was always a fucking tree!' Truth is, John, you looked like a tree! But you did get to say the word 'bastard' in *The Caucasian Chalk Circle*, and I looked up to you for that.

I also went off to a drama school in Woolwich in the evenings, telling my mates back in Blackheath that I was taking guitar lessons, in case they sent me up. As with the Catholic lessons, I was too embarrassed to admit what I was up to.

Bango took the Woolwich evening classes at a place called the Stage Centre in Burrage Road. I didn't know it then but Burrage Road was where I'd end up a drug addict after I left school. I'll tell you all about that later. I enjoyed drama but always felt embarrassed in front of an audience, and still do. Bango usually found me comic parts to play. The other actors were very deep and you could see they could make great actors, but then, what's a good comic if not a great actor? Can you hear that trumpet?

Early in 1967 I appeared in another Gang Show event, a Billy Cotton Band Show on TV, which was filmed at Elstree. In that I had a speaking part and had to say something to Billy. When we rehearsed it struck me how enormous his nose was – it looked like it had been soaked in bottles of gin for years. I also met two very big stars of the day then and was understandably in awe of them: Leslie Crowther and Terry Scott.

By the time the 1967 Gang Show came around I was in the fourth form and something of an old-timer. I didn't have my own spot but I got some of the best parts in the musical numbers instead. Not long after that, I auditioned for the film being made of Lionel Bart's hit West End musical *Oliver!*. Mum took me to meet a lady up in Park Lane who was picking children for audition a few days later for specific parts. She took one look at me, smiled and said: 'Artful Dodger!'

She thought I'd make a better Dodger than anything else so that's the part I auditioned for at the Savile Theatre in Upper Shaftesbury Avenue (now a cinema), where *Oliver!* was running. As before, I arrived with Mum and Dad and waited to have my go.

My audition piece was a disaster and as I was doing it I knew I'd failed. I had to sing 'Alicante', a poxy Gang Show song in too high a key for me. On top of that, unlike all the other kids there, I couldn't dance for toffee. When I heard later I hadn't got the part, but was instead offered a lesser, walk-on part in the film, I turned it down.

The part of the Dodger went to Jack Wild. Years later, I sort of got my own back on Jack for taking the part which was so rightfully mine. His wife was in a trio on *New Faces* when I was on the show, and I beat her!

After the failure of that audition, at all of thirteen,

I decided I'd had enough of Scouts, Gang Shows and show-business and turned my back on all three. Instead I wanted to go fishing and start pulling girls' pants down. I had learned lots of things while I was with the Scouts but I had to get out. I think of the Scouts as a really great organisation and, if I'd ever had the time, I'd love to have been a scoutmaster – and I can still remember how to make a fire out of nothing. Use a lighter! On his grave Baden-Powell has a circle within an outer circle, which means 'Gone home'. It's a great touch. On mine I want 'Told you I was ill'. Alternatively, I wouldn't mind being buried at sea – as long as my mothers-in-law dig the grave!

My footballing days also came to an end pretty soon after show-business got the push. I realised that as much as I still loved football I'd never get any more powerful as a player. I was painfully thin and as I'd now started smoking round the back of the bike sheds, I wasn't as fit as the others and was no longer the football star. For three years I had always been able to kick the ball furthest, but now there were others better than me.

The timing was unfortunate, though. We got a new coach to replace Deathly Doyle and he was a real hero. In contrast to the pedantic Bunny, this man loved the sport and took it all seriously enough to coach us properly. More than that, he even swore at us as he ran alongside, which we thought was brilliant. 'What are you fucking doing, Davidson?' he cried out if I got the ball but played badly.

'Pass it over there, boy!' he'd order. Then he'd push me over for playing badly. 'Don't give me any of this shit!' he'd say. 'Play properly or you're off the pitch, son!'

Gone were the petty days of 'tuck your shirt in' and 'pull your socks up'. Our new coach was much more lenient. If we didn't want to play wearing shin-pads, we didn't have to wear them. In a single week he had boosted morale in the team better than any coach ever had in a year at St Austen's. I remained captain of the team for a short while but eventually I was dropped from the team altogether. It was a sad but inevitable end to my footballing days.

Without the diversions of drama and football, I started

larking about all the more. With a lad called Johnny Rispoli, who had a little upturned nose and looked like a miniature Victor Spinetti, I did impressions of all the masters in a sort of double-act. We could look and sound like most of the teachers, mimicking their idiosyncratic ways. Next I also started to draw caricatures of them and got each one spot-on, apart from Bango Wray.

Bango must have felt left out because he taught me himself how to do him! When I drew his caricature I had him holding a big cigarette in his hand. 'What's this?' he said, pointing to the cigarette. 'I don't smoke.'

'A drug, sir,' I said, and he just laughed. He was just an ardent Pink Floyd fan after all.

The highest I could get then was by going fishing, with or without Dad. That's why I'd tried making myself that tackle box in Mr Davies' woodwork class and that's why, quite soon, I was skipping school. In addition to drawing those caricatures I was also a dab hand at forgery. I sussed that the school had never seen my Dad's signature on anything and made one up for him. Then I started writing notes, as if from him, saying drastic things like 'Jim can't come to school today, he's got pleurisy', or 'Jim's broken his back'.

But instead of lying in bed in agony I'd be off fishing down at Horton Kirby. Sometimes I went alone but more often than not I went with Ronnie or his mate Ray Sparks, who was fourteen, lived near me and went to a different school. Sometimes all three of us would go. We'd skive off day after day to go fishing. Then I started getting guilt pangs and would say to my friends adamantly: 'I can't hop school any more, I haven't been for two weeks! Next Monday I'm definitely going to school.'

When the next Monday morning came around, Ray would be back at my door, a hand-rolled cigarette hanging out of the corner of his mouth.

'Come on, off we go!' he'd say.

Some days I got home with my school uniform wet through or covered in mud. 'What have you been doing?' Dad would ask.

'I fell in the school pond,' I'd say, running to my bedroom

to avoid further questioning. It was a miracle the excuse worked – we didn't have a school pond. Mind you, I don't think Dad even knew which school I went to – except that it was 'a bloody Catholic one'.

We didn't always have Horton Kirby to ourselves. I remember a trio of older guys, who looked like hippies, sitting alongside their rods fishing for carp. I think they were semi-professional because they had state-of-the-art rods and tackle. These three guys would be there for days on end and wouldn't stir until their electronic bite-detectors went off, signalling a catch on one of their rods.

I used to look over at them enviously, thinking, that's for me! I'm sure I caught the fishing bug off Dad, although my brothers were also natural fishermen, and still are.

In my last year at St Austen's, in 1968, I landed the entire school in detention. As Guy Fawkes' Night approached everyone at the school kept letting off bangers around the classrooms, which drove the teachers mad. Fireworks were like currency at that school. One morning in assembly Mr Craddy snarled at us: 'If any more fireworks are let off in the school, you're all on detention.'

Craddy's threat was, to me, just too tempting. Egged on by Danny, I went out and bought an aerial bombshell, a sort of mega-banger. I aimed it at the woodwork shed, lit the blue paper and fled. The explosion was sensational and smashed plenty of the windows in the woodwork room. Out of nowhere Mr Davies appeared doing 'warp nine' on one leg. Even Ben Johnson couldn't have caught him! 'Fire! Fire!' he cried, disappearing into the main school in a flurry. Perhaps he did have a wooden leg after all and was worried he'd half-burn to the ground.

Craddy hit the roof. The whole school was kept in detention, all 400 of us. They say there's a sort of honour among rogues, so every child at that school must have regarded himself a rogue – even though everyone knew it was me, no one said a word to finger me and get out of the punishment.

After half an hour of detention, Danny jumped up and announced: 'Right, I'm off!'

We were amazed at how plucky our Danny was being. The teacher taking detention glared at him and said: 'Scott, where are you going?'

'I've got a paper round to do,' he said. 'I can't sod around here doing this foolish stuff, I've got a living to earn!' He turned on his heels and stormed out. His action that day summed up St Austen's: everyone just couldn't wait to storm out, earn some money and get on with their lives.

In my last year I did at least start to get the hang of courting. I had two girlfriends while I was at St Austen's. Both were cast-offs of my best mate Terry Honeyman, who also lived opposite me in Holburne Road. He went to a school in Eltham Green, so he knew different kids. He'd had a brief fling with a girl called Yvonne Kemp, who was outstanding because she had huge titties.

Yvonne and I started going out together and she scared me to death. She would keep trying to put her hand down my trousers and I'd get really shy, saying, 'No, stop it.' I was petrified. When she got amorous, I got shy because I'd only got a little, bald willy! I fell madly in love with Yvonne, however, and even though we never actually did anything to clinch matters, I regarded her as my girlfriend – until, that is, I left her for a week to go on a camping holiday to the Norfolk Broads with Mum and Dad.

The holiday was dreadful and when I got back remember that two important things happened: The Beatles released *Sgt Pepper's Lonely Hearts Club Band*, which was great, and Yvonne and I split up, which wasn't. I found out that while I'd been away Yvonne, the girl of my dreams, had given another boy a 'wank'. When I confronted her about it she said: 'I'll give you one if you want.'

I didn't, and I split up with her on the spot. I think the truth is not so much that I was hurt that she'd found someone else to play with, but that I was simply too petrified of her.

In Woolwich I found two great truant haunts. The first was a pie and mash shop, called Manze's, and the other was a hairdresser's! Around the corner from Manze's was a salon called Maison Maurice, run by an eighteen-year-old called Malcolm and his slightly younger sidekick.

They ran a really hip shop. They'd always have great rock music blaring out by bands, quite new to me, called The Nice and King Crimson. I remember hearing these albums for the very first time in that long, thin salon knowing I'd actually found the music I could connect with. Rock music. It just hit a chord with me and I probably owe any musical discrimination I developed totally to Malcolm and his mate.

Not only was the music revolutionary at Maison Maurice, but you could also buy trendy things, like cigarettes, Coca-Cola and condoms. I'd hang around chatting to them when I should have been at school and one day Malcolm, who nicknamed me 'Chops', asked me if I wanted a Saturday job as the junior. I jumped at the idea and started turning up every week to work, shampooing and sweeping up hair. For the first time I started earning some money and I loved it. At Christmas I loved it better still, because the customers would bring us presents and leave bigger tips.

Malcolm and his mate were completely mad. If things were quiet they'd line up six unopened Coca-Cola bottles at one end of the shop and bowl another full bottle at them. All the bottles would explode into a fizzing mess and I'd have to go down and clean it up. I thought these two guys were so brilliant I even fancied myself as a hairdresser for a while. I thought that, if Maison Maurice was anything to go by, hairdressing was easier than working and a darn sight less tedious than school.

I told Mr Sankey I wanted to be a hairdresser and he gave me a very strange look. I think, what with my theatrical connections and now my hairdressing interests, he thought he had a budding homosexual on his hands.

I remained a virgin all the time I was at St Austen's, even though, after Yvonne, I had a fling with a new girlfriend called Jane. She was another 'ex' of Terry's, from his school. Jane was slightly younger than me, about thirteen, and had short hair and quite boyish looks. All my life I've had a bit of a thing for boyish-looking girls, but don't tell the current wife, whoever she is when you read this. Only joking, Tracy!

Jane and I started to see each other while she was still dating Terry. Hardly surprisingly, this didn't go down at all well with Terry. After we'd seen each other for a few weeks, I threw a bit of a party at home one night. Mum and Dad went out to the pub for the night and we had the place to ourselves. I'd invited Terry along and, much to my disappointment, he came. Then he promptly punched me in the mouth! The back of my head went through the bedroom window and there was glass and blood everywhere.

It was a landmark incident. It was the first time, but not the last, that a real friend hit me. Losing Terry's friendship hurt me much more than the bruises and fat lip he gave me that night. We never did make up and I still miss his friendship to this day.

A less violent blow came when I turned up at Maison Maurice one day to be greeted by completely different staff. Apparently the shop had been robbed and Malcolm and his mate were suspected of doing an 'inside job'. I knew they hadn't done whatever it was they were accused of but, unfortunately, I never saw either of them again. It was a pity to lose their friendship – and their record collection. They'd been really good mates for the short time I'd known them.

It wasn't long afterwards that my life at St Austen's came abruptly to an end. I simply walked out one day and never returned because a spiteful teacher called Mr Scripture was about to cane me – and he could really cane. 'Bend over!' he demanded.

'No, I'm off!' I said. 'I don't want to play your game any more!' I walked out of the classroom, through the school gates and never returned. I liked school, but in the end I was fed up with being caned all the time. I walked from St Austen's to the little launderette Mum ran in Catford. 'I'm not going to school any more, Mum,' I said. 'It's getting on my tits.'

She must have been very disappointed but mothers stick by their sons and she certainly stuck by me. So, without any great fanfare or fuss, I left school with nothing more to show for it than a certificate for swimming a mile.

I was fifteen and free at last. Although I missed some of my school mates and life at Mason Maurice I was at least still dating Jane. Stay tuned!

3

A Teenage Husband

My first steps into the world of work in 1968 might well have been as a hairdresser, if the money had been better. After Malcolm disappeared from Maison Maurice I was offered the chance to continue at the salon as a trainee. Another man took over as manager and he sent me down for an interview at the sister salon in Welling. The interview went well and the boss offered me a job. 'Yes, you can start straight away,' he said. 'You'll be on £3 a week and for that you'll also have to work every Saturday.'

Now my pal Tommy Hayes had also just left school and got his first job, working in a warehouse up in the West End for £10 a week. So I thought about what I was being offered, turned it down and walked away from hairdressing. Instead, I ended up on £6⅙ as a dogsbody in the Charlton Co-Op supermarket. I filled the shelves, boned and sliced bacon and helped out around the shop. I loved it there and they quite liked me.

At the end of the first week I intended, as is traditional, to give Mum my very first wage packet. It never happened because somewhere between leaving the shop and getting home on the Friday night I lost that wage packet. When I told Mum I don't think deep down she really believed me, but she didn't show it and was always pleased thereafter when I did cough up my weekly thirty bob housekeeping.

Although the work in the Co-Op was routine enough I

liked earning, but I was embarrassed at the fact that by the time I'd started work in the real, grown-up world I still hadn't got my leg over. Jane and I were still seeing each other but nothing naughty had happened. The fact of the matter was that I was paying tax and I hadn't even had a leg-over yet. It just didn't seem right to me – and it still doesn't!

The Co-Op sent me on a two-week course to a big house-cum-conference centre in Oxleys Wood, Kent. There I met a girl from Rochester and for a whole fortnight we were inseparable, and went around everywhere hand-in-hand. I was in love again – great! At the end of the course I arranged to meet her that Sunday at Dartford station. As much as I genuinely liked her, I'm ashamed to say I never showed up for the rendezvous.

I've often wondered what happened to that girl and, if you're reading this book, please turn up at a show one night so that I can apologise in person. If you are reading this and you ever wondered what happened to me that day and why I let you down, well here goes . . .

That same Sunday Jane telephoned me to say that her parents were off to Margate for the day and she had the house to herself. So I went over to her place in Eltham and we did the dirty deed. We actually did it, and it was great, well worth the waiting for and a darn sight more exciting than Father Mars Bar's lessons or a crumpled copy of *Health & Efficiency*.

I remember Ronnie had told me something about sex, with which I was totally preoccupied. He said that once you'd had a leg-over your dick got bigger.

Great! I thought. If I have three or four of these I'll be all right!

After my first sexual encounter with Jane I couldn't wait to see if Ronnie was right. On the way home that night I got off the bus at Eltham and rushed into the public toilets. I stood in the corner, dropped my trousers and had a good look at what I'd got. I was disappointed to find it looked pretty much the same size but cheered myself up by thinking, well done son, you've cracked it! This beats the shit out of fishing! We weren't rude a second time; she left me for someone else before I got the chance.

After three months with the Co-Op I began to get itchy feet. So one day off I went up to the West End and walked into an employment agency in Charing Cross Road. I was interviewed and suggested for a job as a messenger boy with a company called Millbank Travel. I went directly to the company's offices and to what, an hour later, was to become my new work address: 104 New Bond Street, London W1.

I was on my very best behaviour and as polite as could be. The managing director, Mr Tampin (N.B. good name for a piss-take), interviewed me and offered me the job on the spot. When I got home and told Mum the news, she was delighted. It meant her days started slightly earlier, as she had to get me up in time to catch the morning train from Kidbrooke Station to Charing Cross.

The work was a doddle. I fetched and carried the post all day long. At first I just delivered internal memos around the offices and then I was a messenger boy minus the motorbike, running around the West End with tickets and letters.

I worked for a man we all referred to as The Sarge. He came from the Surrey Docks area in east London, fancied himself as a bit of a boxer and in many ways was very like Alf Garnett. The Sarge was always very nice to me, although if he got a bit pissed, he could be scary to be around.

One Friday morning a few days before my sixteenth birthday I shot off my big mouth to The Sarge and the other messenger boys. 'I could drink six pints of bitter in my lunch hour,' I declared. 'No problem!'

The Sarge whisked me off to our local, just around the corner in Conduit Street, and lined up the pints. The first wasn't a problem. After the second my belly felt tight. After the third I'd started to resent myself bitterly. Then Bert, another of the messengers, arrived and helped me with the fourth. In the end I was so drunk and all over the place I had to give up. I was green, both in my behaviour and my gills. I couldn't drink six pints of bitter then and I still can't today. Six pints of brandy maybe, but that beer gets me too drunk!

For my sixteenth birthday I arranged a special treat for Mum. She wanted to see *Paint Your Wagon*, the film of the Lerner and Loewe musical starring Lee Marvin and Clint Eastwood. I booked tickets for the Astoria Cinema in Charing Cross Road. I went in with Mum and sat down expecting to be bored to death, but I wasn't: it was magic. The film got me from the start with its extraordinary sound. It was being shown in Surround Sound, which meant the soundtrack came at you from every angle in the auditorium, and it was fantastic.

First I'd had Malcolm at Maison Maurice getting me with rock music and now Lee Marvin was getting me with a sound system.

Paint Your Wagon has stayed with me ever since that birthday. I rushed out and bought the soundtrack the same week and still play it regularly in my dressing-room. For the rest of its run I kept going back again and again just to listen to the Surround Sound. I've now seen it about seventy times and can even recite the dialogue word-for-word in lip-synch.

The same week I also had an unforgettable fishing triumph. I was now fishing up at Horton Kirby for carp like all the other serious anglers and landed a fish which weighed in at 21½lb. It was a record for the lake and went unbroken for the rest of the year – a week!

At Millbank Travel I fitted in well and continued to excel in my work throughout 1969, in as much as you can excel at being a messenger. Then The Sarge sent me on a succession of printing courses. One week I learned how to use a Gestetner, another week a Rank Xerox (I've still got the certificate from Rank Xerox for completing the course). Better was yet to come: an advanced Rank Xerox course! By the time I got back from that I knew all there was to churning out photocopies and leaflets by the score.

By now I knew and liked all the employees and, as at school, I was proving to be pretty popular. I didn't realise quite how popular in some quarters until the firm's office party at Christmas.

One secretary who worked there, who was older than me, was all smiles. Then, when no one was looking, she threw me across a desk and put her tongue in my mouth. 'This is great!' I thought. 'If this is being grown-up just how grown-up can I be?' I'd had my first leg-over with Jane but ever since I'd been on the look-out for more.

Life wasn't too enjoyable at home. Mum and Dad didn't get on that well – Dad drank very heavily some nights and, when he was pissed, Mum couldn't do a thing right. He'd rant on and on, making her life a living hell. In many ways they started to lead very separate lives. In the week Dad was always in the pub and Mum had the telly and bingo. But when they were together it was rarely peaceful and I thought it was probably how all families lived. In the end something in me snapped and I knew I had to find a way to leave home. So I went to see my brother Billy, now a policeman, who had been a sailor in the Royal Navy for ten years – I think he'd seen it as his chance to escape the crossfire of Mum and Dad fighting all the time. 'I'm off, Billy,' I said. 'I'm going to join the Navy.'

He encouraged me, and the next day, while out on an errand for Millbank Travel, I raced over to the RN recruitment office at High Holborn. I was interviewed and given another date to return for 'tests' a few days later.

When I returned I was given a medical by a doctor who was soon looking up my bum with a torch. I remember thinking to myself, 'What the hell can he be looking for? Frigates?' Whatever it was I passed the medical with flying colours and was told I'd hear from the Navy in due course about enrolment. That night at home I wrote a formal resignation letter to Mr Tampin, explaining that I was planning to join the forces and do my bit for Queen and country.

He wrote me a nice letter back saying he was sorry to see me go, and that I'd been a good employee. He suggested I stayed at Millbank Travel until I was called up. Good old Tampin – a regular guy (geddit?!).

The Navy kept me waiting about three or four weeks, which was more than enough time for my mates to talk me out of the whole Navy lark. Besides, I'd met another girl and we had a grope which meant I was in love again – the Navy would have to wait.

When I did hear from the Ministry of Defence about my call-up I wrote back refusing their shilling. Mr Tampin wanted me to stay on and offered me a better job with the firm, as an air-ticket clerk. Instead of a uniform I got myself a suit and tie and moved up from the messenger room to the air-ticketing department.

Turning my back on that chance to join the Navy is now a major regret of my life. I should have joined up. I think I'd have learned a lot – how to swim, for one thing! People often think I'm a frustrated soldier but I'd rather have been in the Navy for several reasons. For a start, when a commanding officer in the Navy says charge, he's got to go too – and so have the hot water and the beds!

I did another year at Millbank Travel as an air-ticket clerk and thoroughly enjoyed the work. I learned everything about travel from my new boss and mentor, a Frenchman called Pierre. He was a wonderful bloke and taught me two important things I needed to know as an adult: how to eat French bread rolls with chicken and coleslaw for lunch, and how to enjoy gin and tonic.

Although I didn't take advantage of the chance to travel abroad myself while I was there, I did manage to arrange, with Mr Tampin's help, for Mum and Dad to go over to America to see my sister Jean, who'd emigrated over there years earlier.

Eventually I started to get lazy about my work at Millbank Travel. I knew they were a good company and respected all the help they'd given me but I wasn't looking for long-term job satisfaction, I was looking for a lie-in.

I started oversleeping then turning up late for work and, just like school, played truant. In the end I just walked out on the job because, having been absent too many days in succession, I couldn't face Mr Tampin with transparent excuses for my skiving. I was so sure

I'd get a nasty bollocking I just ran away from the situation.

After Millbank I worked in Woolwich with a firm called Sunair Holidays, owned by a great character called Mr Goodman (who later owned Air Europe, then sadly went broke). But the job didn't last – I got bored with it. Next I got myself a £23-a-week job as a Rank Xerox machine operator with Thomas Moore and Company, a copying firm in Chancery Lane. In no time at all I was promoted to manager of the copying department.

When I was just seventeen, early in 1971, I went to stay with a Rank Xerox work-mate, an Australian called Fosci Bianchi, in his flat in Finborough Road, Earl's Court, for about three weeks. While I was there I taught myself to play his guitar. I remember watching him play and feeling sure I could teach myself. I bet him I could learn a tune in an evening and proceeded to do so. He took me through the chords of 'House of the Rising Sun' and I practised and practised hour after hour. By the end of the night I could just about play it properly.

I don't think I had any natural musical talent. I think I forced myself to learn it out of a sheer determination to be able to show off at something! As well as guitar, Fosci tried to teach me how to smoke dope but, although I tried a few times, I didn't take to it. It did nothing for me. Yuk!

Although not a born musician, I was good enough as a bit of a drummer to pick up some part-time work playing drums adequately enough in a Woolwich pub, the Director General.

One weekend another work-mate, a black guy called Horace, had a party and I was lined up to go along with a blind date, an Indian girl called Darleen. She was nice enough but nothing sparked between us. However, at the party I met a girl called Sue Walpole, who I'd seen before hanging around Woolwich. She was very nice – funny and giggly – and laughed at me a lot, which I thought was wonderful. That night I was quite taken with Sue and got her 'phone number from her before she left the party. A few days later I rang her and invited her out. We met and, after a few more nervous nights together, started to go out properly. Stand by Eltham toilets!

We went steady for about six months and even began talking about marriage. I saw it as a way of taking the plunge and growing up, like Danny Scott had done by boldly walking out of St Austen's. I also thought it might be just the chance I needed to turn my back on the ceaseless tears and shouting at 118 Holburne Road.

But Sue and I just couldn't decide whether to buy an engagement ring or go down to Dymchurch, near Folkestone, for a holiday together. So we did the sensible thing and took ourselves off to the seaside. We found a small guest-house advertising a room to let and were shown into a studio – in the adjoining garage! However, the room was bliss for both of us; to Sue it was a bit 'homey', to me it had a bed and all I wanted to do, given half a chance, was make love. Sue had very different ideas. She found rides at the local fair and walks along the sea-front much more appealing than jumping into the sack with me. She never liked doing it as much as I did, probably because I wasn't very good at it.

I think that little garage was probably where Sarah, my first child, was conceived because Sue and I didn't have sex much after we returned to London.

I would often stay at Sue's overcrowded home, a ground-floor council maisonette looking out on Woolwich docks. I got on very well with her mum, June, sister Lesley and her husband Dave, little brother John and even Sheba, their Alsatian. I never felt anything for their two budgerigars, though. Sue's dad had died in a car crash long before we met, and June had been seriously hurt in the accident. Her face was badly scarred and she had damaged her hip, which left her with a limp.

If I stayed over I slept, in theory, on the sofa downstairs, where John also slept. More often than not, though, after everyone else had gone to bed I'd creep upstairs to sleep with Sue in her bedroom. Many times June got up before us and my whereabouts were given away by my shoes on the wrong side of Sue's door.

One evening June and I were in the sitting-room alone and I mentioned how women, if Sue was anything to go by, didn't seem to go to the loo very much. 'Sue hasn't been for weeks!' I said, laughing.

'I know what else she hasn't been for weeks,' replied June solemnly. 'What are you going to do about it?'

'Get married,' I said without hesitation. I went home and spoke to Dad about it – as I was only seventeen, legally I needed his consent to marry. He wasn't at all happy about the idea.

'I'm going to marry her anyway!' I said, in case he started shouting and tried to forbid me.

'OK, son,' he said calmly.

'Where are you going to live?' asked Mum.

'We'll live at her mum's in Woolwich,' I replied.

So it was arranged, and a ceremony at Woolwich Town Hall Register Office was hurriedly booked for Saturday November 6, 1971.

The night before, Tommy, my best man, Larry and Ronnie took me on my stag night and we bounced from pub to pub until we were all legless. We ended up in the Wimpy Bar in Greenwich, from which we were already banned after a previous drunken visit. The big Turkish man who ran the place looked at us and put up his hand. 'I'm not serving you three,' he said, pointing at me, Larry and Ronnie. 'I'm only serving you,' he added, pointing to Tommy.

'Wimpy and chips four times, please!' replied Tommy, quick as a flash.

I got up the next morning with a dreadful hangover and got into the £21 suit and kipper tie Mum had bought me for the occasion from Take Six in Wardour Street. We headed down to Woolwich and straight into the Director General, which was conveniently sited bang opposite the register office. With me were Mum and Dad, Tommy, Larry, Ronnie and all my mates.

'What would you have done if you were me?' I asked Dad, downing a pint to steady my wedding-day nerves.

'I'd have kept the fucking cab going straight on!' he said drily.

After the short marriage ceremony we headed into another pub for lunch then back to Sue's home. I put on a Pink Floyd album and everyone moaned at me. 'Turn that shit off!' said Dad.

'No I won't, it's my wedding day!' I shouted back.

Then Sue upped and went to bed and the whole thing seemed disastrous. I hadn't even been married a day and already I felt lonely. That night we all went down to the Director General again where I got up on stage and had a quick go on the drums.

While I wasn't looking Mum and Dad had a whip-round and gave me enough money to take Sue to the Strand Palace Hotel in the West End for our honeymoon night. We took a cab to the hotel and fell asleep in the strange, somehow sterile, surroundings.

Next morning we got up, had breakfast and Mr and Mrs Davidson checked out. Our honeymoon was over and, by that afternoon, our life was back to normal, living at June's.

At Thomas Moore's things didn't go so well after I got married. I was still manager of the copying department but once again I began oversleeping in the mornings and arriving late, and once again I walked away from the job, too timid to face the music with an angry boss.

My oversleeping was beginning to become a habit I just couldn't break. Instead, when a rep from Rank Xerox suggested I put in for a night job at their Tottenham Court Road premises, I applied for it. I got the job, operating a big, old-fashioned thing called a Rank Xerox Copy-Flow Machine, which churned out microfilm on massive rolls for a Customs and Excise contract. Being night work it was perfect, I started at 5.30 pm, which even I could manage, and finished at 1.30 am.

Six months after my wedding I was eighteen, and Sue was very pregnant with our baby. Poor Sue used to be in agony even when she had period pains, and I was sure having the baby would kill her. She woke up one morning saying the pain was appalling and that I had to take her to hospital at once. I hadn't even passed my driving test by then but I drove Sue the 150 yards to Woolwich's Mothers' and Babies' Hospital. The nurse took one look at Sue and told us both to come back later, we were too early.

We went back home and Sue told me I had to go to the chemist for her, to get some kind of appliance called a sanitary belt. I wasn't too sure what I was asking for – the name alone conjured up ghastly images. I think it was something you strap a hammock on to but I've never found out. Anyway, I went in to the chemist's and started asking for steel combs, toothbrushes and anything else I could think of until I finally plucked up the courage to ask for a sanitary belt. Buying the shop's entire stock of Durex would have been less embarrassing!

Sue and I got ready to return to the hospital again and set off in my ancient Herald. When we got there the nurse took one look at Sue and said, 'Oh, yes! Your wife is going into labour now. Her waters have broken.' More ghastly ideas sprang to mind. Then the nurse said: 'There's no room here, you'll have to go to the hospital in Plumstead.'

So, at 5.00 pm, we headed off for Plumstead in rush-hour traffic. The journey was a slow-moving nightmare with Sue screaming in pain every few minutes. We eventually got to Plumstead and, thankfully, Sue was admitted. 'I'll be back later, dear,' I said as they took her away. I drove to Holburne Road and had something to eat. Then I grabbed a pocketful of biscuits, borrowed some money from Mum and headed back to the hospital. On the way I stopped at a pub in Woolwich to buy a bottle of orange squash and, leaving, promptly reversed into a lorry, smashing my rear light.

I got back to the hospital at 9.00 pm and Sue had already been given some pain-killers to make her more comfortable. She was in labour for hours and I stayed with her throughout. Baby Sarah was finally born at 5.20 am on April 25, 1972.

I took one look at the tiny being and thought 'Oh my God, you poor thing! You've got to go through everything I've had to go through. I wonder how you'll do? And I wonder if I'll be a good dad?' Two decades later, the answer is:

debatable, good on occasions, but must try harder, given the chance.

Sue was exhausted and we had a little cry together before I left, whispering, 'See you later, well done.'

I sat in my car in the hospital car park for a while thinking about the baby. Then I put the key in the ignition, turned it slowly and nothing happened. The battery was as flat as a pancake. So, having just witnessed the birth of my first child, I pushed the car down Plumstead Hill, trying hopelessly to get it to start. I telephoned Dad and he drove over to give me a jump-start, then we drove home in convoy.

Mum placed a big plate of bacon and eggs in front of me, and said, 'Well, you're a man now, son!' I burst into tears: all of eighteen and a quarter and now a father.

I was always very nervous holding baby Sarah but Dad was much more boisterous. 'Give us her here!' he'd say, then he'd throw her up in the air and catch her. 'See, that's how you treat babies,' he'd say. On cue, Sarah would bawl her head off!

When I passed my driving test a little while later I decided I had to have a decent car. A Ford Cortina Mark I to be precise, registration ELN 798C. I bought it from a used-car lot in Feltham. I didn't know the first thing about cars or engines but made out I did. I asked to look under the bonnet and the salesman lifted it. Then he started up the engine. 'The carburettor's whistling,' I said, bluffing.

'It'll save you buying a fucking radio, son, won't it?' he replied. That put me in my place. I agreed to buy it, on hire purchase as I didn't have any money saved, and he asked who was standing as guarantor to the loan.

'My brother-in-law Ted,' I answered.

'What does Ted do for a living?' he asked.

'He's a docker,' I explained.

'Oh no, we can't have a docker,' he said. 'We have to have someone who works. Dockers are high risk, they get ill if they have to move too quickly. Have you got any other brothers?'

'I've got one, Billy, who's a policeman,' I replied.

'Put him down instead. Ted can sign his name for him if he won't,' added the salesman. Later that day I found a quiet moment with Billy and said I'd got some forms for him to sign to guarantee the car loan. He went mental.

'You know I could get the sack for this?' he snapped. Then he relented, signed the forms and I got the car.

Sue and I continued to live with her family but it wasn't ideal. I stayed on at Rank Xerox, working nights, to pay the bills for Sarah. I'd get a lift home at 2.00 am then snatch seven hours' sleep before the noise in the house grew too loud to sleep through any longer.

One weekend I got into bed with Sue in a terrible state. I'd dabbled in drugs again and they hadn't agreed with me one bit. I'd gone with a work-mate called Eddie to a pub near London Zoo, where he bought a £1 deal of dope. He rolled some up into a cigarette and I smoked a little. The drug took hold and I'd never felt as paranoid or frightened before in my life. When I crept into bed with Sue later I was physically shaking. 'Eddie's given me some drugs,' I said to her. 'Help!'

'Serves you right!' she snorted.

I fell asleep frightened out of my life. The effects of the dope scared me and for ages after that I wouldn't touch it, not until my mates started smoking cannabis all the time and I was re-introduced to it. I thought of grass as just a bit of fun but dope always sounded more 'druggy' to me then.

Sue's sister Lesley was very high-spirited, full of life and great fun to be around. Her plumber husband Dave was known in the area as 'Daisy Raven', an odd nickname because he was so tough you couldn't knock him out with a hammer. But Daisy wasn't a bully – in fact he was totally dominated by Lesley.

June, too, dominated her men-friends. She had a fancy for little Indian blokes and they came running around to be by her side all the time. She was nice enough but she had a fiery temper which could reduce even Daisy to a quivering mess. And she ran the household with military precision: none of us were allowed to eat before we'd got down on our hands and knees and scraped up Sheba's dog hairs. The reward dangled before us was always the same – a plate of eggs, chips and beans for our dinner. I think I even began to look like eggs, chips and beans after a while.

One Christmas I played drums in a pub for some extra cash and got home late, slightly the worse for a few drinks. The next morning I went downstairs, hung-over, and the two budgerigars started shouting at me. Christmas morning or not, we still had to get down on all fours to pick up bloody dog hairs. Sheba must have been going bald because now there seemed to be more than ever.

I couldn't face it a moment longer and snapped. I had a bitter row with June and she slung the turkey at me. I told her, and shortly afterwards Sheba and the budgerigars, to fuck off and ran out of the front door. Daisy ran after me, caught up and whisked me into the nearest pub where I cried into my bitter until I'd calmed down.

'You just have to put up with it,' he said quietly. 'They're quite nice, really.' I went back and tried to enjoy the rest of Christmas Day but I wanted something better for Sue, Sarah and me. We had to get out.

A few days later we moved to Mum and Dad's in Holburne Road – out of the frying pan and into the line of fire of Mum and Dad's arguments. Sue and I talked about how miserable we were and decided to split up, temporarily, until I could sort us out somewhere to live. I stayed in Holburne Road and she and Sarah moved back to Woolwich, where I'd visit them both every few days. It was the beginning of the end, really, and we hadn't even been married a year.

I was with Sue one day and sensed something was wrong but didn't know quite what. We weren't talking much, and then she looked away from me. 'I've had enough,' she said. 'That's it. I don't love you any more.'

My pride was dented and nervously I shot my mouth off. 'Sod you then, I don't love you,' I said, and left. It all seemed quite simple: if she didn't want me then I didn't want her. But in my heart I think I rather did. When a little later our application for accommodation on the local council housing list came through, we were given a flat in Thamesmead. Sue moved into it with Sarah and a girlfriend.

I tried putting her and the baby behind me but I really missed them. I thought that, as we now had the chance of a place of our own together, it might still work out. I called to see Sue at the new flat and dropped to my knees begging her to have me back. It cut no ice. She wasn't going to have me back and that was that. I started crying and telling her how I really did love her, but eventually I cried myself dry of emotion. I left and went back home to Holburne Road.

I suppose Sue really didn't need me. Luckily, her family was very close and, with me finally out of the frame, they all rallied around and helped her to bring up Sarah. Sue lived in that little Thamesmead flat for a while with her friends. Shortly afterwards she found a boyfriend called Tony. He was a nice enough man – a West Ham supporter, but nice enough all the same.

When Tony arrived I refused to pay the rent and the council started legal proceedings against me for the arrears. I said I'd only cough up if they would let me rent it for myself.

Tommy, Ronnie and I liked the idea of having the flat for ourselves, but it was not to be. The council swiftly changed the locks in an operation which must rate as the quickest and most efficient service ever carried out by a local authority!

I didn't only fall out with the council. Sue and I had words about maintenance for Sarah. In the end I had to appear before Dartford magistrates who ordered me to pay £3 a week and increased the maintenance after I started making serious money. But, in fairness to Sue, she never felt she had a claim on any money I made later because when we had our time together we were both skint.

Sue made a good mum although she was a bit panicky when Sarah was very young. Her outstanding qualities were that she enjoyed a good laugh and was very confident in herself. She's never changed. Eventually Sue left Tony and went to live with a nice policeman, and had kids with all three of us. She's worse than me! Why don't the papers write about you, Sue?

4

Drugs and the Devil

At nineteen, with Sue and Sarah gone, I instead set my heart on something new in my life – a motorbike. I yearned for a little Honda 175 and repeated the hire purchase trick on my brother Billy, putting him down as guarantor of the loan. Only this time, to avoid a row, I didn't tell him. Sorry, Billy!

Once I had the Honda I felt on top of the world again and my troubles with Sue seemed a million miles behind me. I rode the bike over to Barking one day and got myself a new job, as a delivery van driver with National Carriers. It was a brilliant job and I really took to it. My daily task was to pick up the van from the depot and drive to Ilford to collect little parcels from the train station. Then I had to deliver them to the massive Ford motor plant at Dagenham.

At the time the country's unions were organising go-slows everywhere in protest at Prime Minister Ted Heath's three-day week, which was bringing the country to its knees. Lorries delivering parts to the Ford plant would have to queue up outside the main gates and wait for hours, days even, before they could unload and get away. The 'jobsworths' in the unions at Ford wouldn't have it any other way.

I decided I wasn't prepared to waste my days waiting for the union bods to let me in. So I'd park the van around the corner, find a trolley and load it up with my parcels. Then

I just walked past all the other drivers. They'd all blow me kisses, whistle and laugh at me because I'd grown my hair long and bleached it blond.

But I reckon I had the last laugh. I'd be finished by 10.00 am and skived off for the rest of the day. These were my kind of hours! I'd spend a leisurely day parked up somewhere in the van, dreaming of playing drums professionally and being a rock star. Rock groups then were always made up of three musicians and a drummer. To me, playing the drums was like being able to play a real musical instrument without needing to be talented. All you needed was rhythm. I prided myself on my fashionable hairstyle and believed it meant I was already halfway up the road to a rock career. Whether or not I was a fair drummer didn't come into it – I looked the part and that was all that mattered!

When I was nineteen I dabbled for the first time with LSD. I went over to Tommy Hayes's, where Ronnie had some acid tabs, tiny green microdots about the size of a saccharine sweetener. Ronnie cut one in half and we swallowed a half each, then sat and waited for something to happen. Nothing did.

By now we had our minds set on trying drugs and Tommy drove the two of us to see a friend of his called Shep, who smoked dope.

Shep lived in Woolwich with his very pretty wife, Yvonne, and their young kid, Matthew. The moment we arrived at Shep's the acid started working.

'Ronnie and Jim have taken some LSD,' Tommy told Shep. The two of them proceeded to roll and smoke several joints, but Ronnie and I didn't need a thing more – we were really tripping. We laughed non-stop for eight hours. Everything seemed so funny. We felt so quick off the mark we had what we thought were hysterical one-liners ricocheting around the room at a hundred miles an hour. Oddly enough, though, when Tommy and Shep laughed under the influence of their dope they were miles behind us. Ronnie and I felt we'd become really intellectual, our trip was leaving theirs standing.

After that we all started dabbling more with drugs.

Usually a joint would be passed around and I gradually got the hang of it a bit, though I was never a great fan.

Christmas that year was nothing special. On Boxing Day I went to the Fox Under the Hill pub in Woolwich. I got talking to a girl and asked her back to Holburne Road to watch a documentary about my rock idols, Emerson, Lake and Palmer. After we'd watched the programme, Tommy turned up saying we'd been invited to a party but had to take a bottle of booze. I asked Dad to lend me enough to buy a bottle of whisky but he wouldn't. Instead he taught me a great dodge, which worked a treat.

He took a half-bottle of whisky and poured the contents into a jug. Then he filled the bottle almost to the top with cold tea, topping it up with a tiny amount of whisky. 'Now,' he said, 'when you arrive at the party you must "accidentally" drop the bottle on the doorstep so that it breaks. Then stride in full of apologies and grab yourself your first drink!'

We headed off to the party with our bottle of tea, apprehensive about whether the trick would work. The host opened the door and, as I handed over the bottle, wishing him a very merry Christmas, it slipped from my hand and smashed on the doorstep. There was tea everywhere. It worked a treat. The man behind us on the doorstep, already drunk, was so sorry about what he'd witnessed that he gave me a bottle of vodka! Who says my dad never taught me anything useful?!

The party was pretty boring and the three of us didn't know a soul. Snooping around, we opened a drawer and found a bottle of Valium. None of us knew what Valium did but we knew it was a drug and that was enough for us. We shared out the pills among ourselves, about twenty each, and knocked them back.

To say the rest of the night was a blur is an understatement. The next thing I knew I woke up in bed in Holburne Road the next afternoon, covered in eye make-up! I found Tommy later and we had both lost twelve hours. We did work out that we'd nicked a Mini. At first I thought I'd dreamed a joyride and told Tommy about it, but we couldn't both have had the same dream. We had no idea where we'd taken the car from, where we'd been in it or where it had ended up. I didn't take Valium again after that, apart from when it was properly prescribed for me by the doctor many years later.

In the New Year I got the sack from National Carriers, fired by a man I thought was a complete bastard called Mr Chubb (I used to call him Mr Trout or Mr Salmon, anything to annoy him). One day he called a union meeting and referred to us all as 'brothers'. He called us out on a one-day stoppage and, afterwards, the very same 'brother' sacked me. He called me into his office and just said, 'You're sacked.'

I'm pretty sure I got the push because I really wasn't hard-working, as much as I liked driving the van. I was also too lippy. Apart from that, Chubb probably knew I spent most of my days in lay-bys daydreaming lazily.

I found Tommy, Ronnie and a guy called Kevin who had started hanging around with us. We were all bored and concluded we had to do something with our lives, get a flat together, if we could.

Tommy was working at a warehouse in Erith on quite a good income and Ronnie did bits and pieces. I'd just lost my job so I was no help; nor was Kevin who, being on bail or on the run, had no chance of earning. We spotted an advertisement in the local newspaper for a flat in Woolwich for £16 a week, an absolute fortune then. We asked to see it and set off trying to behave as responsibly as we could.

It was in Burrage Road, just along from the Stage Centre where I'd diligently attended Bango Wray's evening drama classes. The terraced house had a few steps leading up to a front door behind which were two flats, one upstairs and one down. Ours was the latter. It had a living-room, kitchen and two bedrooms, one tiny and one fairly large. It was perfect.

We left the flat and headed to the nearest pub. We mulled over how to afford it and decided, because Tommy was earning quite well, that one way or another we'd find the weekly rent – if we didn't eat.

What we couldn't afford was the obligatory advance of

four weeks' rent needed before we could take it. Several pints later we decided that I would sell the Honda, which I hadn't even paid for, to raise the deposit. So I sold the bike for £100, enough to cover the deposit with about £40 to spare. We moved in immediately. Tommy, Kevin and I shared the one large bedroom and Ronnie, because he owned the hi-fi system, had the small bedroom to himself.

It didn't take long to get the flat exactly as we wanted it, with three posters adorning the walls. One of Alice Cooper, one of David Bowie and the third of a group called Stray which played regularly in a local pub. With the spare £40 we decided to buy some grass to sell to our mates at a slight profit. We weren't trying to be big-time drug-dealers; we thought we were just having a bit of fun and raising a bit of cash.

We occasionally bought grass or dope from some guys in a couple of local pubs. I simply asked them where they got it from and went down to their supplier, who lived in a house in Catford.

For £40 I got what they described as 'a quarter of a weight' – a carrier bag full of the stuff! I took it back to the flat and we chopped it all up, wrapped up little £1 deals and started flogging it in the Fox Under the Hill, now our firmly established local. Pretty soon all we were doing to make money was flogging grass or dope.

We had a meeting one night and decided to go into narcotics in a bigger way and sell amphetamine sulphate – speed. Everyone had started taking speed by then and £1 bought ten pills, enough to last all night and the whole of the next day.

We bought a thousand pills for £40 and planned to sell them ten for £1. In theory we stood to make £60 on the deal. In reality, of course, we swallowed all the profits and turned into right little pillocks into the bargain.

The four of us each had our own little 'manors'. Mine was the Howick pub in Woolwich where Sue, my ex-wife, had started working. Sue was completely ignorant of the seedy business I was getting up to on the other side of her bar. After we'd been to our respective manors we met up again at the Fox, then headed back to the flat and each swallowed a handful of tablets. We'd stay up all night long dreaming of being David Bowie and thought amphetamines were great. We were so high we didn't need to drink and could talk complete rubbish at each other for hours yet find it riveting.

On amphetamines I became very switched on, mentally. I could finish a crossword puzzle in five minutes flat. It gave me great confidence, I used to think it had turned me into the best bird-puller in the world. Wrong – George Best is. In reality, of course, the drugs only turned me into a right dickhead.

Sex on drugs was also great. It wasn't a case of not getting it up, it was a case of getting it to stop being up. The Problem was finding someone to do it with. After a month I had an arm like Arnold Schwarzenegger's!

One night a whole bunch of us retreated to the flat after a night at the Fox. With me, Tommy and Kevin was Dave Murrell, a big chap, a window cleaner called Larry and a couple of others. When we got to the front door we could see a light on in the flat. We knew Ronnie was out for the night, so we all picked up sticks to beat the intruders and ran through the front door. There, slumped on our sofa and completely off his face with eyes like bulldog's bollocks, was a guy called Dave.

Dave was one of the local Blackheath characters. He was known to tell a bit of a fib from time to time – in fact he was a downright liar. He just couldn't stop fantasising about his life. But he wasn't a bad bloke, and he could even be really funny at times. We could see that Dave had taken something while we had been out, because the flat was magically transformed. As any pill-freak from those days will tell you, speed gives you great energy and nothing can stop you working it off. If you've got no one to talk to, you can even find yourself doing the housework. Dave had got so smashed while we were out that he'd not only cleaned to pristine perfection everything in sight, he'd even done our ironing!

He said he'd popped around to buy some pills and been

let in to wait by the man in the flat above. 'Fine, what would you like to buy?' I asked.

'I've changed my mind now,' he said.

'You haven't been at our pill drawer have you, Dave?' I asked.

'No!' he lied. It was a stupid thing to say: his eyes were frothing at the mouth! For not coming clean with us about what he'd taken, we planned revenge.

'Here you go, Dave,' I said, handing him some pills. 'For tidying up the flat so beautifully have a handful on us.' Then we forced him to swallow all of them. He didn't sleep for about two weeks, nor did he ever try to nick our drugs again.

Another Dave – Dave Stillings – was also a bit of a card. He came from Bradford and had a northern accent. He also had an appalling lisp which meant he even had problems pronouncing his own name. He needed a windscreen wiper on the inside of his car. To add to this handicap, he had a bit of a squint in one eye so you were never sure whether or not he was looking at you. He did change his name to Dave Bradford but we insisted on calling him Dave 'Shtillingsh'.

Tommy, Ronnie, Kevin and I became dab hands at drug-dealing but it didn't always go to plan, and there were a few disasters. Once we couldn't get any speed to sell anywhere and a dodgy bloke sold us something called Seconal, telling us they were 'downers' rather than 'uppers'.

I couldn't see the point of something to bring you down so I didn't take any myself. However, that didn't stop me flogging an entire bag of them at the Howick in Woolwich. I told everyone to take just two at a time but they wouldn't listen to me. Some had ten, others twenty. Then they all started passing out on the floor or, worse still, throwing up. By then the mob wanted to kill me and I had to do a quick runner to save my skin.

When the four of us didn't have any pills for ourselves, let alone any to sell, we got terribly depressed. All of nineteen or twenty, we would be sitting around staring at death's door just because we'd run out of drugs. Some days it must have looked like that scene from the film *Whisky Galore*, where everyone is completely despondent because they've run out of scotch.

One day when I was on the up the girl of my dreams walked, or rather teetered, into the Fox. Denise. She was wearing a pair of silver platform boots and it was love at first sight. Silver platform boots – she must be a Bowie fan! I thought. Although I was never that much of a Bowie fan, he was the undisputed leader of pop fashion in the seventies. I was mesmerised by Denise and quickly started chatting to her.

She said she had a boyfriend in Streatham but met me all the same later that week. I was completely smitten. The only girl I'd ever been with for any length of time was Sue, and she was very 'wifey'. Suddenly, here was Denise with her boots. She had such an effect on me that a few days later I went out and bought my first-ever pair of platform shoes to catch up.

Although she was living with her mum in Blackheath, Denise had actually been brought up in St Albans by an auntie. Her mum wasn't well and was prone to doing outrageous things, shouting and screaming hysterically for no discernible reason. For me, the most memorable night of my courtship with Denise was when I took her to see Emerson, Lake and Palmer playing Wembley. We'd both taken some speed and I had everything that night, my rock heroes playing live and the girl of my dreams sitting next to me in her boots. I'd go over to Denise's house most nights and we'd take some pills and flop around. But at the end of the evening I always had to leave and go back to the flat to sleep alone.

I went off for a Norfolk fishing break with Mum and Dad and, when I got back, I found out that Denise had deceived me. While I was away she'd been rude at Blackheath Dips with my mate Dave Franks in his Ford Granada. I never really forgave Denise for that betrayal, or Dave for having a bigger car than me – I only had an old Ford Anglia then, which I'd bought from him anyway. Holidays in Norfolk, I decided, were always jinxed. Yet Denise and I continued to go out together. We'd keep taking pills and listening to rock music.

I don't know where she was the second time I tried LSD, but it wasn't good and proved to be the last. The devil himself warned me off. Ron, Tommy, Dave Stillings and I were at the flat one night and each took a whole LSD tab. We waited for the effect to take hold and, every so often, one of us asked optimistically, 'Anything yet?'

When the LSD did take a grip it was very strong and in a matter of minutes we were zombies. We could do nothing more energetic than sit and listen in silence to a Roxy Music album.

Dave Stillings sat next to me, twiddling with the flex of our one-bar electric fire. Under the influence of the drug, to me Dave suddenly looked like the spitting image of Brian Eno, Roxy Music's keyboard player. His face was lit up red from the glow of the fire and, as he looked around, his eyes seemed to leap into my face. I felt myself drain of any colour and I panicked.

'Quick, put the light on, someone!' I cried out. The light went on and I think Ron and Tommy told me to calm down, but it didn't help. I said I had to get out of there, grabbed Tommy and we went out to get some air. I was so scared I even got Tommy at it. We must have strolled around Woolwich for about three hours waiting for the LSD to wear off. We talked and talked, stopping only to watch the sun come up on the way back to the flat.

When we got back, Dave was still awake but I couldn't bring myself to look at him until he spoke to me. 'You saw the devil last night, didn't you?' he asked.

'Yes. How did you know?' I replied.

'When you screamed it was me who put the light on.'

'But how did you know I saw the devil?' I asked again. 'I haven't said anything.'

'Because I felt horns on my head,' he said.

I've never taken LSD since that day. It was too scary an experience to ever repeat. If one thinks of a graph to measure the effects of various drugs, grass and dope would be an inch-high column and speed, say, three inches. The effect of LSD clears the graph completely and takes you to the moon. It is a very odd and extremely dangerous drug. Today, in retrospect, I think all drugs are dangerous. I've seen too many people hurt or killed because they were married to drugs.

Eventually the four of us at Burrage Road started to get bored with drugs. At the height of our drug-taking I could swallow 250 speed tablets in a weekend, but I'd started to become quite immune to them. And we suffered extreme tiredness and appalling withdrawal scenes coming down from massive doses of the drug. I often felt sorry for the poor publicans who had to put up with us bouncing around, getting over the effects of our drug-taking. Not that there was ever any violence or nastiness from the people on drugs. They just looked awful.

Around the same time drugs started losing their appeal, we stopped dealing in them. The drug barons running London seemed to get seedier and the whole business started to lose its glitter. Anyway, I was about to stumble on a much better way of getting high – until I later bumped into old Charlie Coke – telling jokes.

I was still out of work and window cleaner Larry was on the look-out for something for me to do. One day he was cleaning the windows of the Black Bull pub in Lewisham and the guv'nor of the place, Gerry, told him he needed a comedian for Sunday lunchtimes. Larry told him I was a very good, upcoming comic.

When Larry told me this I was stunned. He said I had to introduce myself to Gerry so I went off to the Black Bull. I strode in – all skinny eight and a half stone of me, dripping wet, as the saying goes – wearing a pair of big silver platform boots to match my new Bowie hairstyle. Gerry was standing behind the bar with his pretty wife.

'I'm Jim Davidson,' I said, instantly abandoning the name Cameron.

'I've heard about you,' he replied. 'What pubs have you already worked, then?'

'The Duchess of York, King's Head and Bricklayer's

Arms,' I reeled off for starters, making up names as I went along.

'OK,' he said, 'Can you do Sunday lunchtime?'

'Yes,' I replied. 'No problem.'

So that Sunday I went to the pub about mid-morning with, for support, Denise, Tommy, Larry and a few friends. We sat around a table in the corner of the pub and had a few drinks. Looking around I saw a beautiful blonde girl unloading a mini-van. She had long hair, a skirt right up to her bum and turned out to be Linda Regan, the pub DJ. Linda went on to become one of the *Hi-De-Hi* girls and for years I kept bumping into her. I've still got a crush on her to this day, because she was the first professional I ever worked with.

I went over to Linda as she set up her records and started talking to her. I was beginning to feel very nervous and went back to the others and told them how anxious I was. 'This'll do it!' said one of the gang, and out came a little cellophane packet of amphetamine sulphate. Old habits . . . We all dabbed our fingers in and took some. By the time I had to go on I felt much better, happily waffling away and somehow feeling quite fearless.

'A big hand for Jim Davidson,' said Linda. I took the microphone and looked out at the audience of a dozen mostly black guys. I managed to make them all laugh, especially when I did a funny impression of a black pal from school. The pub regulars seemed to like me, and then a load of rowdy blokes who had just been to a football match came in. They started heckling me and I gave as good as I got, which went down really well. My first professional engagement seemed to have gone comparatively smoothly, but by the time I left the stage I was so nervous again that my mouth had dried up and my top lip was sticking to my teeth.

I downed a pint of bitter in record time – seconds – and sat down, still uneasy, thinking, this is definitely not for me.

Then a bloke called Trevor came over and said: 'Hello, I'm a singer in the band which works here and I've also got a tobacconist's round the corner. I want to be your manager.'

'Oh yes?' I said. 'Of course you do!' I chatted to him for a while but thought no more about him.

Then Gerry came over, said he liked the act and gave me £6. He offered me the weekly Sunday lunchtime spot, at £6 a time, and I agreed.

After that first time I didn't use drugs again. I didn't need them to give me confidence or make me feel good because I had something much stronger – I had people's laughter, which gave me a more direct hit. With a microphone in my hand I was suddenly important. That was better than any drug.

Five weeks later Gerry also offered me the Saturday and Sunday evening spots for a total weekend wage of £15, an awful lot. When I agreed, he cunningly added a quick rider. 'You'll also have to work behind the bar when you're not performing,' he said.

Trevor reappeared one day, saying he was trying to get me a job at the Montague Arms in Peckham. For donkey's years the Montague Arms had been run by a Yorkshire drummer called Peter Hoyle and a brilliant blind keyboard player, Peter London. The pub had a reputation for very blue comedy and was the starting place for many of today's names, such as Mike Reid and Jimmy Jones. After Oliver Hardy, with his wonderful slow fed-up looks to camera, Jimmy Jones was probably one of my earliest comedy influences. He had perfect timing and, like just a few other stag comics of the time, had mastered a great Chalkie-type voice.

The two Peters used a filthy but popular resident comedian called Mike Kemp, who later devised *Big Break*. But Mike was a bit too blue for the police's liking and they had threatened to arrest the licensees for running an unruly house! So the two Peters reluctantly got rid of Mike and tried me out in his place. I turned up with Trevor, did two spots for them and they offered me Mike's job. Now I was working six nights a week as well as Sunday lunchtime, having Wednesdays off. For this I got £60 a week which, after paying Trevor ten per cent, left me with £54. Not bad!

The work at the Montague Arms wasn't as easy as I'd

expected. If anything it was more scary than working the Black Bull because now I could only do clean gags. Peter Hoyle was still petrified about the risk of losing his licence. He'd even follow me off-stage some nights, really worried, saying things like: 'I think that joke about the Durex was a bit over the top. Best if you drop it from the act.'

But even squeaky clean I did well at the Montague Arms, though I was terribly nervous all the time. I started doing two spots a night and, in between the acts, I got so scared I'd have to go and sit in my Ford Anglia which was parked behind the pub.

One night I couldn't even pluck up the courage to return for the second spot and drove home to hide instead. Trevor 'phoned and said: 'Peter Hoyle's going mental. You've left him high and dry. We've got to go and see him tomorrow.'

We went to see Peter the next day and he took me aside. 'Look, I'd like to have you back and you can come back,' he said. 'But I don't want Trevor involved at all any more. He's not your agent, he's a nothing.'

I agreed to Peter's terms and said goodbye to Trevor. I did another three or four weeks at the Montague Arms and then, incorrectly believing that my apprenticeship was over, cockily walked out on the two Peters.

I had had enough of the Montague Arms but I didn't have any alternative work. I was lost. In desperation I went to see Mum and got her to 'phone pubs and restaurants to try to find me bookings. 'Hello, Astral Entertainments here,' ran her patter. 'I've got a boy on my books and I'm looking for engagements for him.' Half the time, bless her, she'd be trying to book me into a Chinese takeaway!

Then in the newsagent's one morning I discovered a wonderful newspaper called *The Stage*, full of famous people. Listed in the paper were plenty of agents and I rang them all up in turn but they didn't want to know. The next day I got a breakthrough. I rang an agent called Derek Allen, who said he had heard of me and knew I'd done well in the Montague Arms.

'What are you doing Saturday night?' he asked.

'Nothing,' I answered. He booked me to compere a

show with another comic, called Mike O'Mally, and some strippers at Blackheath Rugby Club.

The club was a stone's throw from Holburne Road. I got there on the Saturday and froze in my shoes as I walked through the door. I was all of twenty and about to face an exceedingly drunken rugby mob of 150. Some of the crowd had already seen me work at the Montague Arms, but now I didn't have to be clean so I let rip. I could do what I'd always longed to do – be disgusting and funny at the same time.

The following afternoon Derek Allen telephoned. He'd heard I'd gone down well and gave me a few more bookings, including one in Brighton. Val, one of the strippers at the rugby club night, was also appearing at the Brighton gig and Derek asked me to give her a lift.

I picked her up in my little Ford Anglia from her maisonette at 17 Naylor House, near the Old Kent Road. I drove her to the cabaret and, afterwards, took her home again. I was still going out with Denise at the time but when Val asked if I wanted to go in 'for coffee' I accepted gladly.

Val was about three years older than me, very cute and slightly chunky with short, blonde hair, like a young Mia Farrow. After coffee the obvious took place and afterwards, as she fell asleep in my arms, I thought, Denise is awful, Val is wonderful. I was off again!

In the morning she brought me a cup of tea in bed and I thought I was in paradise. There was no doubting she was a proper grown-up woman. From a failed marriage she had two boys and her last boyfriend had been a black man called George, who'd returned to the Caribbean.

I yearned to get back to the real adult world and to be in a grown-up relationship again. I always longed to be older, I think deep down I was hung up on somehow catching up with my brothers.

Derek Allen booked Val and me to work together on several cabaret shows during the next few weeks and I'd give her a lift to and from work and, when I could, stay over at her place. One night when we got in after working she asked me, casually, if I'd like to move in with her and the boys. It was music to my ears and I hastily accepted in case she changed her mind or the locks (remember Thamesmead?).

We had the top half of the building and the people below us were from Barbados. When our lady neighbour shouted at her kids it was always very lyrical – people from Barbados don't talk, they sing. She probably never realised it, but listening to her scolding her kids helped me come up with several funny voices for the act and helped with my send-up of my black school chum and my Chalkie character.

Val looked after me terribly well. She'd make me endless cups of tea and full English breakfasts or, for lunch, bowls of soup. But she also had a terribly violent temper and could fight like an eight-round preliminary fighter. She had a tendency, on occasions, to get frustrated, then drunk, if I was out on my own. If we worked together she'd accuse me of looking at the other strippers and, when we got home, whack me over the head with a pan. She woke me up one morning by smashing an empty milk bottle over my head.

If she was especially angry I'd hide knives and forks, just in case!

Once she gashed my hand open by hitting me with a full-length mirror. I ran off and hid in the bathroom – until, that is, she kicked the door off its hinges. I ripped the towel rail off the wall and used it, in defence, to hit her on the hand. We both looked like we'd been in a war and I had to drive us to hospital. She had stitches in her hand and I had some in my forehead. Talk about The Odd Couple!

I used to think the violence was madness but that I had to put up with it – like with Mum and Dad, fighting was what adults did.

Once Val frightened me by telling me her flat was haunted. I came to realise that Val was sensitive to unearthly spirits. She said at one time two spinsters had lived there. The youngest had fallen in love with a man who, with the elder sister, had tied her up and starved her to death. Val asked if at night I'd heard the noise of washing being done in the kitchen, when all of us were safely tucked up in bed. I hadn't – until she mentioned it, and then I heard it all the time! I was too scared to explore where the noise was coming from.

One night Val got into bed and told me she'd seen a white crucifix floating over the boys' beds. I never checked that out, either. Val even woke me up, screaming. 'Listen to that!' she said, holding me tight. Someone was banging on our bedroom door as hard as they possibly could. I inched towards the door, terrified and holding my breath. I turned the handle and expected something ghastly to leap at me.

All I could see was our frightened cat, which shot under the bed. I didn't know what or who had been banging so loudly on our door but one thing was certain, there was no way the cat could have done it.

I didn't get back to sleep at all that night. Instead I sat up and drank anything I could find. I convinced myself that, for our own safety, we had to get out of that house. Next morning I ran down to the council offices to demand that we were re-housed.

The woman interviewing me was very stern. She didn't look like she'd ever done many favours. 'We'd like to move, please,' I said.

'Why?' she bellowed. Everyone in the room stopped talking and looked over at us. The prospect, in the silence, of putting into words our spooky little problems suddenly didn't seem such a good idea. On the other hand, ghosts aren't that bad, I thought, and left.

Val and I continued to work together for Derek Allen and I started finding other work on the notoriously blue stag circuit. I called venues listed in *The Stage* and tried forcing myself upon them with varying degrees of success.

One night I went for an audition at the Maybloom Club in Abbey Wood, a smoky pub frequented by plenty of stag comics who loved the great resident comedian, Harry Scott. I was introduced to an agent called Benny Palmer, who used to handle many of the stag comics and was known in the trade as 'The Canceller'. Even Benny's office in Hornchurch, Essex, was known as 'Cancellation House' rather than by its real name, Construction House.

Benny earned his nickname by calling up his long-suffering acts week after week, saying: 'Give me Monday and Tuesday night, and you're also working for me twice on Friday and again on Saturday.' He'd wait a few days then 'phone the acts back to cancel all the bookings.

'What's your name, son?' Benny said to me.

'Jim Davidson,' I replied.

'That's no good,' he said. Then he changed my name without consulting me, introducing me as Jimmy Davies.

It was a tough room to work and the act went down badly. I died on my arse. I came off, feeling very sorry for myself, and Benny practically ignored me. 'Well, keep practising, son,' he said, and I left feeling suicidal.

I found stag work wherever I could and it was while doing the blue nights that I met a man who became a good friend and helped shape my early success – Monty Wells. Monty was about fifty and a clever and inventive comedian. During the day he was a children's clown working for a social services department in south London. At night, in complete contrast, his was the archetypal blue comic.

He had a wonderful end to his stag routine. He'd go into a mime of different people having a piddle to music, using his microphone for a penis. Then he would finish up unable to pee at all because of a slight erection, to the line from the Gilbert O'Sullivan song 'Told you once before and I won't tell you no more, so get down, get down, get down.'

At night, whenever I wasn't working to gain some experience, I started driving Monty to the clubs where he was booked. I liked being with him and I liked listening to as many other comedy acts as I could. I would use any jokes I could pinch from anywhere, just as long as they were funny.

I took Monty to work as a clown once. He was in a classroom making all the children laugh with a puppet show. I watched amazed as he operated the puppets with one hand while, unseen by his young audience, he smoked a cigarette and swigged whisky from his hip-flask with the other. He looked up at me, all rosy cheeks and smiles – a bizarre yet perfect picture of a contented man.

In the summer of 1974 I drove Monty to what, for me, was perhaps his most important gig: Woking Football Club, where a succession of comics had died because the drunken audience was so unrelentingly hostile. Even Monty died when he walked out in front of them. A little later he introduced me to a man standing in the wings, the organiser of the evening, Wally Dent. Wally was a tall man in glasses, suit and tie. Gentle to the point of meekness, he had a very friendly manner.

'Jim's a comic,' said Monty. 'Give him a go. We've all died, what have you got to lose?'

'Well, get out there, son,' said Wally, and I strolled into the spotlight to try to placate the hostile crowd. In no time I had them eating out of my hand. I threw every gag I knew at them and they came round and roared with laughter. I went on to try ten minutes and stayed for an hour and a quarter! As I left the stage, to hearty applause and whistles, Wally gave me a tenner.

'That's all I've got, it's out of my own pocket,' he told me. 'Is there anyone looking after you?'

'My mum,' I said, like a prick.

Afterwards, I drove Monty home and we talked about how much work I was getting and how it was all going. I said I'd picked up quite a few stag nights and that I'd done the act for Benny Palmer once which had gone down like a lead balloon. Monty, encouraging as always, told me not to worry about Benny as I was off to a good start.

I was starting to be in demand on the stag circuit and I won back a regular Sunday lunchtime spot – at Slough Town Football Club. Then I heard from Benny Palmer again. He 'phoned me one evening to say a comic called J.C. Fields had spotted me on the circuit and told him I was good. 'Would you like to come and do a show for me?' he asked.

'You don't remember, do you?' I said. 'I'm the bloke you renamed Jimmy Davies who died a thousand deaths!'

'I don't remember that,' replied Benny. I agreed to try again with a Sunday lunchtime spot in Enfield a few weeks later. It was in front of 700 employees of a firm called Murex. I paralysed the place.

Afterwards, Benny had a smile stretching from ear to ear. 'Jim, are you managed by anyone?' he asked.

'No,' I replied.

'Are you earning £300 a week?' he asked.

'No, I'm certainly not!' I replied, drooling.

'You sign with me and I'll give you £300 a week, put you on *New Faces* and make you a star or my name's not Benny Palmer!' The £300 flashed into my eyes like dollar signs do in cartoons.

'I'll have to ask my mum,' I said, being a prick again! I shook his hand and left.

I rushed home to speak to Mum and Dad about Benny's offer and gabbled on about the £300 a week offer.

'But what about this Wally Dent you also met recently?' asked Mum. Wally had offered to look out for me but hadn't offered me serious money. He didn't have it to offer.

Dad, who could be very wise when he wanted to, suggested my best bet would be to make my manager the man who was honest and didn't promise too much in case he couldn't deliver. I telephoned Wally and told him of Benny's offers, including the £300 a week wage packet.

'Well,' he said calmly. 'I can't promise you that. All I can promise you is my sincerity and my trust.'

I signed with Wally Dent the next morning!

5

Can You Do March 9?

On signing with Wally Dent in 1975 my first gig for him was in Welwyn Garden City and is memorable because it paid £40. I couldn't believe it at the time; this was more than some people took home in a week.

With Wally as my manager I got regular work, mostly stag nights and cabaret spots. But he also got me work in very new territories, such as Northern Ireland. He sent me there on gigs to entertain British soldiers and I was happy to go, not for patriotic reasons but because I got £75 a time. I considered the extra money was certainly worth the risk of entering danger zones.

I also got regular work at a pub in Peckham called the Adam and Eve, which was where I met the man who is undoubtedly the country's best ventriloquist, Roger de Courcey, the vents' vent. Roger worked his unlikely dummy Nookie Bear like magic and was regarded as 'unfollowable' on the stag circuit. He was superb. He often came into the pub at the end of the evening to watch me work but was always difficult to get close to. Moreover, Roger did some work for the dreaded Benny Palmer I'd turned down in favour of Wally.

Roger was always immaculately dressed and confident bordering on the arrogant. He'd keep a wad of banknotes in his pocket like a Lyon's Maid Arctic roll and loved waving it under my envious eyes if he could. 'Want a drink, Jim?'

he'd say when he saw me. 'I've done four tonight for Benny Palmer and, of course, I killed them. 'I must have a fiver here somewhere,' he'd add, peeling off tenners and twenties from the pile to find smaller change.

I decided I'd had enough of Roger rubbing in his success. So I saved all my earnings for about six weeks until I'd amassed enough for a wad big enough to look like a small growth on the side of my leg. For weeks after that I waited for Roger to show up for a drink so I could flash my money under his nose – and he never returned. Bastard!

What with the Adam and Eve and other pubs, as well as the stag circuit, I was earning about £150 a week by now, but I wanted richer pickings, the kind Roger seemed to throw around so easily. I'd got a good reputation as a genuinely funny newcomer but felt real fame and success were passing me by. Towards the end of the year I went to see Wally and pleaded with him to get me a chance to get on television. 'You must get me an audition for *Opportunity Knocks*,' I said. Wally promised he would try, and he succeeded.

The auditions for the Thames TV talent show were being held in Twickenham at the Neller Hall, which in the days of great military bands was where they had all performed. I arrived, a twenty-two-year-old nervous wreck, and looked around.

Sitting behind a large table was the most important man of the show, its host, Hughie Green. He was surrounded by three or four other men but he was the one I couldn't take my eyes off. Seeing Hughie near me, larger than life, made me especially nervous. Then my *bête noir* from the Maybloom Club, Harry Scott, turned up by my side. Harry was also up for the audition, and seeing a friendly face temporarily took my mind off my insecurity. 'Hello,' he said. 'Aren't you Jimmy Davies?'

'Don't you start!' I replied.

Harry was just ahead of me in the auditions and when he was called he gave a faultless performance, finishing spectacularly with a gag which not only got roars of laughter but was also the one I'd planned to close with.

I was devastated. Then, as Harry was whisked away quickly by the director, I was called to go on.

I went out in front of Hughie, his smile stretched across his face, and launched into my funny policeman 'Nick-Nick' routine, reeling off one-liners. After two minutes I had to wrap up but couldn't think of a good gag to finish with. 'I'm sorry,' I said, pathetically. 'I was planning to use the gag Harry just closed with.'

As the words came out I wished the ground would open up and swallow me. I knew I'd blown it. Then Hughie stood up and walked a few paces towards me and stared. I stared back at him, speechless.

'How long have you been doing it, old son?' he asked wickedly.

'A couple of years,' I replied timidly.

'Well, old son, you just go away and practise,' he said. He turned his back on me and ambled back to his seat. I'm sure he wasn't really singling me out to lacerate, but it certainly felt like it.

I went back to Val that evening a broken man. She tried to console me as best she could but nothing could cheer me up. I drank my way through what whisky we had in the flat and slumped into bed, depressed.

I went back to work on the stag circuit but I was feeling disheartened. Still, sweet revenge on Hughie Green was to come along soon enough.

I telephoned Wally and pushed again desperately for him to get me another crack at television. 'Look,' he said. 'I know someone who can maybe get you an audition for *New Faces*.'

New Faces was *Opportunity Knocks'* big rival, made by ATV (now Central Television) up in Birmingham. I rang off hoping he could pull off a second audition. He got me one just 48 hours later and I knew I had to make it work. I thought it was the last chance I'd ever get to make it big time.

The night before the audition, in February 1976, far from calming my nerves, Val was doing just about all she could to shred them. We had a terrible row and the upshot of it was she ripped my Catford-made brown dress suit trousers into ribbons.

Next morning I desperately looked around for something else to wear. I found a pair of white slacks and quickly ironed them as best I could. I wore a white frilly shirt, brown bow-tie, brown shoes and the brown dress jacket. I looked like a Brown Coat, if such a thing existed.

The audition was being held at the Victoria Palace Theatre (another theatre to play a great part in my life when it became home in 1989 to the musical *Buddy*, with one of my sound systems). I got there at 11.00 am, just one of 300 nervous acts pacing the foyer and corridors, each desperately willing the others to do badly.

'Right, on you go,' someone called to me at noon and I walked on to the stage and up to the microphone. The auditorium was dark and empty but for a row of four people sitting in the middle of the stalls.

'Well, it's very nice to be here in London,' I began. 'I have to admit I got a bit lost on the way here. I stopped someone and said, "Can you tell me the way to the Victoria Palace?" ' Then I burst into the funny Jamaican accent, now more finely tuned than ever, thanks to my West Indian neighbour. ' ". . . then you go up de street and around de corner and there it is." '

'I replied: "Thank you, constable!" '

In those days there were hardly any black policemen in the country and from the line of four came uproarious laughter and then a clunk. The producer had found the gag so funny he'd fallen off his chair. Without pausing for him to pick himself up I went on, ending with the 'Nick-Nick' routine and neatly bringing the West Indian back as a running gag.

I'd glided through four minutes of routine and felt sure I must have done reasonably well. I still walked off stage almost paralysed with fear, although I also noticed from the corner of my eye that six or seven cleaners had crept in to the stalls to watch me.

As I waited in the wings a slightly officious, camp little man came over to me. 'The producer would like to know if you always wear these clothes?' he asked.

Fuck, Val's ruined me, I thought. I'd have got the job if she hadn't slashed my trousers last night.

'Well, he wants to see you anyway,' said the little luvvie, pointing to the producer, Les Cox, in the still, darkened auditorium.

I crossed the orchestra walkway and felt my legs start to turn to jelly. Les was a large, plump, silver-haired man in a suit with big, fat fingers clasped around a big, fat cigar.

'I liked your act,' he said, shaking my hand. 'Do you always wear that?'

No! I thought again. They really have got it in for me because of the way I look. Next he'll say 'You were very good, you could have been a star, but Val ripped your trousers so get lost now.'

I looked at him and replied quickly: 'No, no. I've got lots of suits to wear . . .'

Les could see I was squirming and took my hand again to calm me down. 'Can you do March the ninth?' he asked.

Now I looked at him, stunned. He looked bemused and even appeared to be waiting for an answer – as if I'd tell him I was too busy that day to let him change my entire life!

That line from Les was the full orchestra playing the 'Ode to Joy' full pelt. The real break I longed for. I told Les I was definitely free on March 9 and thanked him. I made sure they had Wally's 'phone number and was told to turn up on the appointed day at ATV's studios in Birmingham. Then I ran to the pub opposite the theatre in a trance and 'phoned Mum.

'I've done it!' I said, then broke down crying. I thought I'd have to tell the pub my cat had died there! I had a quick pint then jumped in the car and drove back to Naylor House to celebrate with Val. I knew then I'd made it. All I wanted was this one chance and I'd got it.

Just after the audition I was doing a double for Wally – a stag spot at Woking Football Club followed by a gig for the staff of Debenham's in Guildford.

When I finished the stag routine, Wally introduced me to an ATV casting director called Alec Fyne who, unbeknown to me, had been at the audition, and an agent called Laurie

Mansfield, from International Artistes. He handled some of the biggest entertainment names of the day, including Cleo Laine, John Dankworth and Peters and Lee. Apparently, after the audition Laurie had been 'phoned by Les Cox and Alec. Both enthused that they'd 'just seen the next Jimmy Tarbuck' and both urged him to quickly sign me up before my TV debut.

Many years later, Laurie confided in me that as soon as he saw me work the Woking audience that night the hairs stood up on the back of his neck and he knew he had to do a deal. Before I'd even finished the spot Laurie and Wally, surrounded by half-naked strippers in the wings at the football club, had agreed a deal. Wally remained my manager but Laurie would come in as agent. I was all Gary Linekered up!

When I met Laurie that night he was very enthusiastic and promised the deal was in my best interests. Then Alec Fyne left and Laurie came with me and Wally to the next gig, for Debenham's.

Only Wally came with me when I went up to Birmingham to do *New Faces*. It was being recorded at ATV on a Tuesday, for transmission as if live the following Saturday. The two of us arrived on the Monday night and met singer Rose-Marie, who Wally also managed and who was also on the show.

Wally really cocked things up. Even though we had a big day ahead of us he booked us into really cheap digs, the alcohol-free Compton Hotel in the centre of Birmingham. We were all nervous and all needed a drink, but the hotel was run by Methodists and was completely dry. Not quite what Rose-Marie and I needed before a terrifying first time in front of television cameras!

So we went out for a drink in a pub. When it closed we bought up all the miniatures we could afford and sneaked past the porter to our rooms to drink on.

The night before the show I felt sure I'd win. I knew it was all a big deal now but I wasn't really frightened, not until I got to the studio the next morning. The first news to greet me on arrival was that Les Cox, the producer and my fan from the audition, had left the show and another man, Albert Stephenson, had taken his place.

The next blow was identifying my main competition, a three-piece group called Canned Rock. I was sitting in the auditorium as they rehearsed their number for the cameras. They performed 'Bohemian Rhapsody' brilliantly and their version was easily as good as Queen's. I was convinced I'd met my match and the new producer came up and quietly sat next to me. 'They're good,' he said, 'but I've heard you're better.'

Then he slipped away. I tried to believe him but Canned Rock still had me very worried.

After I'd rehearsed my spot, the rest of the day was spent hanging around with Rose-Marie until the show got underway at 7.00 pm. I couldn't eat anything before the recording started – I was frightened I'd bring it all back up.

At last the show began. I was on third but Canned Rock weren't on until last. Rose-Marie went on ahead of me and was slagged off badly by panellist Lionel Blair for, as much as anything, wearing dreadful clothes. As he tore into her I realised that all this was for real.

When I went on, in my invisibly repaired brown dress suit, I was fired up by adrenalin and on a roll, shooting off the routine perfectly, if not a little too speedily. It ran for two minutes and forty seconds – fifty seconds shorter than it should have been.

When I stood for the panel's verdict my heart was almost coming out of my dress jacket. They liked me, but Canned Rock were still to perform and, when they did, were note-perfect.

As well as Lionel Blair, also on the panel were Alan Freeman, Arthur Askey and Martin Jackson. At the end of the show all of the artistes were gathered in front of the cameras for the voting. First the panel gave marks out of ten for entertainment value and content, then star quality. As the votes were cast it soon became clear that Canned Rock and I were running neck and neck for first place.

For entertainment value and content Canned Rock and I

both got straight tens. For star quality I got 10, 9, 10, 10 and Canned Rock got three tens on the trot. Only Arthur Askey was left to vote for them and I felt sure I'd lost. He quickly glanced up at the scoreboard, did his maths and gave Canned Rock eight. He swung it for me to win by just one point! I was totally euphoric.

After the recording finished I went straight down to the payphone near the dressing-rooms to ring Mum. Teasing her, I sounded very sorry for myself: 'Mum, it's Cameron.'

'Never mind, love,' she said. 'There'll be other times. You know you've done well. You know you're good.'

Then I whispered: 'I've won it, Mum!'

After that I got drunk with Wally and tried to give Rose-Marie one while her husband wasn't looking. No chance, he had eyes like a Dogger Bank cod!

That Saturday I watched *New Faces* at Naylor House surrounded by all my friends. Val's kids went into a state of semi-shock when they saw me, their surrogate dad, on the screen. And as soon as the credits rolled the 'phone began to ring and the fun and games started. The first call was from a man called Gill Lucas.

'I'm Gill Lucas from The McGill Five,' he said. 'I book the pubs for Kenny Scott, the Dun Cow and the Green Man, can we book you?'

'Yeah!' I replied.

'Right, it's £75 for a Sunday lunchtime. I'll put you down for some.'

Later that night I was working at a club for Wally at the old price of £35. I noticed the different reception I got at once. Because most of the audience had seen me earlier on the box I was suddenly a star to them. And for £35 the club got itself a real bargain. Mind you, I've been out for a lot less since – but they're called charity shows.

The following week I was booked to do my own regular spot at the Dun Cow pub in the Old Kent Road. But it wasn't only the work which started rolling in after that one television appearance. Suddenly girls who until then would never have even talked to me started queuing up outside the dressing-room to give me a blow job! They always said the same thing: 'I'm not just doing this 'cos you're famous.'

And I always answered: 'Of course not, my dear!'

When I returned to Birmingham for the next *New Faces* both Wally and Laurie came with me – and this time we stayed in a decent hotel. I won the show by a mile the next day. The maximum mark available was 120 and I scored highest with 117.

We arrived at the studios for the rehearsals and found out that the judges were Mickey Most, Jack Parnell, Jess Yates (Paula's dad) and Danny La Rue. When Danny whisked in for the run-through – he never walked anywhere, he always whisked – he stopped the show. He oozed star quality. To me he was one of the biggest talents Britain had ever produced and I was totally in awe of him, and I still am.

Danny always acts like a star and usually behaves impeccably although, admittedly, he can be rude. But that's a failing of all of us. We all tend to take it out on those closest to us, our families or our employees. Danny confided in me much later that after my rehearsal he had said to the director, 'This Jim Davidson is fantastic! Fantastic! I'm going to give him 100 marks.'

'Don't give him 100, Danny,' the director told him. 'Give him 99 or 98 or something like that.'

'How dare you!' Danny had snapped back. 'I'll give him a hundred and fucking twenty if I want!'

During the rehearsals some of the other comics had spiced up their acts with really blue gags but I hadn't. When we were all getting ready just before the show started a message came around to all of us forbidding anyone to 'go blue' in the recording. I went on and did my spot, the West Indian/Chalkie gags and Nick, Nick routine. It went quickly and seemed fairly slick.

Then it was time for the panel to give their verdicts. The comments couldn't have been nicer. Jack Parnell said something upbeat then handed over to Jess Yates, who said something I've dreamed since that moment will come true. He said: 'I've been in the business forty years and I guarantee this young man will be in the business forty years.'

'Yeah, I liked him,' added Mickey Most. 'I'd prefer not to hear the Irish jokes because we hear so many of them but, yeah, good.'

'I love the running gag you just did,' enthused Danny. 'The "Ooh-Ooh" stuff is just great . . .'

'That's "Nick-Nick" Danny,' said Jack Parnell, correcting him.

'Yes, "Nick-Nick",' said Danny. 'And let's hope he doesn't get Nick-Nicked!' I was though, many times!

I spent the rest of the show waiting in the green room. Then we were all herded together at the side of the studio as Derek Hobson turned to the panel for their votes, Danny's last. 'And votes please, Danny La Rue,' said Derek.

He dished out marks in the eighties and nineties for the others then looked up at the gallery where the director was sitting.

'. . . and Jim Davidson 100!' he said. It was the glance to the gallery which spoke volumes. It was Danny's way of showing who was in charge, his way of saying 'Don't tell me how many marks I can give out. I'm a star. I've got twenty-seven years of feathers up my arse!'

I think what he really wanted to do was give me 99 in the show and one in the dressing-room later. Only joking, Danny! Take away all the feathers and deep down you're left with 'Danny Boy' – a bloke, and a great bloke at that.

After the show I was unstoppable. Laurie was anxious to shake off any conceptions in the industry that I was just another blue stag act. He wanted to establish me in mainstream entertainment, lining up TV guest spots, summer seasons and winter pantomime runs. He assured me I was destined to be a big star and that he'd help me get there sooner and stay there for longer; the only person who could fuck it up was me. Charming! He also tried teaching me to be patient, but he never succeeded on that point – I always want everything yesterday.

Perhaps one of the most important things Laurie taught me in those early days was that to be a big star making a lot of money I had to be prepared for others to also make money out of me. That was how show-business survived. No one wanted mean celebrities; sooner or later their selfishness was their downfall.

After several guest spots on TV shows, the first big break Laurie got me was at Thames Television with a producer called Mark Stuart, who had many successful shows to his credit, such as *Please Sir!* and *The Benny Hill Show*. He soon became my sort of guardian angel and the one man in the business whose views I respected more than any other. Mark was putting together a weekly forty-five-minute quick-fire *Rowan and Martin*-style revue show called *What's On Next?*. I went along with Laurie for a meeting with Mark. Later he told Laurie he thought I was a story-telling comic who wouldn't be any good at acting out one-liners in the show. Laurie quickly took Mark out for lunch, convinced him otherwise and I was signed for my first television series.

The *What's On Next?* team were an eccentric bunch to be around. I was very much the junior alongside Bob Todd, Barry Cryer, William Franklyn, Anna Dawson, Hinge and Bracket, Sandra Dickinson and Pam Ayres. The funniest among us had to be the late, great Bob Todd. He was in his mid-fifties, overweight, balding and with baggy eyes. He was actually a farmer who had started in the business quite by chance after turning up in London to look for work. He was so inherently hysterical he landed a never-ending succession of acting jobs.

Bob was just brilliant to work with and one of the kindest gentlemen you could ever meet. He knew all there was to know about comedy and taught me how to mimic cartoon movements and timing. But Bob's real speciality was playing a drunk, a part he spent a lifetime researching. There was never any point in asking whether Bob was pissed, you knew he always was. But the drink didn't make a jot of difference to his work because he was naturally funny. Plucky, too. When we were out filming Bob would always offer Mark undying devotion.

'If you want me to, I'll jump off that bridge for you or climb the outside of that building,' he'd tell Mark, waving his arms in all directions. Bob had a bit of Charlie Drake in him – he liked to do his own stunts if he could no matter what the risks were.

Mark often lost patience with Bob because he was often impossible to work with, making everyone laugh so much that no one got any work done. If we were in a pub Bob couldn't resist playing jokes. He perfected two. In the first he used a blast from a soda siphon to mimic sicking into an ashtray or on to a carpet to get people leaping from their seats in disgust. The second was equally funny – and equally disgusting. He'd put a cockle up his nose and leave the yellow bit sticking out of a nostril. Then he'd walk up to the bar and wait. Sooner or later someone would come along who couldn't resist pointing out that Bob had something up his nose. 'Oh, thank you so much,' he'd say, pulling it out of his nostril and eating it!

Bob drank all the time but never had a penny to his name. He tried borrowing money from anyone and everyone. He'd walk up to people with an old, dirty cheque made out to his wife, Monica, for £50. 'You couldn't possibly cash this for me, could you?' he'd ask in a terribly polite voice.

'I'm afraid I couldn't,' came the usual reply.

'Well, do me a favour,' Bob would respond. 'Iron the fucking thing for me, will you?'

The others in the show also made me feel very welcome. Some, like William Franklyn, gave me crash courses in television and camera techniques. Barry Cryer became a good mate on the series but I could never feel completely at ease in his company. I think that was because as well as appearing in the show he was also one of its writers, and had the inherent quality most writers have of dreadful self-doubt bordering on over-protection of their work. I've often found writers difficult because they're as insecure as performers. In rehearsals, as you read their lines they mouth them with you and if you point something out as not being very funny they're mortified and retreat back to their shells – or to the whisky bottles. Barry was a good comic as well, so I suppose he had the best – or worst – of both worlds.

Hinge and Bracket were very nice but they kept themselves to themselves. Pam Ayres was sweet. We were all amazed that she was even in show-business, but frankly, so was she. She did have terrific timing and various cute expressions. Barry said she was Benny Hill in drag because she had his talent for looking both innocent and guilty at the same time.

Anna Dawson was a great professional but one afternoon, during rehearsals, she threw a real wobbler with Mark. It was the first time I'd ever seen anyone raise their voice to him and he dealt with it very calmly. We'd all been working long and hard to get the week's show right when Anna cracked. 'Mark, why are you doing this to us?' she pleaded with him, bursting into tears. 'We're really trying our best and you're killing us.'

'Go outside and come back when you've stopped crying,' he said. Anna left for a few minutes, to calm down, then came back in and apologised to Mark. 'Good, let's carry on,' he replied. Mark really was a quality director.

I turned up late for a rehearsal with him once and nearly burst into tears because I'd let him down. I'd been in Hereford the night before and hadn't left until dawn, planning to get back to London in good time for rehearsals at 10.00 am.

But the car broke down on the way back and I turned up two hours late. As I walked into the rehearsal room Mark shot me a glance which could have killed me and I was never late for him again.

Everyone in the show wished me luck when I went off to Birmingham that July to take part in my third and last *New Faces*, the winners' gala final. This time I was much more confident than before but somehow I knew I wouldn't win. Roger de Courcey was also in the show and I knew he'd be tough to beat. Moreover, the winner of the show was to pick up a trip to appear in Las Vegas. It was obvious to me that my Nick-Nick routine wasn't the stuff of Las Vegas cabaret but Roger and his beloved Nookie Bear were. Everyone believed Roger would win.

I remember arriving at the rehearsals in the afternoon and finding out that on the panel was Tony Hatch, who could lash some acts if he didn't like them, and Bernie Rothkopf, the executive director of a big Las Vegas hotel.

I immediately struck up a friendship with a Geordie comic in his late forties called Johnny Hammond. Johnny was different from the rest of us; he wasn't at all anxious about anything. He'd been in the business thirty years and didn't seem to have a care in the world. I still felt nervous but I also felt myself caring slightly less about winning. It didn't seem as important now that my career had already taken off at full speed.

At lunchtime I went off to a pub with Johnny for a few beers during which we plotted pranks against Roger. We decided to safety-pin Nookie's mouth closed so that when Roger brought him out of the box during the rehearsal he'd be stumped. Touching a vent's props is one of the worst things you can do to them and I was so scared of Roger that we didn't do it in the end.

With an hour to go before the recording, I told Johnny I was still feeling anxious. He told me to go to hospitality to get myself a whisky. When I got back to the studio he said: 'Did you have that brandy?'

'Brandy?' I asked. 'No. You told me to have a whisky.'

'No. Not whisky,' he said. 'That makes you worse. Go and have a brandy.'

So I went back to the bar, downed a brandy and found Johnny again back in the studio. 'Did you have that gin and tonic?' he asked.

'Gin and tonic?' I said. 'No. I had a brandy like you told me.'

'Brandy?' he said. 'No, not brandy. That makes you worse. Have a gin and tonic.'

Off I went again and it dawned on me just what was going on. Johnny was trying to get me pissed to improve his chances in the show. The rotter!

When the show was up and running Johnny was on ahead of me. He brought the house down with a lampoon of the Telly Savalas hit 'If', called 'If in F'. He sang the song, adding an imaginary echo, 'If, if, if a picture, picture, picture . . .', etc., etc., etc. Johnny was so original he deserved to win in many ways, but we all knew that the time wasn't right for a man so late in his career to scoop *New Faces*.

When Roger went on with Nookie he stole the show. The audience loved him. I went on second from last and did well, but I knew I hadn't done well enough. Roger came first and, thanks to Tony Hatch giving me his highest vote, I came second.

After the show we all went to eat together in a local restaurant. The wine flowed and we all relaxed. Roger got up to go to the lavatory and, while he was out of the room, the director stood up to make a speech thanking everyone for their hard work. When Roger came back to the table, the producer handed him a bronze statue of the show's mascot, the little busker with his star-shaped guitar, as a souvenir of the show.

Roger remained standing and launched into a big speech of how he'd worked hard all his life and how wonderful it was to win the show. Then he rambled on about what a great honour it was for him to be given the statue which would always take pride of place in his home.

'Sit down, you cunt!' someone shouted. 'They're all getting one!'

As my big year ended Tommy Scott, the brother of my close friend Kenny, died. He'd been diagnosed with leukaemia, treated and given the all-clear. When he got out of hospital we had a party for him to celebrate. Two weeks later he was dead.

The doctor who had treated him approached me to help form a new charity, in Tommy's memory, and I agreed. We called it ELF, the Elimination of Leukaemia Fund, and it had the express intention of paying for the actual treatment of leukaemia sufferers, rather than raising money for research into the disease.

Humphry Berkeley, who had been Conservative MP for Lancaster in the sixties, became the director of the charity. He's one of those blokes who you can listen to forever – and invariably have to! To overcome a few early hiccups we reformed the charity, naming it after a little girl called Sharon Allen who had leukaemia. She was only a tot when I first met her and had just been through gruelling treatment. She didn't have any hair but she did have bags of courage.

The Sharon Allen Leukaemia Trust's namesake has been in a period of remission for several years now and we're all delighted. Today she has grown into a young lady.

I'm founder life president of the trust and Princess Michael of Kent is our patron. With Humphry's help we've built up an impressive list of vice-patrons, including Baroness Falkender (Harold Wilson's former secretary), Sir John Gielgud, Sir Alec Guinness and Lady Wilson of Rievaulx. Lord Olivier was also a vice-patron and, when he died, his wife, Lady Olivier, took his place. Two more recent vice-patrons are Jim Bowen and Laurie Mansfield.

Over the years we've staged many shows and fund-raising events around the country and paid for the treatment of patients and vital hospital equipment. Our proudest moment was years later, in 1989, when we helped open a new leukaemia unit at Charing Cross Hospital in London.

On Christmas Eve 1976, I opened very much the new boy in my first-ever pantomime, *Jack and the Beanstalk*, directed by Alan Curtis, at the Alexandra Theatre in Birmingham. I was playing Idle Jack, dolled up as a Bay City Roller, alongside Frank Ifield and Patrick Cargill, who was playing the dame. Also on the bill were a singing cabaret act called The Cox and Webb Twins, two sets of twins married to one another.

I got on very well with Frank and came to like him a lot. I think he's a great performer and he taught me a make-up rule I've always followed: it's just as important to make up the backs of the hands as the face.

Patrick Cargill wasn't so easy to get on with. He was a very plummy actor and, thanks to the success of *Father, Dear Father*, a very bankable name who had to be revered. Patrick had thinning hair but even this was in fact an extremely expensive toupée. For the panto he had to take off the hairpiece in order to get on the various dame's wigs. And every night he'd make his entrance by roller-skating on-stage, stopped by me rolling a barrel underneath him.

One night I missed him completely and he didn't stop. His dame's wig fell off to reveal his complete baldness to the entire audience. For days after that he wouldn't speak to me – well, only if it was scripted!

Revealing Patrick's bald pate was the least of my problems during that panto run. I came a real cropper myself on-stage up a ladder about three weeks into the run. I'd got to know the stage crew really well by then and, that night, like every night, I had to leave the stage and return a few minutes later with a clothes-horse complete with clothes. While I was off the four twins did a bit of the business on-stage and I was meant to come back on with the props and climb up the ladder.

I left the stage to fetch the rail from the wings. The trusty crew were sitting around playing cards and I couldn't see the rail so I asked where it was. No one looked up from the card game. 'Oh, it's over there Jim,' said one. 'Get it yourself, will you, I've got a good hand here.'

I needed to break wind and thought I'd do it into their card game, for a laugh. I started then followed through with the most disastrous results. I felt the back of my trousers and there was a yucky, damp stain about four inches in diameter. Before I had the opportunity to do anything, I got my cue to return to the stage.

'Idle Jim? Idle Jim?' came the call from the stage.

'Idle Jim's shit himself!' I thought, grabbing the prop and running back on. I couldn't let the audience see what I'd done to my costume so, when I had to climb the ladder, I tried doing it backwards. It was a struggle getting up the steps and when I looked into the wings I could see the entire company looking at me in disbelief and wetting themselves with glee.

When I eventually left the stage, which felt like hours later, I was the butt of everyone's jokes. I was so embarrassed by what had happened I couldn't even face the wardrobe mistress with the stained trousers. Instead, after the show I smuggled them out in a duffel bag and threw them out of the car window on the way home. They are probably still rotting in a ditch now next to Birmingham's Spaghetti Junction.

The next day I went to the wardrobe mistress and told

her the costume had been stolen. Fortunately, she must have been the only member of the company who hadn't watched me from the wings, and she believed me.

That Christmas I got my first taste of adults-only panto-mime when we staged a charity midnight matinee. Director Alan Curtis was the driving force behind the idea and he also got along Eric Morecambe and Danny La Rue, who was appearing in the Night Out in Birmingham.

The show struck me as being an ingenious formula for laughs. We kept fairly closely to the script but, being late at night and with only adults in the audience, it was four times as funny. It gave me the idea for *Sinderella*, which finally got its first run in Ipswich seventeen years later. Thanks, Alan!

6

Get Yourself Some Class

In February 1977, towards the end of *Jack and the Beanstalk*, I noticed a poster for a club in Birmingham called the Dolce Vita. Appearing for a few days was none other than Johnny Hammond, my mate from the *New Faces* winners' gala show. I caught his act one night and he had me in stitches. The act was unbelievable: he'd play a dreadfully out-of-tune piano with perfect comic timing. Afterwards I saw him and promised I'd be back to support him the next night.

I got everyone from the panto to come along the following evening to see Johnny's act, including Frank, Patrick and all the dancers. We took over a couple of tables and Johnny came out beforehand to meet the gang. As I was introducing him to everyone he broke into a sweat and had palpitations. I quickly sat him down and when the manager came over told him Johnny wasn't well enough to perform.

So I got up in his place and did the spot. Afterwards the manager tried to pay me and I told him to give the money to Johnny. We thought Johnny might have been having a heart attack but it turned out to be a panic attack. It was the first time I'd ever seen one, although I've had a few in my time since, mostly at altars!

Johnny and I have remained good friends since that day. He wrote to me once, saying: 'This is not a begging letter but give me some money for fuck's sake or give me one of your PA systems or give me a job. Do you want any writers? Do you know anyone who wants a really funny comic?'

The final line was the best. He wrote: 'Fucking hell, I can't even write a begg . . .' just as the biro ran out of ink.

When the panto run ran out, my next job was a week-long tour in the early spring for Birmingham's Bernard Parr Agency. It was to be a wholly misnamed 'Midlands' tour, taking in Birmingham, Southampton, Aberystwyth, West Ham, Kidderminster, Luton and Hereford! Also playing the gig were Wout Steinhouse, a lovely Dutch guitarist, and an all-girl singing group called The Kaye Sisters. I fell madly in love with the youngest of the sisters, Jilly.

On the first night in Birmingham one of the partners of the agency turned up and introduced himself. His name was Clive Brandy and he became one of the biggest wayward influences in my life. Clive was a large man with square features and the spitting image of Jack Hawkins. He looked and behaved like a millionaire but he never had a tanner to his name. He was perhaps the rudest man I've ever known but he did like a laugh, even if it meant having to go completely over the top.

Clive had worked in Australia, where he'd tried his luck as a comic before successfully turning manager for British singer David Whitfield. It was while Clive was in Australia that he earned his name by drinking so much brandy. That night after the gig I knocked back the brandies while, ironically, Clive demolished endless vodka and lemonades. He told me that in the days when he was the turn he'd received a call from Wallamaloo Rugby Club. 'Are you the pommie comic?' the club secretary asked him.

'I am indeed,' he replied, and was promptly booked to appear that Saturday.

Clive flew up from Sydney in a little plane to Wallamaloo and was met by the club secretary, who drove him to a tiny building. 'It's very small in here,' said Clive, puzzled.

'No! No!' said the secretary. 'You don't do it here, this is where you come for your bit of tucker afterwards. We'll take you up to the gig now. Have you got a coat?'

'Yes,' answered Clive.

'Put it on, son,' he said. 'It's a bit cold where we're going.'

Clive was driven through the darkness to a vast field with hundreds of cars parked in it. They pulled up at one end next to a caravan sliced in two lengthways – the stage. An old-fashioned microphone was strung up above it and a couple of small lights pointed at it. 'What's this?' asked a horrified Clive.

'The latest thing,' he said, 'Drive-in-comedy! They listen to you on little speakers in their cars.' Without further ado the secretary got out of the car, walked up to the microphone and introduced Clive.

'Ladies and gentlemen, Clive Brandy – The Pommie Comic!' he said into the darkness. Silence.

Clive took the stage and nervously cracked his first joke. Nothing. He couldn't hear himself on any speakers and he certainly couldn't hear any response from his audience. He was looking out to an icy stare of blank windscreens.

With no applause or giggles to slow things down, Clive got through his forty-minute act in half the time and left the stage with no idea of how well he'd gone down. Then all the cars started flashing their lights.

'You've killed them,' said the surprised secretary. 'Get back on, look at those lights!'

Clive did a ten-minute encore and left the stage again. The car lights flashed and horns sounded.

'Strewth,' the secretary told him. 'That's a standing ovation. I've never had anything like it, son. You've killed 'em! I've had flashing lights before but never bibbing!'

Clive had a gift for talking his way out of situations. When we got to Aberystwyth he went to take a shower backstage in the club. The club organist, Billy, was also in the communal showers and whereas he was extremely well endowed, poor Clive wasn't. 'Fucking hell, Clive!' Billy said, 'Who do you satisfy with that?'

'Me!' said Clive.

During that tour I became very fond of Jilly indeed. In Wales we all stayed at a country club in acres of its own beautiful grounds, including a lake. After the show we all went back to the hotel for drinks then turned in. But when I got back to my bedroom I didn't want the night to end, so I climbed out of the window and slid down the drainpipe to Jilly's room and asked her to come for a walk.

We ambled romantically arm-in-arm around the lake and grounds and stayed out until dawn. After that we cuddled all the time but were never rude. Shame!

At Hereford we played the Labour Club. After the show Clive and I got very drunk. The others all left and soon we were the last two there with the resident steward, who didn't hide his annoyance at having to serve us so late. By about six in the morning he was furious and started hurling obscenities at us. We listened for a few minutes then Clive staggered to his feet.

'You're fired!' Clive told him. 'We've had quite enough of your rudeness, you're sacked and that's the end of it!'

'That's the best fucking news I've heard!' replied the steward angrily, throwing the keys at us and storming out.

'We've gone a bit over the top, Clive,' I said.

'No, fuck it!' said Clive. So we continued drinking, going behind the bar to help ourselves and conscientiously keeping a list of what we were taking.

We stayed up drinking until about 9.00 am, when the club secretary arrived.

'Look, it got a bit out of control here last night,' started Clive. 'The steward was very rude . . .'

'What time was this?' he asked.

'I don't know, I wasn't watching the time,' said Clive.

'What happened?' asked the secretary.

'Well, I've sacked him!' answered Clive. 'He threw the keys at me and I've locked up to the best of my ability. But I didn't know how to set the alarm so we've had to stand here drinking all night to protect the place!'

Far from being furious, the secretary thanked us. Apparently they'd been trying to sack the steward for months and our binge had done the trick.

Next Clive and I had to drive to West Ham, in east London. The final night of the tour had been cancelled and Clive moaned about it on the way. So I came up with an idea I thought might please him. 'I've always been really big at Slough Town Football Club,' I told him. 'I used to play it a lot on the stag circuit, even did a weekly Sunday spot for them. They'll take me at short notice.'

'Great idea!' said Clive. He rang the club steward and offered them me for two days later at a price they really couldn't refuse.

We wondered what sort of business the club could drum up in two days and, as we pulled up, Clive looked around gleefully. The car park was jam-packed. 'I can't believe it!' said Clive. 'For the first time in my life I've taken a gamble and it's paid off! I've never seen so many cars – we've made it!'

Then a whistle went and the car park emptied as everyone buggered off home after a match. I went on that night to a lousy thirty people!

Clive turned up a few weeks later, when I was working back in Birmingham. He found me tinkering about with my car at the back of the hotel. He'd driven up from Southampton and looked very worried. He was having dreadful problems with a Norman Wisdom tour which was losing money hand over fist and no one had been paid for weeks. Clive had remortgaged his house in Southampton to keep the show on the road and stood to lose the lot.

I had my head under the car bonnet of my battered Triumph 1100 and he immediately took charge of the situation. He looked under the bonnet and started tinkering himself. I sounded the horn in fun. He banged his head and I've always remembered the look he gave me then. It was just like Oliver Hardy's most fed-up look to camera.

'You've got to get rid of this filthy thing, Davidson!' he told me. 'You're meant to be a bloody star now, you can't go around in this crap. Get rid of it and get yourself a Rolls-Royce!

'And while you're at it, get yourself some class. You can't drink shit like Veuve de Vernay any more – that's only for council-house weddings. Drink sodding champagne from now on!' he said. A seed was planted . . .

Later that night he came back to the hotel. Ordering drink

after drink on my tab, Clive explained how desperate he was for money. He stayed over and next day walked into the dining-room while I was having lunch.

'What's that you're eating?' he growled.

'Gammon,' I explained. 'Gammon steak.'

Without saying another word he grabbed my plate between his huge, podgy fingers and walked away with it to the waitress. 'What's that?' he snapped at her.

In broad Brummie, she replied: 'That's gammon steak, that is.'

'That's not gammon!' he countered. 'That's a filthy piece of burned bacon.'

'Well, it's not my fault.'

'Isn't it really?' he said. 'Well, whose fault is it? I didn't bring it in myself. You served it up! And it's very cold in here,' he added.

'Yes, all the staff are cold as well,' she spluttered.

'I'm not concerned with your problems!' he said rudely. 'Get Mr Davidson a real gammon steak and either get the heating put on or bring me an army blanket!'

That night after the show Clive and I went back to the hotel for late-night drinks and in came two on-duty uniformed policemen with a dim, rookie cop. I knew one of them and all two and a half joined us at the bar for a drink.

Then Clive left the room and came back and said that there was an inspector outside. The two full-grown policemen fled out of the room to hide but the young rookie didn't move, instead he pointlessly froze to the spot in front of the bar and put his helmet over his number, as if that would have protected him if there had really been an inspector about, which of course there wasn't.

He ran off and Clive and I found two policemen's helmets, belonging to the others. We stripped the badges off, then placed the two bald, felt hats on the bar and fell giggling into the casino across the road. Clive borrowed £70 from me and made straight for a roulette table.

'Always have a bet on Twenty Black,' he whispered to

me. 'Bet on the other numbers, too, but make sure Twenty Black is always covered.'

And with that he proceeded to win a fortune. After a good number of small wins he plonked the lot on Twenty Black and up it came. As the piles of chips were pushed his way I kept grabbing handfuls to get them cashed. When I'd cashed the last one, I pulled Clive away from the table and, just as we were leaving, the two policemen came in – wearing bald, felt hats like pantomime cops! They were all soft at the edges. We gave them back their badges and they were great sports about our prank.

When Clive and I got back to the hotel we counted his winnings. There was over £4,000. The next morning he drove back to Southampton, paid Norman and everyone else in the tour and cleared the second mortgage!

I was working with Mark Stuart at Thames Television again on a second series of *What's On Next?*. He took me aside on the first day and said: 'Jim, you're a very clever lad and you should have your own television series. But I don't think you've got enough switch-on power yet so we'll do another series of *What's On Next?* and then talk about it again.'

Starting work on the new series, Bob Todd was just as delightful. One day after rehearsals he took Barry and me with him to a drinking club in the West End called Marie Lloyd's. Toddy introduced us to all the locals, who were at varying levels of consciousness. They reminded me very much of politicians and judges.

The three of us left the club having had a skinful and decided to crash the never-ending queues, stretching from Leicester Square to Portsmouth, for the year's box-office hit, *Close Encounters of the Third Kind*.

As we got nearer the cinema, everyone stared at us. They all knew who we were and Barry and I shot each other a nervous glance which said, Oh shit, now what are we going to do? But Bob had it all planned.

'Hold this,' he said to me, giving me his jacket. Then he strode past all the patient punters, into the foyer and up to the duty manager.

'Is the manager here?' said Bob. 'Bob Todd, from Thames Television. Our tickets please – Davidson, Cryer and Todd.'

'Please come this way,' said the duty manager, doubling the bluff without hesitating and handing us complimentary tickets.

Now Bob was stumped, he'd been geared up to create a bit of a scene to get the tickets. So, not to be deprived of his fun, he went into his fake fit routine.

Bob threw fake fits for his own amusement as much as for anyone else's. He coughed and spluttered, went red in the face then heralded the end of the fit with his favourite, wonderfully metallic sound-effect: 'Phedang!'

Bob had got us in, but his 'Phedang!' almost got us thrown back out. It was a blatantly silly noise which easily gave his fraudulent fit away. Barry and I gathered him up, thanked the duty manager and quickly took our seats before he could ask for the tickets back!

Bob was just as impossible when we were in the TV studio. He was the worst straight man in the world because he laughed all the time. In some of the skits it nearly hurt to feel him concentrating so hard on not laughing. He'd stare blankly ahead, trying to throttle any hint of a smirk. There was one sketch Barry, Bob and I tried to do many times and each time was a disaster. We'd stand before the audience pretending to be in a shop, in which Bob was a customer trying to buy a solitary sock.

'I'd like to buy a sock, please,' Bob would slur.

'A pair of socks, sir?' I'd politely inquire.

'No, one sock,' replied Bob. 'Have you got a customer with a wooden leg?'

'Yes but . . .' started Barry.

'Well, he only needs one sock and I want to buy the other, please,' Bob went on. And so did the sketch – or so it was meant to. He never actually got much further than that because by then all three of us were in tears.

Another time Bob tried it in a French accent and it made it even worse. 'Ello, I'd lak to buy a suck, pleeze . . .' he started. We crumpled. We were on our knees, crying uncontrollably, until Mark stormed down from the gallery to tell us off. Then we laughed even more. It got to the point that the mere mention of the word 'suck' could send us into hysterics – and Bob back into a fake fit.

In the end Mark had to concede defeat to Bob in that sketch and it was scrapped. I'm sure if Mark hadn't given in we'd still be trying to get it right for him now!

In July 1977 I opened in my first summer season, four months at the North Pier in Blackpool in a variety show with Little and Large, Frank Carson and Norman Collier. I had the worst spot you can have if you're a comic – opening the second half of the show. The audience always drifts back late after the interval and takes ages to settle down. If they don't take to you, they talk all through your act.

It wasn't only the spot that didn't do me any favours. The audiences didn't like me. I was too cocky, too clever by half for them. Some nights I could actually feel their hostility towards me.

I rented a house up there opposite the Central Pier and moved up Val and the boys to be with me, but it wasn't very comfortable. The northern way of life grated on me all the time. I started spending most of my spare time hanging around with the show's musicians. I could relate to them, because they were just as bored as me. We formed a drinking club and would tour the pubs in Blackpool trying to out-drink each other and win a little £2 cup. A mundane existence, to say the least!

Although Val and the kids were with me I still missed London and got homesick for my mates at the Dun Cow.

So for six Sundays on the trot I chartered a little plane to fly me back to London so that I could do a quick spot at the Cow and then fly back. On the last visit I bumped into a little guy called Kevin, who promised to visit me up in Blackpool.

Kevin duly turned up and came out drinking with me for several nights running. Then I asked him to stay on and work for me as my roadie and driver and he agreed. Now, when I drank too much after the show, Kevin was there to keep an eye on me and get me home safely – no matter how far I was from home.

During the summer season I had to appear on the Isle of Man for the very first time and flew over from Blackpool, having downed several large drinks to pluck up enough courage for the trip in the tiniest of planes.

I did the show over there and afterwards went back to my room at the Casino Palace. A useless Welsh comic was appearing at a function there and I was greeted with the news that he'd banned me from watching him work, in case I stole his gags. I think he had ideas above his station.

It was an unwelcoming start. Things looked up when I found my mate Clive Brandy, thank God. He'd already been at the Palace for a few days and was clearly in his element, gambling non-stop in the hotel's casino. A few nights earlier Clive had fallen into the casino, pissed, and won £6,000. The next day he'd bought a horse with his winnings, got drunk again and ridden it into the casino!

He rode up to the gaming tables on his horse and demanded: 'Put this on Twenty Black and, if it comes up, send thirty-five horses to my room!' Not surprisingly, Clive and his horse were thrown out on their ears.

'You look glum,' he said to me. 'Come on, we're going gambling!'

He signed me into the casino, where we were served champagne – in elegant china teapots! Several cups later I started playing cards, so far gone I couldn't remember if I was playing blackjack or pontoon, and lost a fortune.

Then a £25 chip slipped through my fingers and rolled off the table. I got on my hands and knees to try to find it. In the next few minutes I apparently had everyone in hysterics. I crawled around the entire room after that chip and, every so often, my little head popped up paralytically from behind a table or chair to whoops of laughter.

One angry bouncer told Clive to get me out of there at once and he blew his top. 'What's the matter with your casino?' asked Clive. 'Last night you kicked me and the horse out and tonight you want to kick my friend out. Remember, a casino is run by cunts to cater for fucking lunatics – and don't forget it!'

Clive stormed off alone and I went downstairs to a bar

and had a few drinks with two guys from the band Hot Chocolate.

Half an hour later two bouncers from the casino strutted in and started pushing one of the musicians around. Next they began punching and kicking him. I leaped on the back of one to pull him off. Then another casino heavy arrived, grabbed me and threw me out of the casino. I stormed off to the police station, furious at what I'd witnessed.

'It was unbelievable,' I told the duty officer. 'These blokes at that casino are real thugs. It was a completely unprovoked assault of the first order.'

The policeman heard me out, then asked: 'Do you want to make a complaint?' The tone of his question said it all; it said, 'You're wasting your time'.

'No, stuff it!' I said, and left. I vowed there and then to leave and never return. When I got to Manx Airport I'd just missed the day's flight to Blackpool, but I knew I wasn't staying another day.

I 'phoned Kevin, who was waiting for me in Blackpool, and told him to hire a plane to collect me. He arrived and as we took off I told him what had happened. 'I hate this bloody place. In one night I've lost all my money, seen a mate get beaten up by real bastards and effectively been told to fuck off by the police.'

I turned to the pilot and offered him an extra £500 if he'd fly a victory roll over the casino.

'If we do that,' he said, 'all the fuel will go up our noses.'

I've been back to the Isle of Man only once since then, and loathed it just as much. I turned up to take part in a charity football match and an awful bit-part actor from *Eastenders* picked a fight. He was such an unpleasant shit I'm surprised he didn't ask for a job in that casino!

One weekend I agreed to take part in a charity football match in Blackpool. I got changed into my kit and looked a real weakling with my white, skinny legs and knobbly knees. Just before I was about to leave, Val, to make me look a bit healthier, gave me some false tanning lotion to spread on my legs. Now I looked like Pele!

Halfway through the game someone threw a bucket of water over me and, to my intense embarrassment, my legs went all streaky. 'It's the first time Jim Davidson's legs have run all match!' announced the commentator. And as I came off at full-time, looking more bedraggled than ever, he called me 'The Vagrant' – because I had no visible means of support!

Afterwards I went for a drink in the clubhouse and met a singer called Jane Beaumont who had dark, pretty looks. She was in a group called January, which was appearing at the South Pier. Jane was very bubbly. We went our separate ways and I drove back to Val and the kids in the horrible, rented house asking myself why I couldn't have someone lovely like Jane for a girlfriend. By the time I got home I decided that indeed I could. After all, I was on television and now I had plenty of money to splash around on the good life.

I couldn't get Jane out of my mind after our first meeting and set about trying to woo her, even though Val and the kids were with me. When Val took the kids out for the day, I'd surreptitiously take Jane for lunch. Across the lunch table I fell for her hook, line and sinker and, after a while, I think she'd fallen for me.

One night Jane came with me to a party at the South Pier, where I met the late, great comedian Les Dawson for the first time.

'Who are you?' he asked.

'I'm Jim Davidson,' I answered. 'I'm on at the North Pier with Little and Large, Carson and Collier.'

'What do you do?' he said.

'I'm a comic.'

'Oh,' he said, having another sip of his whisky. 'Mike Reid died on his arse up here so you've got no fucking chance.'

'Thanks a lot!' I said, and walked off.

Next day I met Les again in a bar. 'I'm sorry if I upset you last night,' he said. 'I was pissed.'

'That's OK,' I answered.

'But I fucking meant what I said!' RIP Les. I loved you even if you were a shit.

Jane and I clinched our feelings for one another towards the end of the season after another lunchtime rendezvous. I got back to the rented house one day. Val was in the lounge but I didn't say anything to her. I put on a record of soppy love songs by Bread and rang Jane. The two of us sat on our 'phones, simply listening in silence to each other breathing and to the lyrics of the love songs playing in the background.

To me, those long, meaningful silences were the Susan Sergeant flashing lights syndrome all over again. I'd come around full circle. After that call I decided I had to do one of the saddest things I've ever done. I came clean to Val about Jane. She had had no idea that anything was going on between us – not that anything actually had gone on between us by then, but we were in love.

I told Val she'd have to return to Naylor House and she started crying. Then the boys came in and started crying as well. We all got upset and I felt lousy about what had to happen. Val had known our relationship was heading for the rocks when I'd first started drinking heavily at the start of the Blackpool season. But neither of us had wanted to own up to the inevitable.

She and the boys left Blackpool reluctantly and I finished the last few weeks of the run. Jane and I saw each other several times but we never got around to anything more amorous than kissing and cuddling.

By the time the season finished I was very much in love – and so was my driver Kevin, who also had a new girlfriend. Wally ordered me to take a holiday and sent me and Kevin off to a hotel in Guernsey owned by a friend of his. On landing the two of us rented a car, found the hotel and then fell straight into the bar.

This wasn't a holiday! We both had long, miserable faces. I was full of remorse about Val and the kids yet missing Jane, who was still in Blackpool. And Kevin was missing his girlfriend.

We decided to go out to see a movie to take our mind

off our troubles and cheer ourselves up a bit. *The Greatest* was showing, the film about boxer Muhammad Ali, and a moving love scene reduced Kevin and me to nervous wrecks. We came out of that cinema gutted men, and fell into the first bar we could find.

Next morning I had to get back to Jane. I bought a diamond engagement ring on my credit card, hid it in a cigarette packet to smuggle through Customs and flew back, with Kevin, to London. We caught the first available flight back to Blackpool, where I found Jane after her show and proposed to her. She accepted and I slipped the ring on her finger.

Several of our friends came back to the hotel for a celebratory drink and I 'phoned Wally to check in with him. For all he knew I was still in Guernsey on holiday. He asked how everything was going and I said I was thoroughly enjoying myself.

'You little bastard!' he said. 'What's the tower like?' He either knew or had guessed that I'd flown back to Blackpool to be reunited with Jane.

When she finished her season, I was about to go off on my first big tour for British troops in South America. I lent Jane my little MGB and she drove off happily to her parents' home in the glorious-sounding Heckmondwike in Yorkshire.

Jane's parents, Barbara and Don, were wonderful and always made me feel very at home.

In October 1977 I flew off on a ten-day visit to our lads in Belize, Central America. I put together a small band with my keyboards player Alan Rogers, and also on the tour was singer Frank Leyton and a juggler called Richard de Lord.

We flew out with the RAF to Airport Camp, Belize. First we did the show for the troops, who were watching from the backs of four-ton lorries.

It was really hot out there and the electricity supply kept coming and going. Poor Frank had problems being a singer. It's hard enough for a male singer to perform in front of an all-male audience, but with electric keyboards which kept losing their power supply, and therefore sound, it was virtually impossible. All the same, we had a fantastic evening. Then we went off to do another show in the sergeants' mess.

A few days later we flew down to a remote and tiny town called Punta Gorda, halfway between Airport Camp and the Guatemalan border. Gorda was bang in the middle of a jungle clearing with five empty grit roads running into it. We were met by army personnel and driven to a military base five miles away, home to a single company of soldiers.

When we arrived Frank and I played volleyball all afternoon with some of the lads and got extremely sunburned. In the evening we did the show and then had a few drinks in the sergeants' mess, where I met a Brummie sergeant called Percy. 'Do you fancy coming down town to meet Gobblin' Jenny?' he asked me.

'Who?' I said.

'There's a bird down in Gorda called Gobblin' Jenny – so I've heard,' he replied.

'What do you mean "so you've heard"?'

'Well, I'm a fucking married man like, but I thought you might like to go down there,' he explained.

'Who's this Gobbling Jenny?' I said.

'She's great,' he replied. 'Beautiful. Fucking beautiful. She'll be in the disco bar in Gorda.'

'Right!' I said. 'I'll have that! Are you coming, Frank?'

'Yes,' he said.

The three of us needed an excuse to leave the base and I found the major at the bar. 'After we've had a drink, we're going to go down to the town to have a look at the scenery,' I told him. 'I've heard it's very beautiful down there on the coast.'

In his plummy accent he replied: 'Ah, you're going off to see Gobbling Jenny are you, Jim?'

Sergeant Percy, Frank and I were driven in an army Land Rover to Gorda. When we got there, we found that the 'disco bar' was no more than a Nissan hut with ultra-violet lights in it. All you could see were teeth! I met Gobblin' Jenny and she was horrible.

The disco was full of locals, mostly men, drinking pints out of grotty glasses. Some came up to us and tried to sell us drugs and, after a little while, Frank and I decided we'd rather drink in the officers' mess.

I asked the sergeant where the Land Rover was and he said it had gone back to the base. We were stranded. Then, as a prank, the sergeant, yelling 'Take me to the camp!', jumped on the back of a complete stranger outside the disco. Unsurprisingly the stranger wasn't at all happy about it and neither were his mates.

The sergeant was floored and the gang jumped in, punching and kicking him while he was down. I tried to stop the fight and one local pulled a knife on me. It got very ugly and, in the commotion, the sergeant just vanished. We left, smartish.

Hiding behind a rusting corpse of a car, Frank and I could see the locals getting out torches to come after us. We picked at random one of the five roads leading out of Gorda and ran into the dark, thick jungle.

By the time the grit roads turned to mud roads it was very, very dark, and we were very, very lost and scared. It's been said that you should suck a pebble when your throat is dry so I picked one up, put it to my mouth and it bit my lip. I'd picked up a land crab by mistake!

Frank and I were both shitting ourselves and, thinking tactics, I smothered his nice white shirt as well as our faces and hands with mud in an attempt to camouflage us. Then we heard more footsteps in the distance and kept running until we heard only one person behind us. I thought it could be the badly beaten sergeant and dived into a muddy ditch to hide until the footsteps caught up with us. Then I whispered: 'Psssst! Sarge? Hello, Sarge?'

No reply. Instead the footsteps got faster again, then fainter. Frank and I waited until we were sure no one else was around then walked on cautiously until all the stars had disappeared. I could just make out the massive silhouette of a mountain, and from that I tried to deduce a route back to the camp.

Three hours later, at dawn, we arrived at the gatehouse of

the base, looking like we'd been through hell. We found out that the sergeant had made his way back earlier, sporting a black eye.

The single footsteps we'd heard on our tail turned out to be those of a Gurkha soldier also dragged into the fracas. When he got back he'd told everyone he'd heard mysterious voices in the jungle – the nervous croaks from me and Frank.

Fifteen years later I arrived at an army base in Vitesse, Bosnia, after a hellish eleven-hour night-time drive. We'd dodged sniper fire along the way from Split, in Croatia, and I arrived shattered and fed up. As I got out of the Land Rover, before I could even have a stretch, a voice spoke to me from the darkness. 'I bet you don't remember me, do you?' it said.

'Yes I fucking do!' I replied. It was the Sergeant.

When I got back from the Belize trip I went straight into rehearsals for the 1977 pantomime, *Babes in the Wood* at the Wimbledon Theatre, with Windsor Davies and Don Estelle. I got on very well with Windsor but Estelle is pushy and I never took to him.

The panto wasn't the only thing about to start running in December – I'd picked up my very first dose of VD – not from Jane, I might add. I went to the little social club next to the theatre to ring Mum for the 'phone number of the family doctor, Dr Joffe.

'You haven't got crabs, have you, son?' she asked.

'Good gracious me, Mum,' I said. 'Don't be so filthy! I've got a dose!'

As I said it I could feel her making the sign of the cross on her chest. She said she'd try to track Dr Joffe down for me but she didn't have much luck. So that Sunday I drove to the doctor's house where I found him tinkering with his car, smothered in grease and oil. He didn't examine me, which was just as well given how dirty he was, but he gave me some tablets and told me to see him again if they didn't work.

After several days it was clear the pills weren't working and I tried calling Dr Joffe a few times but he was never around. So I 'phoned the ever-faithful Clive Brandy for advice.

'What's the problem?' he asked.

'I've got a dose,' I said.

'That's not a problem.'

'It is!' I insisted.

'You've got to go down the local clinic to get treated,' he said. 'Don't worry, I'll pick you up early tomorrow morning from Emily's and take you myself.'

'You won't tell anyone, will you Clive?' I asked. 'Mum's very embarrassed about it and would hate our neighbours to find out.'

'Am I your pal or what?' he said. 'Don't worry about a thing.'

The following morning, bright and early, Clive turned up at Holburne Road in his Datsun estate car with Kevin. He sounded his horn like a blasted ice-cream man. Mum looked out of the window and sharply drew in breath. Running the entire length of the car was a bold hand-made sign: Clap Clinic Special!

I ran to the car, jumped in and told Clive to drive away as fast as possible. He took me to a hospital in Greenwich and stayed in the car with Kevin while I boldly went where most men have anxiously gone before, into the special clinic, to wait with several other worried-looking men.

When I went in to see the doctor the man was a torturer. He started prodding my corey and asked lots of questions.

'Name?' he said.

'Stan Dallas,' I replied.

'Occupation?'

'Lorry driver.'

'How's the panto going, Jim?' he asked, not even looking up from my corey.

All went smoothly until I had to give a urine sample. I couldn't, so I had to go to a local café to drink cups of tea until I could. I went back and performed properly and then the doctor shoved a needle in me for a blood sample. Right then I decided I'd never return to a public clap clinic like that again and never have. Well . . .

Just before 1977 ended I landed myself in a punch-up with a smarmy copper called Sergeant Terry Lawson, ironically when I was on my way to perform at a function being held at my brother Bill's police station at Shooters Hill.

Lawson had stopped me in my car along the Old Kent Road. I had three friends with me and when he looked inside the car he clearly recognised me.

'Name?' he said, although he knew.

'Charlie Kray!' I said.

For that I was hauled before Tower Bridge magistrates to face assault charges and charges for minor motoring offences. Lawson claimed I'd sworn at him (which I had) and head-butted him twice in the face (which I hadn't).

I was cleared of assault and given a conditional discharge for causing an obstruction and, for the minor charges, I had to pay fines and costs.

But I was back before magistrates a few months later, in May, after being nabbed doing 100 mph on the M23 near Brighton. I'd given the police a fair run for the £100 fine I got – they'd been on my tail for sixteen miles! When they stopped me they produced the breathalyser bag which I blew up, and popped it, honestly. I was banned from driving for three months and also fined for other minor offences.

I had every Sunday off during the pantomime and one night I was booked to appear at Jenkinson's in Brighton, one of those clubs where I'd earned a kind of cult status and always did well. Also at Jenkinson's was a French barmaid I fancied called Pascale. I'd never got anywhere with her before, but that night she came back to my hotel suite in the Grand Hotel.

Kevin was there with an ugly bird he'd picked up and a good eighteen or so newly met close friends. When Pascale arrived she said she was going to reception to make a private 'phone call but would be back shortly.

While Pascale was gone I took Kevin's rather rough-looking friend into the bedroom for a few minutes, then took her to join the party in the sitting-room.

When Pascale returned I jumped up to get her a drink.

We chatted for ages, and when I tried getting amorous with her I got the brush-off.

'Don't think you can ferk me after you have been ferking 'er!' she said, in her sultry accent. Of course, a few minutes later I did.

Later still Kevin said we needed more drinks and called room service.

'You know,' I said to him. 'I'm sure the hotel reckons there's an orgy going on in here.'

'Well, I'll soon sort the hotel out,' he said, in between ordering the drinks. He then stripped naked and waited for the old night porter to arrive. When he knocked on the door, he was greeted by Kevin in his birthday suit showing off his dented tent-peg!

The porter took one look at Kevin and went white. Then, and it seemed to happen in slow motion, the glasses of whisky started to slide off the tray. One glass smashed on the floor but he saved the others. 'Sorry, sir' he said, handing Kevin the tray and quickly closing the door.

A few minutes later there came a second knock at our door. Kevin opened it again and this time the porter's arm came around the door, blindly waving a whisky miniature to make up the order. After that a good night was had by all. Stand by Clive and the Clap Clinic Special again . . .

Early in 1978 I was back on the road and appearing in Workington at a club called the Rendezvous. I was there for the week and I'd died on my arse three nights running. On the Thursday night the manager found me in the dressing-room as I was getting ready. 'You'll be all right tonight, Jim,' he said. 'There's a good crowd in this evening.'

I went on and started doing better than the previous nights, when suddenly Prince Charles strolled in at the back, surrounded by an entourage of mayors, councillors, detectives and a bevy of beauties.

Every eye in the place turned from me and fixed firmly on to His Royal Highness instead. I finished the act to polite applause and was invited to meet him.

He was sitting at a table with four lovely Miss Wherevers.

I went over and shook his hand. I addressed him politely as 'sir' throughout, and every so often, for good measure, bowed my head a bit.

'You're a Cockney, aren't you?' he asked.

'In fact, sir,' I explained, 'I'm not actually a Cockney, I'm from south-east London. I can look out of my bedroom window and see your house.'

Then one of the girls, let's say Miss Workington, got up to go to the lavatory. He leaned over towards me a little and whispered quietly. 'Don't these girls go to the loo a lot?' he asked.

'Yes, sir,' I replied.

'I've been here hours and haven't been once!' he added.

As he said it I wished he'd gone while I was on. It would have given me a chance to get my audience's attention back. What a way to be upstaged!

It turned out that the girls could hold their drink perfectly well. They were all local and thrilled to have been invited into the club with the prince. They kept leaving him to ring their friends to say 'Guess who I'm out with?'

Not long after that I officially met my first royal, Princess Anne. She came to Blazer's nightclub in Windsor, her local! Neil Sedaka was topping the bill and I was supporting him. Because of HRH we fell out badly. He was a great performer but, off-stage, something of a prima donna. And that night he excelled himself.

Long before the show started the princess invited Neil and me to join her for supper on the top table. Princess Anne was with her lady-in-waiting, Lady Victoria Legge-Burke. Over supper I sat opposite Lady Victoria, and kept trying to wind her up. I came out with every saucy innuendo I could, in an attempt to make her drop her slightly aloof cool. Nothing worked. Then, under the table, I put my foot on the hem of her dress. 'I'm very sorry,' I said. 'I'm standing on your dress.'

She replied, trying to be as risqué as she thought I was: 'I'll have to tuck it in my knickers then, won't I?'

We were all talking politely, keeping the tone of things very jolly, when Sedaka got up in a huff and walked briskly from the table. I didn't storm after him at once but a minute or two later I excused myself from the table and caught up with him.

'What was all that about?' I asked.

'I don't like being seen by my public before a show!' he said.

'Well, neither do I,' I answered. 'But Her Royal Highness has invited us to dinner, you could show a little bit of respect.'

He ignored me and swanned off for a drink before getting ready. I thought it was very tacky behaviour then, but eventually realised Neil wasn't showing any disrespect. He was just showing what all performers have – a nervousness of meeting the audience before you've entertained them.

Laurie devised a three-year plan for my next spate of seasons. I could top the bill anywhere I wanted, but I couldn't guarantee to fill a place night after night for three months. So for the 1978 season I was booked to appear with Roger de Courcey and singer Bernie Flint in Margate. During the run Laurie convinced Thames Television's head of Light Entertainment, Philip Jones, that I just had to have my own show.

In those days in television, if you were young you usually had to wait a long time for your own show, and I was only twenty-four. But Philip agreed to take a gamble on me and I was signed for a new quick-fire comedy series, *The Jim Davidson Show*.

Until then Laurie had always managed to get all my new television work purely on the back of my previous television appearances. He knew if the television types saw me doing the uncensored stage show, which is what the public really wanted, only the swear-words would register. They wouldn't see as far as any comedy, even if the audiences were rolling in the aisles.

At the end of the Margate season I started work on the series, and Johnny Ammonds, the producer-director, told Laurie he wanted to see me working in a club live, to take a look at the sort of thing I did in my act.

Johnny had worked with Morecambe and Wise for the

BBC and was very much of the 'old school'. He was at the top in television terms and, before that, had been in radio. To him the words 'bloody' and 'damn' were racy.

When I got out on stage at Blazer's and delivered the act at a hundred miles per hour poor Johnny could not believe what he was hearing. His eyes came out like organ stops. Afterwards, apparently, he leaned across to Laurie and said: 'I don't know what to say to you. If I hadn't already signed the contract I'm not sure I would have done. I'm not sure where to go with him.'

Where we did go was into the studio to record six half-hour shows, quick skits and jokes. The first show would hit the screens on January 6 1979.

Pantomime that year was a lovey-dovey affair. I appeared with Jane Beaumont in *Cinderella* at Wolverhampton. I played Buttons and she made the sweetest, soppiest, most adorable fairy. We had a great Christmas that year and I was still very much in love. We both worked in the business and understood the trials of living out of suitcases and working irregular hours.

As we toasted in the New Year together we were joined by the patter of tiny feet – a Chihuahua puppy's! We called her Cinders and she's still going strong, living in Heckmondwike with Jane's parents, where she never stops eating.

7

Mrs Davidson Number 2

When Jane and I finished in Wolverhampton we rented a little house in Twickenham and, in addition to our dog Cinders, heard the patter of more feet – those of my roadies, Kevin and Stukie.

Stukie was a tall, skinny man who always got his words muddled, so we nicknamed him Mr Malaprop. If he wanted to say he was standing in a 'bracing' wind, he'd call it an 'embracing' wind . . .

The television show was deemed a great success, and I signed for another series with Thames Television, and for the 1979 summer season I was at the Princess Theatre, Torquay, supporting Peters and Lee. The work was easy enough and with days to waste in Torquay I looked longingly at the sea. I felt drawn to the sea, slightly frightened of it, but drawn all the same. So I bought myself a Fletcher speedboat for £2,000. Laurie was with me for the start of the season and I got one of the roadies to drive the two of us over to Paignton to collect the boat.

The salesman's parting words were: 'Don't forget, you have to run the engine in slowly for ten hours.' Laurie and I set off bound for Torquay at 20 knots all the way. We still had our suits on and looked like a couple of ridiculous characters from *Tales of the Riverbank*.

That was about the most sedate I ever was in that boat. My

daily routine soon revolved around it. Starting in the pub by mid-morning I'd get pissed, stagger on to the boat with one or two of the lads and the occasional Doris and then continue pissing it up out at sea.

We'd head back to land only when it was time for me to do two nightly shows at the theatre. Then we'd fall into a pub, get pissed again and (as long as Jane wasn't around) I'd try to pull every girl in sight. I couldn't do it now, I'd never pass the medical!

I nearly didn't live to do anything again when I smashed the speedboat up in mid-season. I was out with, among others, my very drunken saxophone player, Tony Harper, who looked just like a musician from *The Muppet Show*.

We were larking about and crashed into another boat. Its propeller ripped our hull wide open, missing my head by inches. When the boat came to a standstill I was in agony. I'd broken my collar-bone. Then, as we started to sink in the wreckage, Tony uttered six immortal words to me which only a great piss-artist musician could muster: 'Hey man, the seats are floating!' he said.

We were towed back to shore but before I could get to hospital for treatment, I had to do the first show. When I told the audience I'd broken my collar-bone they fell about. They thought it was part of the act. Afterwards I was taken to the hospital and got back to the theatre for the second show.

That night I nearly killed myself again – with an acrobatic barmaid. I dragged her off to bed at the hotel and forgot for a moment about my collar-bone. My screams were so loud that the people in the rooms next to me must have been extremely impressed!

Next morning the tabloids picked up on the story, printing the line we'd fed them to lessen the seriousness of the incident that I'd broken my shoulder after unfortunately crashing into some rocks. That was the end of the Fletcher, so I replaced it with a £4,000 Zeus speedboat – slightly bigger, slightly faster but just as doomed.

One Sunday I dashed back to London to appear in a royal gala night, a tribute to ENSA in the presence of Prince

Charles, at the Theatre Royal, Drury Lane. I turned up for rehearsals and was pretty unenthusiastic about the spot I had. Prince Charles arrived and the show got underway, but soon it was overrunning like mad. The director was in a bit of a panic and I offered to give up my spot to keep the show on schedule. So instead of getting ready to go on I kept myself in the background, watching the others from the back of the stalls and drinking in the bar. Naturally, I didn't put myself in the line-up to meet Prince Charles at the end of the show but apparently, when he met everyone, he asked pointedly: 'Where's Jim Davidson?'

'He stood down because the show was overrunning, sir,' he was told.

Later that night I met the current Miss United Kingdom, Carolyn Seaward. She was reputedly having a fling with Prince Andrew at the time, so I thought, 'This'll do me!' I invited her to come back with me to Torquay to go out on the Zeus. We drove through the night to get there, arriving at the hotel at about 4.00 am. In the bedroom she disappeared to the bathroom for about 25 minutes and I fell asleep waiting for her.

She woke me up, saying: 'I want to go for a walk on the beach.'

'See ya!' I said, and fell back into an even deeper sleep.

A day or so later I received a letter from the Palace, thanking me for standing down to prevent the gala from running all night. So I did myself more good by not appearing!

One day I took the Zeus out again with Kevin and headed for Brownsea Island at Bournemouth, one of those places which immediately takes me back to my childhood, even though I'd never been there. Brownsea was the birthplace of the Boy Scouts in some respects because it's where Baden-Powell took his lads for some of the first camping trips. The island is still run by the Baden-Powell organisation for year-round camping visits, and that's why I look on it with great affection. Having served my days with toggles and knots in the Cubs, then the Scouts, I regarded the island as part of my own heritage and a monument to the

valiant notion of service above self inspired in generations
of eager young Britons.

As Kevin and I got near Brownsea, disaster struck. The
hosepipe came off the engine and the Zeus started to fill
with water. As the back of the boat started to sink into the
water, to save life and limb I headed straight for the island
– nowhere in Britain should have been better prepared for
a bit of an emergency!

I had visions of Kevin and I, now wet through, stepping
off the boat to be greeted by hundreds of Boy Scouts
wrapping us in blankets, ladling coffee down our throats
and sitting us around a warming camp fire. We approached
dramatically enough, at a forty-five-degree angle to the
shore. A nice man, obviously well-versed in Baden-Powell's
ideas, came running towards the boat.

'You can't moor here,' he shouted aggressively. 'This is
private ground!'

I replied, in my best nautical terminology, 'I'm fucking
sinking! I'll moor where I want, you shite!'

Kevin and I scrambled ashore and the boat was in a
terrible mess. I arranged for someone to collect us and the
Zeus was picked up later, but even though I got it repaired,
I never really bothered with it again and it got rusty. In the
end I gave it to a friend as scrap and found out later he had
done it up and sold it. Cheers!

At the end of the season I flew to Jersey to appear in
a Variety Club gala, and fell out with the creep Paul
Daniels. I was appearing in a benefit night over in Jersey
for the Variety Club. It was a good-humoured, glittering
event. Morecambe and Wise topped the bill, marking Eric
Morecambe's return to the stage after a heart by-pass
operation. Also taking part were The Three Degrees,
The Krankies and even the current Miss World – Gina
Swainson, Miss Bermuda.

After the show we were all invited to a VIP dinner being
hosted by Lady Butlin, Billy's widow, where the guest of
honour was the Duke of Edinburgh. On the way to the
dinner, in a minibus, I had Gina on my arm and with
us were The Krankies and Paul Daniels. The traffic was

chaotic and jammed the 500 yards to the hotel. Daniels had been showing off to Gina, mouthing off offensively, for most of the journey.

'Do us a favour. Shut up, will you?' I said eventually.

'I'm not doing that, she really turns me on,' he said, referring to Gina.

'Any fucking chance of you turning him off?' Ian Krankie asked her in broadest Glaswegian.

Then Daniels started making unpleasant remarks, to which we all took exception, about Arthur Askey, who by then was not well. I had a soft spot for Arthur because he'd helped me make it on *New Faces*.

After a while Daniels got fed up with us all telling him where to go, snapped, got out and opened the back of the minibus to grab his case. As his head appeared looking for his case, the reigning Miss World came out with a triumphant put-down. 'Who is that boring little shit?' she asked. He glared at us and left, and I haven't spoken to him to this day. Who says there isn't a God?

In order to surprise Mum, over many weeks I taught myself to play 'Clair de Lune', the classical piece Uncle Bill had played for her in Holburne Road while I was being born. I knew she loved it very much and wanted to play it just for her, to please and impress her. Having mastered it fairly well I turned up at home one day to find Mum. I told her I had a surprise for her and nonchalantly sat down at the piano, cracked my knuckles and started playing.

I looked round, feeling very pleased with myself, and Mum was crying. I didn't know why and stopped at once. Mum didn't tell me why the tune prompted her tears and for fear of upsetting her further, I didn't ask. Instead I slipped away from Holburne Road, disappointed that the tune I'd spent so long mastering to make her happy had had quite the opposite effect.

In the autumn I turned the club act into a much bigger affair for a sixteen-week nationwide tour. I got myself a permanent backing band, with the help of keyboards player Alan Rogers, and my own sound and lighting people which, in those days, was unheard of for a common stand-up comic.

I knew if I felt insecure I'd have plenty of my own people around me – a staff of sixteen, in fact! And having my own roadies meant I had everything I needed with me in the dressing-room, including my hi-fi stack and record collection (*Paint Your Wagon* soundtrack et al).

One night of the tour was at a club called Bailey's in Leicester, which I'd already played several times, so I knew all the staff well. On this occasion the club was hosting a promotion for Rothmans cigarettes and, before I was due to appear, David Hamilton was to make a quick presentation.

In the afternoon one of the Rothmans girls, Julie Gullick, came to find me. She had shoulder-length blonde hair with pretty, dolly looks and a pair of sexy black velvet trousers hugging her slim, shapely figure. 'Would you mind if David Hamilton and a model use your dressing-room when they arrive tonight?' she asked me.

'Yes, quite frankly,' I said. 'My lads have set up my hi-fi system in here and all my other gear's in here, too.'

She saw my point and walked away. Later that night, when David Hamilton walked out into the spotlights, Julie sat in the audience. I ran up to the balcony to the follow-spot operators and grabbed one of the lights. I moved its beam off David and on to Julie. She couldn't work out what was going on but knew something was afoot. I didn't speak to her before I went on but when I came off-stage I sent Kevin to go and find her. 'Ask that Julie if she'll come and have a drink with me,' I told him.

'Right,' said Kevin.

'Back in the dressing-room,' I added.

'Right,' said Kevin again, disappearing into the crowd.

A few minutes later he returned, accompanied by Julie. I took her to my dressing-room, poured a drink and put on a record. As I chatted to her, one of the band put his head around the door to say a limousine was waiting for me at the stage door to take me back to the hotel. He added that the band and crew were heading back to their own hotel for drinks and invited me to join them.

I asked Julie to join me and we set off through Leicester to the band's hotel. An hour later everyone was pissed and decided they wanted to go swimming. I was the only one staying in a hotel with a pool so they all moved on to my place, where we ordered more drinks. In the early hours the place was alive, and the pool was full of drunken musicians and their fleeting girlfriends skinny-dipping.

Julie and I left them to it and slipped away to my room to fall into bed. Afterwards, I fell asleep thinking, 'This'll do me!' In the morning Julie left but said she'd come back to the hotel to have lunch with me. When she arrived I persuaded her to return to the bedroom. I tried getting her back into bed but she left, saying she had to go to do a promotion in the city somewhere. On the rest of the tour I slept with loads of one-night stands, when Jane wasn't around.

When I appeared in the Royal Variety Show in 1979, at the Theatre Royal, I did a few quick jokes then finished with the song 'My Way', with a running echo gag. It was a routine I'd worked on during the tour. I did the song and at the end, having spent five minutes singing about going, an echo shouted back impatiently 'Piss Off!' For the Queen's benefit we changed the pay-off to an apologetic 'Go Away!'

After the performance I stood in the line-up waiting to shake Her Majesty by the hand. When she got to me my heart was beating very fast and I had 'dry mouth'.

'Thank you very much for doing it,' she said. She made me feel as if I was the only person there. She must know, deep down, that for many people meeting her is one of the greatest thrills there is.

That Christmas I opened in *Cinderella* at the Bristol Hippodrome. This time, unlike in Wolverhampton a year earlier, Jane and I weren't able to work together which made the season seem to last longer.

Back in London in 1980 I recorded another series of *The Jim Davidson Show* and then went off to Margate for a summer season as exciting as the Bristol pantomime run. The only bright spot was a visit from Laurie. He rang to say he was on his way up and wanted me to meet him at his hotel. When I walked into his room he took a bottle of champagne from the fridge.

'I've got good news for you,' he said.

'What's that?' I asked.

'You're appearing at the London Palladium this Christmas in pantomime,' he said.

'Great,' I said. 'Who's top of the bill?'

'You are, you prick!' he said and passed me my bubbly.

Laurie had soft-soaped Louis Benjamin, boss of Stoll Moss which owned the Palladium, and had assured him I was a big enough star to top the bill. And that my reputation for being a bit of a blue comedian wouldn't get in the way of his family show and box-office receipts.

Lionel Blair was directing the rather formal, traditional production of *Dick Whittington* and had hoped to play Dick. But Laurie had convinced Louis I really was a better Dick. Thanks, Laurie. Lionel's nose had clearly been put out of joint and the part of High Sheriff of London was hastily written in for him to play.

At the end of the summer season I moved back to Jane and our house in Twickenham. We were still together but not as close as we had been. Towards the end of the year at the Boat Show at Earl's Court I bumped into Julie Gullick again. Behind Jane's back I took her out for supper and then on to a nightclub before dropping her off at her hotel, the Vanderbilt. When the Boat Show left, so did Julie, and I didn't hear from her.

When rehearsals for Dick Whittington started I began playing hard at night. I became a regular at a private restaurant club in Berkeley Square called Morton's, and if I wasn't drunk in there I was getting drunk in Tramp or Stringfellow's.

In December I was in Morton's when a massive punch-up broke out. I was nothing to do with it but, as you'd expect, the only one to be arrested.

I'd gone in with a friend, Denny Laine, and Terry, a minder who was working for me. Terry had a row with The Sex Pistols and fists started flying. It soon turned into a real bar-room brawl and everyone seemed to join in. I showed my true colours by taking my jacket off, rolling up my shirt-sleeves and quickly diving for cover under the grand piano in the corner.

Next thing the place was awash with police. The fighting stopped and I stood next to Denny, who was cut and bruised. The chief inspector asked who'd started the fight and when the finger was pointed at Terry my tongue rallied to his defence. 'Terry's fucking innocent,' I shouted.

'If you swear again you'll be arrested!' snapped the officer.

'You what?' I said. 'Are you fucking mad? There are people being bashed to fuck here by these thugs The Sex Pistols and you're arresting me? I haven't fucking done anything but hide!'

'Mr Davidson, if you swear at me again you'll be arrested,' he announced.

So I said, and I quote verbatim, 'Fuck, bollocks, arseholes, shit, prick, pooh.'

It must have been the pooh that did it. It landed me in the pooh proper, and I was carted off to the West End station in nearby Savile Row. Laurie was called and nearly had a heart attack when he heard what I'd said. He could see the Palladium panto heading straight out of the window, sure that if a policeman stood up in court and reeled off what I'd said, Louis Benjamin would pull the plug and quickly pay me off.

Then another agent, Peter Prichard, came to our rescue. Coincidentally, he was a special constable based at the station and he had words. I had to apologise at length and was eventually told to quickly get lost. Thanks, Peter!

The panto opened as scheduled on December 22 1980, for a sixteen-week run. The rest of the company included Windsor Davies, Melvyn Hayes, Mollie Sugden, Clive Dunn and Victor Spinetti.

Windsor, Melvyn and Mollie were charming, and I was in awe of Clive because he had a sublime ability to ad-lib about absolutely anything for ages. It was probably in Victor's dressing-room that I spent most time because he is a spell-binding story-teller. I don't know what the

Welshman is on but it should be bottled and sold to the rest of us.

The production was slightly formal because Mr Benjamin wanted it to be terribly authentic. In the plot Dick travels to London and befriends Tommy the Cat. King Rat steals some jewels from Alderman Fitzwarren, but Dick gets the blame and is banished. With faithful Tommy by his side, Dick walks to Highgate Hill and falls asleep, then dreams he will become Lord Mayor of London and, spurred on, returns to the city, duffs up King Rat and enters local government.

Possibly the highlight of the production, certainly for special effects and goose pimples, was the dream sequence set amid smoke behind a gauze. When I fell asleep a double took my place in order for me to rush off for a quick change. When my double woke up on-stage he mimed my line, pre-recorded in my voice and played on tape, to the cat: 'Come on, Tommy – we're going back to London!'

Tommy was played by a little hen-pecked man called Derek Holt. He had a funny relationship with his wife. She used to moan at him all the time as if he really was a cat. He would always stand in the wings with his cat-head in one hand, a bottle of beer in the other and chat up the dancers. His wife caught him one night and the fur really flew!

Another night, thanks to Tommy, I fell out badly with Lionel. We'd played the panto very straight but, a bit bored, I decided to have a joke. As the show got underway, Derek made his first appearance as Tommy. 'Hello, you're a handsome cat, isn't he children?' I said.

'Y-e-e-e-e-e-s,' squeaked Derek in meow-speak.

'My name's Dick, what's yours?' I asked. Derek, as the cat, did a Tommy Cooper impression so I would suggest 'Tommy'. Not this night.

I looked into the pit and the musical director, Gordon Rose, was smiling. As a prank, I named the cat after him. 'Gordon!' I said. In blind panic Derek spat 'Meow, no! Meow, no!' and tried the Tommy Cooper impression again.

'No, no!' I said, 'Gordon. That's your name.'

Mum's mum - very Irish and very Catholic!

Me, as a baby, trying to master how to give a V-sign to my first photographer!

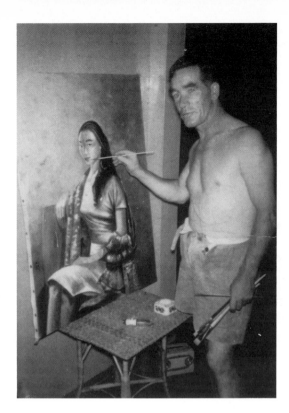

The only picture there is of Uncle Bill.

The legendary Tibby Tibbs - he's been with me all my life.

In hospital with my cherished Tommy Steele guitar. When, years later, I actually got the chance to meet Tommy, I blew it!

Butter wouldn't melt in my mouth!

With Dad on holiday in Great Yarmouth. In the very last show I did for Thames I sang 'Cat's in the Cradle' and dedicated it to Dad. This photo was shown at the end and it brought tears to the eyes of the nation!

Mum, Dad and our dog Deno on Dad's sixtieth birthday in 1971. When Dad died Deno cocked his legs on the wreaths. When Mum died we had to have him put down because he pined for her so badly.

Backstage at Ralph Reader's 1966 Gang Show - sponsored by Wayfinder shoes.

My very first performance at the Black Bull in Lewisham - on drugs!

Wife Number One and Child Number One, Sue and a grown-up Sarah (right).

Me with Val and her boys in Blackpool for my first summer season in 1977.

With Jane Beaumont - I sneaked back from the Channel Islands to Blackpool to propose to her.

With Wife Number Two - Julie Gullick.

With Julie and son Cameron at Wentworth in 1986 - it wasn't all smiles!

With Tricia Duskey on holiday in Marbella, Spain. The Red Devils brought us together!

With Wife Number Three, Alison Holloway, on our wedding day. The smiles didn't last long - and she could throw one hell of a punch.

With Wife Number Four, Tracy Hilton, the final wife.

I bought *Afghan Plains* to impress Tracy. It didn't work - she puts boating on a par with caravaning!

Tracy with Charlie and baby Freddie.

**Meeting Princess Anne at Blazer's in Windsor -
her local cabaret club!**

**Meeting the Queen in November 1979 at the
Royal Command Performance, Drury Lane.**

Princess Michael of Kent and her children with me and the rest of the company of *Cinderella* - the clean version! - in Bradford.

Electioneering for the Conservatives in March 1992 with Cheltenham candidate John Taylor.

Presenting PM Margaret Thatcher with a cheque for leukaemia research in July 1986 at Number 10 Downing Street.

With PM Margaret Thatcher and little Sharon Allen. Mrs Thatcher opened a photographic exhibition staged at the Barbican for my charity, the Sharon Allen Leukaemia Trust.

Croatia trip, Christmas 1992 - me and the upturned
UN truck.

One very proud man! Fishing remains one of my
greatest escapes - if only I still had days to waste at
Horton Kirby.

With my agent Laurie Mansfield. One of the first things he taught me was that if I wanted to be a success I couldn't do it alone. I had to let people make money out of me.

A very proud mum with an equally proud son in 1980.

to

James Cameron Davidson.

on his

FIRST

VERY

birthday

Nothing like this you've had before,
All I can wish is many more.
As you sail life's sea with a merry heart,
and be welcome on any far-off shore.

**Uncle Bill's hand-painted
picture, which says it all.**

I looked back to the pit, where Gordon Rose was in tears along with the rest of the band. The percussionist, Gary Catell, was laughing so much he almost fell off his stool. You can always count on the orchestra for laughs at any slight deviation in a script – they get so bored each performance. It's a lifeline to them.

Then Tommy and I went into our song, and wherever I was meant to sing 'Tommy' I substituted the new name, Gordon. When Mollie came on, laughing, she kept up the joke and said hello to 'Gordon'.

Just before I left the stage I looked again at Gordon Rose. He shot me a glance which said: 'It's funny but you aren't half going to be sorry for this later!'

Windsor, Melvyn and Victor also joined in the joke, calling for Gordon to do this and Gordon to do that. All was fine until we got to the dream sequence, when the joke quickly fell apart. My double took his place and only as I started making my quick change did I realise the clanger to come.

'Come on, Tommy – we're going back to London!' the tape boomed around the auditorium. The entire audience started murmuring loudly. It was all the children asking the adults who the hell Tommy was.

As the curtain came down on the finale one of the crew came over to me. 'Beware!' he said. 'Lionel's crawling up the wall!'

A few minutes later Lionel arrived and called me into his office. 'What have you done?' he demanded tetchily.

'I called the cat Gordon,' I said. I knew I'd gone over the top. What I'd intended as a harmless joke had backfired on both me and the production.

'Louis Benjamin's heard that you've changed the name of the cat,' he said. 'He's 'phoned from New York.'

It was rubbish, of course. Louis had no idea. Since then, whenever I'm directing and something goes terribly wrong or someone fucks up I shout: 'Louis Benjamin's 'phoned from New York!'

I wish that Lionel had given me a bollocking there and then and got it all off his chest. But he didn't. As he stood there fuming at me I guessed he'd probably find a way to get back at me and land me in the shit. He did, in a roundabout fashion, as will be seen . . .

A few days later, when Lionel and I had kissed and made up, he brought a friend to my dressing-room and introduced him. Johnny Miller was a huge, likeable Scot and Lionel actually introduced him, wrongly, as an 'ex-SAS man' (every ex-soldier I've ever met claims to have been in the SAS at some time). I asked Johnny where he worked.

'I'm minding a rock singer called Alex Harvey, from a band called The Sensational Alex Harvey Band,' he said. Alex had a fantastic band but an appalling habit of lashing his audience with really mean language and getting nasty with people. Hence the minders.

Johnny joined Windsor, Lionel, me and my roadie Stukie for supper at Stocks, a restaurant in the King's Road. The PR man there was Roddy Llewellyn's brother Dai. He was a nice enough chap but I always suspected he was also dreadfully devious. Whenever he smiled at you, you felt that he probably wanted something, and he usually did.

Dai hovered around as we had an aperitif at the bar. I asked Johnny what he planned to do when he finished working for Alex Harvey. 'Quite frankly,' he told us, 'I'm going to kidnap the Great Train Robber Ronnie Biggs.'

'Of course you are!' I said. He went on to explain that Biggs was behind a plan to get himself 'kidnapped' during his imminent extradition from Rio to Australia. The financial rewards would include a TV documentary and an 'in-on-the-act' book.

I knew vaguely of Ronnie Biggs and the Great Train Robbery but it all sounded too far-fetched to be taken seriously. 'Sounds great!' I said, dismissing Johnny as yet another crank. I was wrong – as I would soon discover to my own cost.

Dick Whittington did terrific business all holiday and I pretty much ruled the roost from the best dressing-room, the Yul Brynner Suite, complete with jacuzzi.

But things weren't so wonderful at home. Jane wasn't stupid and had a good idea I'd two-timed her more than once. I'd really enjoyed being with her but I knew our relationship couldn't last. My career was pushing ahead and, since the end of the summer season, we'd drifted further and further apart. She wanted her own life and had given up on me, and I can't say that I blamed her.

The night we broke up she came to the Palladium with Carl Wayne's wife, Susan Hanson, who'd played Diane in the TV soap *Crossroads*. 'See you!' said Jane, skipping off into 1981 with Susan.

When I got back to the house in Twickenham all her things had gone. A week or so later I bumped into her again briefly and we both agreed she'd done the right thing. 'Look,' I said. 'You might be upset now, but once you've gone to bed with someone else you'll be over me totally.'

'I have and you're right,' she answered. I'm not sure if I was as convinced by my own advice. Once she'd left I started to wish she hadn't and became very restless. I got depressed if I had to head home alone to that empty house. I hated it.

I'm such a nervous person that I rarely get much sleep at night, five hours at the most. With Jane gone, sleeping alone night after night turned me into a restless insomniac. Once again I found it difficult to accept that I could be famous, rich and desperately lonely. I was in my third series of my own television show and now topping the bill at the world-famous London Palladium, playing to 2,500 people a night, yet I was dreadfully lonely. Not surprising though, is it?

Anyway, absence makes the heart grow fonder and I started to feel incredibly over-sexed. Rather than sleep alone, night after night I began falling out of the theatre and into Stringfellow's to pick up and bed almost anyone in sight. For once those tabloid tales of my bedroom escapades actually were spot-on. I was fucking myself stupid.

Not only that, but in Stringfellow's I tried cocaine for the first time. I went to the loo and someone cautiously unwrapped a folded piece of paper to reveal the white powder. I promptly coughed and sent the lot flying into the air, a small fortune's-worth! But the next time I was offered it I made sure I didn't cough. Coke made me buzz and, like the speed I took as a teenager, it turned me into what I thought was the best, coolest bird-puller in the world.

In Stringfellow's one night someone produced a huge bag of the stuff, and we all tucked in using folded beermats to scoop and sniff it up. But because I'm so hyper the cocaine used to wear off in minutes, and it wasn't the sort of thing I could get hooked on – I didn't have the nose for it.

Backstage at the Palladium during that panto was awash with great entertainment names. I met John Le Mesurier and Arthur Lowe when they called on Clive Dunn; Donovan, a slightly weird individual was backstage one night.

Paul McCartney turned up with his kids and pointed me out to them. 'Hey, look!' he said. 'Here's Dick.' (Charming!) I liked Paul because he was a very good family man and I never was. I'm only just learning how to do that now.

The biggest star to stroll through the stage door after the show was Omar Sharif. I'd never met him before and had no idea he was coming. He found me in my dressing-room and invited me to join him for supper that night. Omar was the most stylish, handsome man with a very powerful persona. You knew he'd be charming even if he was in an appalling mood. Over supper he explained he was appearing in a play called *The Prince and The Showgirl*. He asked if I would watch it and tell him if I thought he was funny or not. I couldn't believe it. 'Omar Sha-fucking-rif' was asking for *my* opinion!

So a few nights later I saw the play. Omar's co-star was a beautiful and talented girl called Debbie Arnold, who played the Marilyn Monroe part brilliantly – better than Monroe could have done. I'd seen Debbie around in Stringfellow's but we didn't know each other.

After the show Omar took me, Debbie and her friend for supper at San Lorenzo's, a very smart and extremely expensive Knightsbridge restaurant. It was the first time I'd ever been there and I was very impressed. This was real style.

'You must have pasta!' he told me as we sat down at our table, proceeding to order for all of us.

Great, spaghetti! I thought. I love spaghetti.

When the food arrived I was mortified. Until then, if it didn't come out of a tin I didn't eat it. When the pasta arrived it wasn't like a tin of soggy Heinz spaghetti, it was the real McCoy and covered in funny bits.

I told Omar I genuinely loved his show. All he wanted to talk about that night was his genuine love – gambling. 'One day you and I will buy a racehorse and win lots of money,' he said, but sadly we never have.

'Do you go to the races much?' I asked.

'Yes,' he said. 'Sometimes I have £20,000 on every race. And sometimes I win!'

'Yes, but sometimes you lose,' I told him.

'That's why I've made the odd crap film,' he said. 'Sometimes I lose badly and 'phone up my agent, saying "Get me a film." "When?" he asks. "Today!" I say.'

Gambling was Omar's life and, if he has his way, it will also be his death. 'My ambition is to win the British Derby and die on the same day,' he told me morbidly.

We had several more suppers together. I remember once we were talking around the supper table and one of the ladies said something. 'Do you mind,' he snapped at her. 'The men are talking!'

Until he said that I only thought of Omar as the great film star. Suddenly I also saw the man, Omar the Arab. I've always loved the Arabic race because they are very courteous, polite and proper – to me, anyway. They enjoy a kind of inherent brotherhood the British race just doesn't have. Like Jews, Arabs have a great reverential pride. It's a shame they don't seem to get on.

I can't put my finger on what I learned from those suppers with Omar, but I know I became a better person for having met him. Thanks to Omar I also got to know his co-star, Debbie, well. She was very holdsy-handsy and 'love you forever', and we saw a lot of each other for several weeks, but never went the whole hog, to bed.

'The worst thing about kissing Omar,' she said once, 'is that his false teeth click.'

'You wicked cow!' I replied, telling her it was bad taste to even notice such things.

Debbie loved going to Morton's so we practically became residents for a while. She could work a room better than anyone I've ever seen and I used to joke with her that she should get a rubber neck fitted so that she could do it in half the time.

One Sunday in February the Palladium also played host to the first-ever Children's Royal Variety Show, in the presence of Princess Margaret. She arrived with her lady-in-waiting, Lady Anne Tennant. I asked Lady Anne's permission to tell the following story, on television, about her visit that night and she said she'd rather I didn't. So, instead, here goes in print.

The cast of *Dick Whittington* was to perform a scene from the production and I was also doing my own solo spot, a routine with a voice harmoniser which made me sound like Pinky or Perky. Also on the show were the great Billy Dainty, Rod Hull and Emu, The Krankies, Suzanne Dando, Adam Ant and the dreaded Paul Daniels.

The big hit of the evening was Billy Dainty, who'd brought the house down by putting on a wig and tights and doing a ludicrous ballerina routine. Backstage was a riot. We were in and out of each other's dressing-rooms, swapping jokes and gossip. Ian Krankie kept pouring beers down Rod Hull in an attempt to persuade him that Emu had to knock Paul Daniels' wig off when he met the princess.

During the finale Ian stood just behind Daniels. At the very end of the song, in true light entertainment tradition, we all had to throw up an arm. Ian kept flicking his arm near Daniels' head and the rest of us expected his syrup to fly into orbit any second. Keeping a straight face was virtually impossible.

After the show we all got ready to meet Princess Margaret in the line-up on stage. At this point I'd started to get slightly anxious because of something Victor had mentioned. Princess Margaret was very friendly with Victor; she used to confide in him and they were agony aunts to one another.

I'd told him just before the show started that I was slightly nervous about getting on with the princess. 'I've had a word with her,' he said, straight-faced, just before the royal party arrived. 'When she comes along the line to you, it's straight out with her, into the car and off to the Palace!'

When Princess Margaret reached me I had the beating heart and dry mouth symptoms. She shook my hand and looked me in the eye. 'Were you in it?' she asked me, with a mischievous smile. Mollie Sugden, who was standing next to me, roared with laughter.

'Yes,' I said. 'I was Dick Whittington.'

I never did find out whether she was winding me up but I think she was. Next it was my turn to laugh at Mollie. After the princess had moved along, two behind her was Lady Anne.

'You were wonderful,' she said to Mollie.

'Thank you, thank you very much,' she replied.

'You must be very fit,' Lady Anne then asked her.

'I beg your pardon?' said Mollie, puzzled.

'Your legs,' she explained.

'Excuse me?'

'You were just wonderful – the way you flitted across the stage,' she said. 'It was very, very funny.'

Then it suddenly dawned on Mollie that the lady-in-waiting thought that she was Billy Dainty! I roared with laughter.

Months later I went to a charity greyhound racing event, where I met Lady Anne again. We got talking and the conversation inevitably turned to Princess Margaret.

'Do you know what one of her stupid ladies-in-waiting said once?' I asked her.

'No, what?' she replied.

'She actually said to Mollie Sugden . . .' I started and, as I did so, two pennies dropped at once.

'That was me!' she interrupted. 'I remember that night. I remember suddenly saying the wrong thing and just getting deeper in it. I was really digging a hole for myself. You will apologise to Mollie, won't you?' she asked.

'I don't think *you* need to!' I said.

Another big star to find me during the Palladium panto run was Tommy Steele – and I was, unintentionally, very rude to him. That night the 'phone rang as I got into the dressing-room and when I answered it my heart skipped a wee beat. It was Julie Gullick. I was thrilled to hear from her and while we were giggling and talking, Tommy was politely shown into my ante-room. I waved to him through the doorway and he waved back then waited for me to hang up. But I couldn't hang up, not on Julie.

Eventually Tommy gave up and left without either of us having said a word to each other. Sorry Tom, I should have spoken to you and told her to wait – then I'd be as rich as you now. During that call Julie told me she was coming up to London shortly to work at a trade show and wanted to meet again. I told her I had to see her sooner.

8

'Come On Parky, We're Going to a Wedding!'

Julie Gullick had me hooked. I arranged an immediate rendezvous at a motel called the Saxon Inn in Northampton, and she looked even prettier than I remembered. We had a few drinks and, thinking I'd got *carte blanche*, I took her back to the bedroom and tried to undress her.

'Oh no!' she said. 'This is not right. I don't like all this, you're not using me like this.'

So I didn't. I was enthralled and happy to play the game whichever way she wanted, as long as I could see her again.

A fortnight later she came back to London, for the trade show, and I took her out most nights. Then she left to go to Aviemore in Scotland, on a skiing promotion, promising I could see her again when the panto run finished.

A few days later I arranged to meet Laurie for a drink in Morton's. I had very little cash on me, just enough for a half of lager until he arrived. I stood at the bar and in came two darling girls. One had short blonde hair and the other was very dark and pretty. They walked up to the other end of the bar and ordered a glass of champagne and a spritzer.

'And a large gin and tonic please,' I added, even though I didn't know them. They ignored me totally.

As they walked past me, the blonde banged a large gin and tonic under my nose. 'Thanks very much,' I said.

I knocked half of it back and then went over to speak to them.

'Thanks, I didn't really mean it,' I said. 'I was only joking, you know.'

We started talking and the blonde asked: 'How's the pantomime going at the Palladium?'

'Fine, we've got about a month to run,' I said. 'What's your name?'

'Angie,' she said.

'What do you do?'

'Nothing,' she said.

She was covered in gold, so I retorted: 'You must have a rich husband.'

'Sort of,' she said.

'Who's your husband then?'

'Guess.'

I went through everyone. Did he do this? Did he do that? Where was he from?

'He's not English,' she said.

'Where's he from then?' I said. 'He's got to be an Arab.'

'No,' she said.

I continued reeling off a string of names. I mentioned everyone I could think of in show-business, every actor, every singer

'Try football,' she said, and I knew at once.

'You're Angie Best, aren't you?' I said.

'Yes,' she replied. I didn't try to chat her up; I like George and he's much bigger than me! So I started talking to her friend, who turned out to be her sister, Lindy James. I invited them both to see the panto. Angie declined but Lindy took me up on the offer. Two nights later she strolled through the Palladium stage door, looking stunning.

'Fucking marry it!' said my roadie, Rick Price, after he met her.

A few meetings later Lindy started coming back with me to Twickenham for nights of passion. She was marvellous and used to wear silk lingerie, which was all new to me. Lindy tagged along with me for the next two or three weeks and put me in a right quandary. As much as I liked Lindy I was also more than smitten with Julie. I had to make up my mind about which one I wanted on my arm and decided, for my sins, it had to be Julie.

Being a bit of a coward, I started ducking and diving Lindy's calls on the telephone until she turned up at the Palladium in person. We went out for supper and she asked to see me again the following night. When she arrived then I sort of half-hinted at what was coming. I was wearing a big, thick gold chain and took it off. 'Here's a souvenir of me,' I said, giving it to her.

Without saying a word, she knew that it was a going-away present. She never 'phoned again after that and I haven't seen her since.

With Lindy gone I started plotting my next meeting with Julie. Talking to Lionel's mate Johnny Miller, the would-be kidnapper of Ronnie Biggs, had planted a naughty seed in my mind. I decided that as soon as the panto was over I would take Julie off for a truly romantic holiday, even if I had to kidnap her!

I couldn't work out where to go and finally rang John Ashby, friend and manager to Cilla Black and Petula Clark. He always had exotic holidays and I thought he'd have some good suggestions.

'You've been to the Caribbean quite a bit,' I said, 'Where can I go for a really good holiday? Laurie's suggested the Virgin Islands but what do you think?'

'You don't want to go to the Virgin Islands,' said John. 'Go to Barbados. There's a great hotel called the Sandy Lane, you should book yourself into it. You'll have a terrific time, it'll be perfect.'

During the last few days at the Palladium, Stukie told me he was going to see Alex Harvey in concert. Good old Johnny Miller had organised complimentary tickets. The next night Stukie stormed into the dressing-room in a mood.

'That bastard never left me a ticket!' he snorted.

'Who?' I asked.

'That Johnny Miller bloke you met,' he said. 'Lionel's pal.'

'Well, where is he?' I asked.

'He's not working with Alex Harvey any more, he's in Brazil!' he replied.

He was for real! I thought, and when I turned on the TV news, there was a picture of him on the screen. He actually *had* kidnapped Ronnie Biggs!

As the panto ended in March I made all the Barbados arrangements for Julie and me. I persuaded Rick to fly to Scotland to find her, get her on a shuttle back to London and finally on to the plane bound for Barbados.

I met Julie on the plane in first class, handed her a glass of champagne and asked her to marry me. We flew off cuddling and kissing.

When we arrived in Barbados, it was a tropical paradise. We got to the Sandy Lane Hotel and went straight down to the golden beach to have a drink and stroll along the shore at sundown. A bird shat on me and I should have realised then that it was an omen.

I felt very happy and we got pissed. Then, in a bid to make Julie giggle, I walked into the sea in my suit. (Anyway, I wanted a pee!)

The next day we met Michael and Mary Parkinson, who were also at the hotel. Michael loved comedians and we got on like a house on fire. We quickly became big fans of the hotel's resident entertainer, a put-upon, fat, effeminate West Indian called Egbert. 'And now will you welcome, for your entertainment, Egbert de Juggler,' someone would say off-stage in a laid-back West Indian accent. Out would come Egbert, dressed like Ali Baba, proceeding to juggle for the bemused guests for ten minutes. Then he left the stage and, after a short interval, there'd be another introduction.

'And now, will you welcome, for your entertainment, Egbert de Limbo Dancer,' said the compere. Out would come Egbert, this time dressed as a limbo dancer and proceeding, despite his wide girth, to wobble uncomfortably under the low rod for a few minutes. Then he left again.

By this time Michael and I were creased up. Just when we thought it couldn't get any funnier, out came Egbert again.

'And now will you welcome, for your entertainment, Egbert de Fire-Eater!' came the introduction.

He clearly didn't take to the fire-eating bit and, in a flash, the poor bloke was on fire. What a way to make a living!

One morning I opened the local papers and couldn't believe what I read. Ronnie Biggs was being held in a Barbados prison and Johnny Miller and his gang were also on the island. I quickly found Parky and showed him the paper. 'I've just met this bloke Miller. He's a nutter,' I said.

Later a note was slipped under my bedroom door. It said: 'From John Miller to Jim Davidson and girlfriend. Am getting married at Hilton Hotel, would you be best man?'

It was very weird. I'd only met him twice, but as I'd seen him on the news I found it all slightly too intriguing for my own good. I went and found Parky again. 'Come on, Parky!' I said. 'I'm going to go down to the Hilton to take a look. Are you coming?'

'No, not me,' he said, and I should have known then I was doing the wrong thing.

I got down to the Hilton with Julie and waiting in the packed lobby was the world's press and a television crew. Johnny rushed up to shake my hand and a split second later photographers' flashguns were going off everywhere. I'd walked right into a viper's nest. Johnny Miller not only had his own press manager, he also had a make-up artist standing by.

Johnny said Biggs had lost his bottle a bit but they'd moved him from car to 'plane then boat and had been making good progress when the engines broke down. They'd made it to Barbados, where police boarded the boat, arrested Biggs and destroyed the video tapes they'd made.

'What are you going to do?' I asked.

'Well, Biggs will probably be allowed to go back to Brazil and at least we'll get the book out of it,' he said optimistically.

He was in a jovial mood and I agreed to be photographed with him although I politely declined to be his best man since I still didn't know him. After the ceremony the champagne flowed and everyone got drunk. About twelve hours later I got an anxious call from Laurie back in London. 'Jim, what have you done?' he asked.

'Nothing,' I replied. 'I haven't done a thing. Why?'

'You're on *News at Ten*!' he said. 'Julie Gullick's dad has gone mad because she's meant to be in Scotland skiing, and suddenly she's a terrorist in Barbados and splashed all over the news!'

The next day things got even worse. Dai Llewellyn had also seen the news and clearly thought he had an angle worth a few bob to the tabloids. 'I heard Jim Davidson, Lionel Blair and Windsor Davies planning to kidnap Ronnie Biggs,' he told them. 'They were discussing it when they came to Stocks one night.'

Laurie 'phoned again to read me the story and I couldn't believe what I was hearing. 'Just get on to the papers and tell them it's not true,' I told him.

'It's too late,' he said, 'The whole of London's under-world hates you!'

Since I'd grown up around the Old Kent Road I knew a bit about London's underworld. I decided that if any of them came up to me about the Biggs saga, I'd just explain I had nothing whatsoever to do with it.

When Julie and I got back to Britain, I took her home to her parents. I put the record straight and they didn't blame me, although they must have wondered what the heck their daughter was getting herself into.

Lionel had dismissed Dai's story as rubbish and I don't think he had any problems. But Windsor received threats after the story named him. There can't be anything more unlikely than Windsor Davies plotting to kidnap Ronnie Biggs!

I was advised by several people to go into hiding, which I did. I checked into a hotel, very miserable at getting blamed for something of which I was quite innocent.

At Kempton races with Stukie, Rick, Julie and her dad, I met someone who really saved my life, and eventually enabled me to come out of hiding again. At the racecourse a smart little grey-haired racing spiv known as Jimmy The One, started talking to me. He introduced me in turn to a man he referred to as his guv'nor, nicknamed 'The Milkman', who was immaculate, good-looking, five or six years older than me and fearsome.

He was obviously influential and held court in a small circle of friends who were all cigars and champagne. The Milkman looked across at me and then blanked me. I asked Jimmy The One what the problem was. 'He doesn't want to speak to you because of your involvement with Ronnie Biggs,' he explained.

I downed a large glass of champagne for courage and went over to The Milkman. I told him exactly what had happened in Barbados but he insisted he'd heard differently and, as far as he was concerned, I was in it up to my neck.

'I swear,' I said. 'You have to believe me, I've told you the truth. You can ask the friends of Ronnie Biggs, they'll know that Miller and Biggs set the thing up.' I knew Biggs' boys wouldn't be annoyed and could vouch for my being an innocent bystander.

After the races I went back into hiding, hoping I wasn't in worse trouble. In the morning the 'phone rang early. It was The Milkman. I had no idea how he'd got my telephone number.

'Yes, Jim,' he started. 'I was wrong. I've made a few calls and I'd judged you wrongly. Leave this with me, I'll have words with a few people and find out what's what.'

To make amends, he gave me a tip for a race that afternoon and hung up. I backed the horse and it won. After that things were fine, although I still got occasional trouble from some of the London gangsters who weren't in the know.

Being dragged into that messy Biggs affair is one of the biggest regrets of my life. I still wouldn't know Ronnie Biggs if I fell over him. I could have met Buster Edwards a few years later, when the film *Buster* was released, but I ducked the chance. I was frightened he'd call me every name under the sun but, then again, perhaps he knew the truth. Eventually Johnny Miller 'phoned me, and my mum, to apologise for all the problems he'd caused.

After The Milkman fixed it for me to come out of hiding,

I set off on another tour round the country in the run-up to a summer season in Bournemouth. Gary Catell joined as my percussionist and was hysterical to have around, a complete nutcase who performed in a German helmet.

One night during the show we could hear a terrible humming noise. No one could work out what it was. It sounded like feedback from the PA system. It wasn't. It turned out to be Gary, drunk and fast asleep on a kettle drum resonating in C sharp minor! Gary was totally fearless, greeting everyone, actors and directors alike, in the same optimistic, chirpy way. Thumb up, he'd ask, 'All right? How's it going? All right?'

Throughout the tour he would sneak into my dressing-room when no-one was around and climb into my wardrobe. He'd hide for ages waiting for me to come back with visitors, then he would step out of the wardrobe and look around the room, apparently puzzled. 'I feel much better for that,' he'd say, and leave! He was magic to have around, like a young Bob Todd.

I arrived in Bournemouth in need of a holiday but plodded on. I was at the Winter Gardens and Julie came with me. With a few days' warning for our families, we decided to get married in Poole Register Office on July 23 1981. Although we couldn't take a honeymoon because I had the season to do, the wedding was still a swell affair.

The night before we all checked into a hotel in Bourne-mouth. Julie stayed in with her friends while I went out with my mates on my stag night. We got leglessly drunk and ended up in a horrible nightclub where I picked up my last final fling, a Welsh girl. I sneaked her back to my room at the hotel and all I can remember about her was her nickname – it was 'Thank God'!

When I woke up in the morning I felt like death. There's a surprise. I dragged myself into the bathroom and got ready. Then my mates turned up and took me to a pub on the way, for a drink to steady my nerves.

Absolutely everyone was on their way up from London for the wedding. Amazingly, even Dad was coming. By then he was too old and usually too pissed to get out much. I arrived at the register office alongside my witnesses, my keyboard player Alan Rogers and roadie Stukie. I can't remember which one actually passed me the ring during the ceremony, but I know I forgave them later. Whichever one it was I wish now he'd kept it in his bloody pocket!

I was determined that this wedding wasn't going to be an anti-climax like my first one, when I'd been bollocked for playing Pink Floyd and my new bride had rushed off to bed – not for a leg-over! After the quickie service Julie and I went back to the Carlton Hotel, a wonderful five-star place overlooking the Bournemouth cliffs, for an excellent wedding breakfast and plenty of champagne.

Dad stayed at the bar drinking whisky until he was so pissed we had to force a ham sandwich down him and put him to bed for the rest of the afternoon.

I went off, very pissed, to do the show, and then we had another party at the theatre. I just didn't want that magical night to end. So we all decided to go to a nightclub – except at that point Julie threw a wobbler. Mum's brother Uncle George tried to cheer her up and offered to take her back to the hotel where I turned up a little more drunk a little later.

Julie and I lived together all summer in a little rented house in Poole and my life felt perfect. In my private life I'd just tied the knot again but in my professional life changes were afoot. At the same time as the wedding, Laurie took over completely from Wally and also became my manager, buying him out fairly.

In Bournemouth that year I met a wonderful British businessman, Bob Braithwaite. He owns Sunseekers, a company with an international reputation which builds beautiful motorcruisers. He showed me a fabulous new two-berth 31ft Sunseeker boat. We went out for a test spin and she went like shit off a shovel. As we came ashore I was drooling, despite the £31,000 price tag.

I went straight back to the house and 'phoned Laurie to ask him if I could afford the boat.

'No!' came the reply.

Then I 'phoned my accountant and asked him the same thing, could I afford the boat?

'No!' came the same reply.

So I went and bought it. I rang a broker who arranged a loan.

I named her *Dishby Doo*, after the Swedish chef in *The Muppet Show*, who could always make Laurie and me laugh. We launched her, and within three days she was back out of the water with a bloody great hole in her side. I'd pranged her in the Channel near Poole harbour, hitting a submerged obstacle.

When we got *Dishby* to Sunseekers she was put on stilts and I went along to see the extent of the damage. She looked a sad sight and I vowed never to be so reckless in the water again – unless it was in a bath with someone.

Towards the end of the season Julie and I went to see Clive Brandy, now married to the singer Iris Williams and living in a fabulous house in Sunningdale. They threw a barbecue, and Clive used real coal instead of barbecue bricks and smoked us all into the house!

The kitchen had two fridges the size of butcher's, one full of food and the other crammed with champagne. 'If an army turns up I want them fed!' Clive joked as he dived into it. Soon he'd persuaded me I should buy a house in the area and become his neighbour.

Julie and I looked at a house that afternoon. It had a pleasant little entrance hall, four bedrooms and an outdoor swimming pool. I put in a bid, for £180,000, which was hastily accepted by the estate agent – an easy sale.

We went back to Bournemouth to finish the season then moved to the rented house in Twickenham before, at last, moving into Wentworth. Some nights Julie and I would go out for supper locally with Clive and Iris. We favoured two local restaurants in Sunningdale, the Chinese and the Indian.

At the Chinese, Clive would take care of the drinks by ordering in bulk: an entire case of wine for the four of us, which we'd see off.

One night we all went to the Indian with Rick Wakeman. This was long before Rick gave up drinking and our party was completely sloshed and raucous, which the waiters clearly didn't like. Eventually their bad karma (or was it korma) got to Rick, who lost his temper. 'How much?' he demanded of the annoyed head waiter.

'For de bill?' he said. 'No. You have behaved so badly I don't want your money.'

'No,' said Rick. 'For the restaurant!'

And on that note we paid up and left.

Julie had stopped working and quickly made a lot of friends around Wentworth. All the women there were the same – heels too high, too much jewellery and a bit too much make-up. The Wentworth Wives. Rich ladies who had very long lunches together and then went back to each other's houses to while away the rest of the afternoon.

I hated that scene. Julie suddenly went from being a nice, sweet wife in her twenties to a forty-year-old nag. Before my eyes she actually became one of those funny women who wear too much make-up to hide the fact that underneath they're all stretch-marks and Femfresh. Like her Wentworth contemporaries, Julie had to have a housekeeper. Soon she'd got her own life going with her friends in Wentworth and decided the last thing she wanted was a little drunk coming home to her for his boring chop and chips. I could never eat any of the fancy meals she used to practise cooking all day. She started to spend most of her time with The Wives. So I'd go and find Clive instead.

Over the Christmas holiday, breaking with the tradition of pantomime, I appeared at the Circus Tavern, Purfleet. As we toasted in 1982 Julie and I had plenty to celebrate. She was pregnant with our baby. To please her I had a new kitchen fitted. It didn't make much difference. The pregnancy tired her out and made her grumpy all the time.

Just after the kitchen was fitted, Clive and his mate George Savva, who ran Blazer's in Windsor, picked me up for an evening at Windsor races. Julie wasn't coming and, as I set off, she made it clear she wasn't happy at being left alone.

At the races the three of us studied the form and spotted a horse in the final race of the afternoon called Hippo Disco, which just happened to be the name of a Barbados nightclub I'd liked so much I'd tried to buy it.

I knew I'd bet on Hippo Disco later and, in the meantime, I picked a horse for the next race and won £500. I put the lot on a horse in the following race and that, too, came in first. I couldn't make a wrong move on the next few horses, and after the penultimate race I'd won £4,000. I decided I just had to put the lot on Hippo Disco. At odds of 11–2 I stood to make £22,000 if it won.

On the way to place the bet I spotted a payphone and decided to call Julie quickly to check how she was. It's said bad things often come in threes, and they certainly did that time. When Julie answered the 'phone, she was still in a dreadful mood. Then she started an argument which was costing a fortune in change my end.

The third and final blow was the cruellest. 'They're off!' the race commentator hissed over the tannoy.

Julie was in mid-yell as, horrified, I hung up. I ran to watch the race and Hippo Disco romped home by a mile.

I thought I'd probably explode I was so frustrated. When you get that frustrated there really is only one answer, to get thoroughly pissed. We went from the racecourse to Blazer's, which Mike Reid was working that night.

By the time I got home I was staggering all over the place. But Julie was still up, waiting for an argument. She started nagging me about wasting money.

'You want some money?' I shouted. 'If you want money, you can have bloody money!' I threw the untouched £4,000 at her, notes flying everywhere.

'I don't want your money!' she snapped back, which was news to me, as Julie wanted everything and the more expensive it was the better.

'Well, if you don't want my money then you won't want the new kitchen it's just bought, will you?' I said. Before she could reply I'd stormed into the kitchen and started demolishing everything in sight with my bare hands. I pulled cabinets off the walls and hurled them through the windows, kicked doors off hinges and even tried wrenching out the kitchen sink.

I was in such a furious temper that I trashed the whole kitchen, gashing open my hand and thumb in the process. I made an attempt to bandage the hand before collapsing in a drunken heap on to one of the spare beds upstairs.

Next morning I left the mess to Julie and went straight to Clive's for the day. After that I never bet again with serious money on the horses. I've still got a scar on my thumb to help me remember the lesson.

When the summer season started in Torquay Julie, very pregnant, again came with me. In a little over a year she'd gone from being a lovely new bride to a grumpy wife and mother-to-be. She hated the idea of being pregnant. Julie believed childbirth to be beneath her, and probably still does – she's never had another baby.

My old mate Kevin was already living in Torquay, where he was married to a dancer called Elaine, and he came back to work for me. *Dishby Doo* was conveniently berthed just by the theatre at Torquay and I went out on her most afternoons. I decided to take her to Bournemouth with Kevin one day, and the night before we planned to anchor up just outside Torquay harbour for an early start next morning.

But first we went to a nightclub and happened to meet a couple of girls. We invited them back to the boat, then for a ride, if you'll pardon the expression. They waited, giggling, at the quayside as Kevin and I got on to the boat to get her ready. As I was untying the front rope I looked up and spotted a third, more familiar pair of ankles next to the girls'. I followed the legs up and there was Kevin's wife Elaine – with her parents.

'Caught you have I, Kevin?' she bawled in Scouse at him.

'Let go for'd!' he said quickly.

'Let go aft,' I cried. The two of us sped off at Warp 10, leaving Elaine and her folks standing with the two girls we'd picked up. Kevin and I decided to head straight for Bournemouth. All I had to steer with was a compass, maps and a fair amount of guesswork, but I thought we could get there.

I called ahead to the Portland coastguard on the radio to announce *Dishby Doo* en route to Bournemouth.

'Can you tell me what speed you're doing?' asked the coastguard.

'Forty knots plus,' I replied, knowing full well we were going too fast.

'There's a thing here called the Portland Race,' he said anxiously. 'It's a very choppy piece of water, with big holes in it.'

'Oh yes,' I said, 'We've just flown over it.'

We berthed in Bournemouth and Kevin was cowering at the thought of having left Elaine, furious, in Torquay. So we both drank the night away trying to forget the problem.

A few days later Kevin came up to me looking rather worried. He told me Elaine had told Julie I was seeing a Swedish girl called Tin-Tin. It caused a massive row between Julie and me. As much as I found Tin-Tin stunning, and would have loved to have been rude with her, nothing had happened. But Julie laid into me all the same and called me everything under the sun. Kevin also went home to a blazing row with Elaine over the trouble she'd stirred up between Julie and me.

Then, to cap it all, my two sisters, Jean (on a flying visit from America) and Eileen, came to stay with us. It came as no surprise when I got back from work one night to find Eileen still up.

'Don't panic, but Julie's been taken to hospital,' she said. 'Her waters have broken.'

I knew at once Julie would be furious – she'd planned for the baby to be born back in London at Queen Charlotte's, where the Queen had hers. As I drove to the Torquay hospital I was chuffed that our baby was being born in a nice, ordinary British NHS hospital.

I arrived and found Julie. She was having contractions and hated every second, and she looked at me as if she also hated me. But she was fine once Cameron came crying into the world in the early hours of August 12 1982, and she saw him for the first time.

Julie was out of hospital a few days later and as soon

as she was home she employed a nanny. Julie had made it abundantly clear that she was going to avoid all the messy business of bringing up baby. As soon as she got her figure back she was into the mini-skirts and back on top of the world.

Back at Wentworth, I still didn't have any idea what I really wanted. I wasn't any better than Julie with our baby son and couldn't change a nappy. I couldn't have anything to do with baby's pooh, and I still can't.

'It's different, son, when it's your own,' Mum told me.

I said: 'It's not my own, Mum, it's his!'

A new routine started to shape my wintry days off. I'd invariably meet up for a buck's fizz with Clive and George Savva. The three of us wasted more days at the races, trying to win a fortune. After a losing streak we decided that our problem was we didn't have any trainer's insider information and would have to buy a racehorse. Well, we couldn't afford a horse so we opted instead for the next best thing – a greyhound dog.

Clive searched through the Yellow Pages and found the nearest breeder. On a dark winter's night Clive, George and I drove to the man's house and knocked him up.

Clive's twenty-stone filled the door frame, George was wearing a thick overcoat and looked like a Russian henchman and I was in a sheepskin coat. We must have looked like the local mafia; in fact, we *were* the local mafia!

'Are you a dog trainer?' said Clive.

'Yes,' he replied.

'Well,' said Clive. 'We want to be the Robert Sangsters of the dog world. Sell us your best dog!'

He took us into the yard at the back of his home and sold us, for £2,000, a greyhound called Academy Lad.

A few days later we three proud owners turned up at the track at Wembley and entered Academy Lad in the first race.

'And now, the 450 yards hurdles,' said the commentator.

'Hurdles?' I said to Clive.

'Hurdles?' he said to me.

'Hurdles are for horses, not dogs!' said George.

The race started and Academy Lad not only jumped the hurdles, he did somersaults as well. He was so slow that the other dogs could stop, shit, bury it and still lap him. We'd poured £2,000 straight down the drain.

Another £2,000 later we bought another dog, Gaily Doll, this time from an Irishman called Adam Jackson. 'If I'd known you were going to buy Academy Lad from the other bloke,' he said, 'I would have told you not to bother. I sold it to him and I was very glad to get rid of it.'

Gaily Doll did quite well, but then Clive and George decided they wanted to go a stage further and bought several cheap dogs to run at Slough races. Clive took one over to Slough one afternoon and asked another trainer if the dog might win.

'No chance,' he told him. 'This is the dog which will win.' He pointed to another dog which Clive promptly backed with a £2,000 bet. The other dog didn't even win a place – and Clive's came first. To add insult to injury, Clive had to collect a cheap trophy from the stewards worth all of thirty bob.

Meanwhile, I was back at Blazer's with George. Clive suddenly stormed in twiddling his little cup in his podgy fingers. 'That's my fucking lot!' he said, and that was the last he had to do with dog racing.

I did dabble a bit more. I bought a third dog called Ceili Lass for £5,000 and got Adam Jackson to look after her for me. She was, and remains, a world record-holder for the now demolished White City stadium. Ceili Lass could lap anything and beat a record by a second and a half.

Once I entered her in the Harringay races and bumped into Jimmy The One, The Milkman's man, who arranged some bets for me. Ceili Lass won the first race easily. She was so magnificent she could have romped home with a gas stove strapped to her back. This put her 8–1 favourite to win the prestigious Oaks race later.

I got greedy and arranged, through Jimmy, to put £8,000 I didn't have on her to win outright. This time she came last and Jimmy looked at me ashen-faced.

'Come on,' he said. 'We've got to get out of this shit. We've got to bet more to get the money back.'

I bet everything I could and lost that, too.

I found Adam Jackson and asked what had happened. Why hadn't Ceili won? He gave me a dodgy answer and I decided I'd had enough. 'Fuck it!' I told him. 'Sell the dog.'

With that I left the track.

The dog was sent to Ireland to breed but I don't know where she is today, probably alongside Shergar somewhere. Perhaps that's why hot dogs are so expensive in Ireland.

By the end of the year I practically became a resident at George Savva's club, I was booked there for the whole Christmas holiday. It meant I could spend plenty of time at home with Julie and baby Cameron, and we also got the chance to visit Julie's parents in Hinckley.

On New Year's Eve I had to be back down at Blazer's, but by lunchtime in Hinckley I was pissed. So Julie drove back, through thick fog, and we got to the club really early.

Julie set about trying to sober me up. I got through so much coffee and mineral water that by the time I had to go on I was completely sober. I don't know why I bothered. Everyone else was completely drunk: the band was drunk, the audience was drunk, everyone under that damn roof was drunk, except me.

I started the act and decided that I'd better join them all, so I knocked back enough brandies to catch up. After the performance I threw a big party backstage for everyone to welcome in 1983 with a bang. I even hired a piper to play for us.

An incongruous couple turned up at the bash, a little Indian man and his wife, who seemed to take offence at me. 'Do you mind not swearing?' she said suddenly.

'Who the fuck is this?' I shouted to Rick Price. 'Get rid of this woman.'

'I'm afraid you'll have to leave,' Rick told her.

'I beg your pardon?' she said.

'Well, it's my boss's dressing-room,' he explained. 'Surely

he can swear in his own room if he wishes? If you don't like his language I suggest you leave.'

'I will!' she snapped, grabbing her little husband and storming out.

George Savva said loudly: 'Do you know who that was, luv? He's the richest man in Windsor. He has three oil wells.'

'Well, well, fucking well!' piped up Clive, and we fell about.

9

Mrs Thatcher Was Mum

I have a real phobia about heights and flying. I hadn't made my first trip in an aeroplane until comparatively late in life, when I was with Val and her two boys. We took a flight over Great Yarmouth and I was really anxious.

I can be very specific about what frightened me – falling out of the plane and landing messily on the ground below, a nightmare which has haunted me many times. I'd never have my own little plane, I know it would be the death of me. Coming down with a desperate dose of get-home-itis is bad enough in bad weather with a boat, but with a plane I know it would be fatal. Too many people have already been killed that way because they think they'll be fine, the weather will improve for them and for their light aircraft. My rule of thumb is the professional pilots' – don't leave the ground if there's the slightest risk.

Needless to say, therefore, I was a little drunk early in 1983 when for charity I agreed to make a parachute jump. Actually, I was more than a little drunk, I was completely mad.

I was in Aldershot with Terry, my minder. He introduced me to several guys from the Parachute Regiment, including a man called Bob Harman, a parachute instructor who organised charity jumps at the Aldershot base for novices in a crash course. He tried persuading me to jump a week later, with his next group of students.

I thought if I agreed I could always do the ground training and back out at the last minute, feigning a sprained ankle or something. With this in mind, I challenged Terry. 'I'll do it, if you'll do it,' I said.

'You're on!' he answered. A week later I really wished he hadn't.

Terry and I turned up at the base mid-morning for the jump. Bob was training seven of us, six blokes and a girl. As soon as I saw the girl I knew I had to go through with it. If she had the balls to do it then so did I.

We were all kitted out with parachutes and struggled into them. Bob ran through the training and everyone seemed to be taking it all in, except me. I was asking myself what the hell I'd been drinking a week earlier to have got myself into this fine mess.

We each had two parachutes, one on the front, another on the back. I asked Bob why we needed both. 'The one on your back is in case the one on the front doesn't open,' he told me.

'If you know the one on the back is sure to open why don't we just wear that one on our front?' I asked him.

Next came the physical training, and I passed with full honours. I had to run with the parachute on. Next was jumping from a two-foot high wall, landing and rolling. Cake, piece of! I felt much more confident after the wall. As long as the plane didn't fly higher than a couple of feet off the ground I'd be fine.

Bob ordered us to remove any false teeth. And he told us we had to shout out a drill the moment we jumped: thousand and one, thousand and two, thousand and three, thousand and four. Check canopy!

Counting thousands in the drill gives you exactly enough time to ensure everything's going properly. If it isn't, that's when you find out if the 'chute on your back's all it's cracked up to be.

One of the students was a little man called Shaun Day. He later appeared in a great television series called *The Paras* and had the whole nation feeling sorry for him because he lost his bottle on an assault course and refused to jump across a bridge sixty feet off the ground. Well, the day of that parachute jump not only did I not take to him, I hated him, for winding me up terribly.

Just as we were getting on the plane he walked up to me and sniffed my spare parachute. 'That parachute smells of death,' he said.

We boarded the plane and took off – with the door wide open! I panicked and felt like death. Perhaps Shaun had a point.

The girl jumped first, wearing special knickers to stop her whistling on the way down, and I went second.

'Thousand and bloody one,' I said quickly. 'Thousand and bloody two, thousand and bloody three, thousand and bloody four. Check bloody canopy!'

I looked around and it was open. Great, all was going well and I felt totally exhilarated. My heart was pounding furiously and I looked around to see Terry and the others behind me. The view in all directions was spectacular. This is the best feeling I've ever had, I thought to myself.

When I hit the ground I rolled perfectly, stood up and was unharmed. Not only that, I was only a short distance from the target landing site.

I took in a long, deep breath and felt wonderful. Then I gathered up my parachute and rejoined the others. Terry got told off loudly by Bob for not shouting the thousand drill.

'I forgot to take out my false teeth!' he said. 'I couldn't open my gob or the whole lot would have flown out!'

It wasn't the first time Bob had come across the problem. A week earlier a man had jumped with his false teeth in. They came out but fell at exactly the same speed, so he just grabbed them back in mid-air and put them in his pocket before landing!

I was so excited by completing the jump I had to 'phone someone to talk about it. I 'phoned Mum, but she wasn't home. I called Laurie, he'd left for lunch. Everyone was out. Talk about an anti-climax!

At Thames Television in 1983 we'd come to a bit of an impasse. I'd done five series of *The Jim Davidson Show* and we all thought it was beginning to run out of fresh ideas. There just wasn't enough good clean material. The replacement devised was a sitcom, *Up the Elephant and Round the Castle*, with me cast as a chirpy Cockney layabout. In addition, Thames still wanted me to do comedy shows for them.

Laurie now set about renegotiating our contract and the deal struck gave them six half-hour sitcoms and three one-hour comedy specials, and put me, at the age of twenty-nine, among the top ten earners on television. Spending the money was never a problem, I'd got the hang of that by now. Putting our differences behind us, Julie and I used some of the money to throw a second anniversary bash the like of which had never been seen in Wentworth.

We invited 300 guests and spent £30,000 on a party on a par with anything Hollywood could mount. We had three huge marquees set up in the floodlit grounds. In the largest a special stage was erected for a band and there were 200 seats. Then we had a burger bar, champagne bar and even extra Portaloos to help cope with the numbers. A maître d' ran it all for me and it was *the* party which went on forever.

The most memorable moment for me was Keith Emerson, my all-time favourite rock hero, not only turning up but also playing for my guests. I'd met him one night in Tramp and invited him but didn't expect him to make it. He started playing and stopped the party. All 300 guests crammed into the 200-seater marquee to catch his performance.

Wizzard singer Roy Wood came along with Sam, his Brummie wife. He also got up on stage and did a wonderful set for us all. Then he drank two bottles of champagne and a bottle of vodka. By the end of the night just about every guest was paralytically drunk. There were heaps of people dotted all over the place. I remember spotting Roy Wood on his hands and knees, crawling towards his car, followed by Sam and their driver.

'Shall I give Roy a hand?' his driver asked Sam, in thick Brummie.

'No, don't. Leave him,' she replied, in equally thick Brummie. 'He doesn't know he's drunk – yet!'

In June I was off with a concert party for a ten-day visit

to the Falklands. I took keyboards player Alan Rogers, drummer Francis 'Franny' Hayward, bass player Joe Fagan (who sang the theme song for *Auf Wiedersehen Pet*) and a great girl singer called Val McKenna.

The CSE (Combined Services Entertainment) organised the trip and supporting acts, including a neurotic girl ventriloquist from Manchester called Julie Craig, underweight and slightly overage, and two singers called Bizzy Line, a boy and girl. We nicknamed the bloke 'Shithouse Rat', because if anyone so much as glanced at her he'd spot them, even around corners!

We met at RAF Brize Norton and flew to that wonderful, warm, dirty rock, Ascension Island. My first steps on the island were really magical. Although the war had finished a year earlier, there was still a lot of activity going on. We took photographs of everything. If we saw a helicopter carrying a load underneath: click! If it moved: click! If it didn't move: click!

Our first show wasn't until the following night, so, on arriving, we were able to take a really good look around. The first night we stayed at American Camp, made up entirely of Portakabins. Our party was split up for sleeping arrangements – boys in one place, girls another.

The next day, as we got ready for our first show in a little club, a man from the CSE found me. He asked me to cast an eye over a cable he'd received from on high.

It was about racist material in my act and asked that I watched very carefully what I said about race because there were all creeds and colours on the island: Hispanic, African, you name it.

'No problem,' I said. 'I've never felt myself racist, anyway. I just tell jokes. If you don't want me to do anything with an accent, then I won't.'

Joe, Val and the band started the show then I went on for the first time and did about ten minutes of squeaky clean material. I introduced Julie Craig, and she came on in a blue frock with a tasselled skirt. If ever she died on her arse – which she invariably did on that tour – she'd quickly spin around to reveal stockings or, as the troops called them, 'all the webbing'.

Julie did a bit of patter and then brought out her first dummy, a chimp in a hat with the word 'Chico' on it.

'Hi, Chico,' she said.

'All right!' said Chico, in a voice sending up the locals.

'Why do you like it here?' she asked.

Chico looked about a bit, then said: 'There are some of my relatives here!'

I couldn't believe it! The MoD thought I was the one who needed gagging and it turned out to be Julie who dropped us right in it! Mind you, no one really took offence, they were having too good a time.

After that show I noticed Julie started to get a bit awkward, a bit demanding. She wasn't mucking in like the rest of us, she had to have special drinks and attention.

She had all the squaddies running around after her, fetching drinks and looking after her wretched props box full of dummies. In no time at all she and her box had a reputation for being pains in the arse, and even the squaddies didn't take long to tumble that she was awful.

Joe was having an affair with Val so he sneaked into the girls' quarters to see his beloved. And Julie grassed him up. I heard about it and immediately had a row with her about being such a rotten sneak.

'Why did you tell tales?' I asked.

'Well, I didn't think Joe should have come round,' she said. She was plain jealous, that's all, and it was a nasty trick to have played on Joe and Val.

'I don't want you to come to the Falklands now!' I said, still furious.

'I promise I'll be good,' she whined. I let the matter go.

At 5.00 am the next morning we got into our 'plane, a slow Hercules C130 (a Pickford's van with wings), and took off, bound for Port Stanley thirteen hours later. Soon we were all asleep.

Six hours later the pilot woke us up. He was about to practise a fuel transfer from a Victor jet and wanted us to watch. To me it seemed an impossible feat. The jet's slowest speed was faster than the Hercules' fastest speed.

'How the hell are you going to do this?' I asked. 'What's the Victor going to do, throw the fuel to us in bags?'

'No,' he answered. 'Watch this.'

We climbed to 23,000ft and met the Victor. Then both planes went into a dive. The jet threw on its airbrakes to decelerate and we accelerated, catching it up. Then both planes really were falling together at the same speed!

The manoeuvre was practised a few times and then the Victor flew away. Next we did a mid-air refuel for real, but thankfully with another Hercules, which wasn't quite so nerve-racking.

When we landed at Port Stanley there were Harriers and Phantoms buzzing around everywhere. Wherever you looked you saw soldiers, boats and plenty of activity. The weather was colder than I was expecting but that was made up for by a warm reception. I was met by the commanding officer, Group Commander (soon to be Air Commodore) Pat King, a really nice man in charge of the RAF out there. I introduced him to everyone in the show and Julie instantly threw one of her wobblers. 'Can you get my dummies off that plane?' she asked Pat. 'They've been bouncing up and down and I'm worried about them.'

He quietly ordered someone to fetch her silly dummies but instead of being pleased Julie piled it on thicker still.

'I don't feel very well,' she said. 'I think I need a lie down.'

Turning to me, she added, 'Can I have the car, Jim? You can go in the bus. I'm not very well at all.'

I watched amazed as she boldly got into the car and drove off with the CO, leaving me to travel on the bus with all the others – not that I minded that one bit.

In the evening we were taken to Government House to meet General Keith Spacey and his wife. He was a little wiry man from 3 Para who looked extremely tough. But he was very gentle and had a general's air, remaining slightly above everything.

We were given drinks and then tucked into a very

welcome buffet. While Pat King and I were talking to each other, I caught Julie's eye. She knew I knew she was trouble.

Mrs Spacey came over to me, all smiles.

'Jim,' she said. 'You will do me a favour, won't you?'

'What's that, madam?' I replied.

'We don't like the Billy Connolly sense of humour out here,' she said. 'All that toilet humour, blowing off and making noises. It's not what the troops want. They want some nice, clean entertainment.'

Christ! I thought. That's my whole act gone!

'I agree,' I answered. 'Will you be coming to many of the concerts, Mrs Spacey?'

'As many as I can,' she said. My heart sank. Fortunately, the general was near and had heard his wife's comments.

'With all due respect to my wife, Jim,' he whispered, 'you know the game. You are down here to entertain the troops. Do whatever jokes you want.'

'Thank you, sir,' I said.

'There's one thing I would ask you, though,' he continued.

'Anything,' I said.

'Well, the troops have started to call the islanders Bennies,' he replied.

'Why's that?' I asked.

'I'm not sure,' he said. 'I think it's something to do with a character from *Crossroads* on television. I don't understand it. Anyway, I find calling someone Benny bordering on the racial.'

He was quite right. 'Leave it to me, sir,' I said. 'I promise I won't.' And I didn't, for the whole trip.

As I was leaving Government House that night I said goodbye to the general and his wife, thanking them for entertaining us.

'Good luck, Jim,' said Mrs Spacey. 'Have a good tour. Oh! And don't forget take the micky out of the Bennies!' The general went white!

The next show was at Goose Green, in the very hall in which the islanders had been imprisoned by the invading

Argentinians. We were all farmed out to stay with islanders and my host was Eric Goss, the Goose Green settlement manager, who'd been on British TV after the invasion.

Eric and his wife Shirley came along to see the show and we all had a great night. No one wanted the evening to end, so we all sat around, singing and playing squeeze-boxes and guitars.

I went back home with Eric and Shirley and shared some rum. We talked for ages about the very remote Falklands way of life. I realised they'd had a very cut-off existence. They'd gone straight from wireless to video and never had television, for example.

The next day we went out to meet some of the islanders. I loved them. We also went to see the war graves, to pay our respects, and to the place where Colonel H. Jones had been killed. General Spacey laid on a helicopter for me to go to see another of the islands, and the wrecks along the way.

I went sightseeing with some of the soldiers and, at one point, was up to my waist in water in the middle of a river. I'd never been quite so cold before. My nuts turned to Findus peas.

We flew back to Port Stanley where we stayed on a thing called The Costelle, 400 Portakabins wedged on to a big floating hull. We were doing two concerts that night on a ship at anchor just outside Stanley harbour, the Royal Fleet Auxiliary *Fort Austin*.

RFA *Austin* was a big ammunition ship and as we boarded the captain saluted us.

'Can you get my dummies, they're in my special box,' Julie whined at him.

The captain told me the ship had eight full storage decks – full, that was, with condoms, apples, pears, catapults and bombs of every kind.

For our first show, HMS *Southampton* docked alongside with another ship. The place was packed. Flags were hanging off everything as, too, were some of the blokes. It felt like a scene from an old black and white war film.

In the audience for the first show was the captain of HMS *Southampton*, Captain Sam Salt. He had been the captain of HMS *Sheffield*, lost in the war, and I felt quite a close bond with him, even though we'd never met. I recognised him from the TV reports a year earlier and to me he was a real hero.

At the end of the show Captain Salt presented me with a plaque and one of the ship's flags, then the two ships pulled away. There was a break between shows and the arrival of the next two ships.

I realised that our drummer, Franny, was nowhere to be seen. He was a great drummer, but he was also a great drinker. I went looking for him and found him plastered in the crew bar with all these funny blokes who weren't quite masculine. They were pissed and having a great time, sending themselves up.

'Hello, love,' one of them said to me.

'Hello men!' I said.

'Does your drummer want a drink?' he asked.

'I don't know,' I said. 'Ask him.'

'I don't know his name. What is it?'

'Franny!' I replied.

'What?'

'Franny,' I repeated. 'Fanny with an "r".'

He walked up to Franny and, sending me up, asked him, 'Would you like a drink, Crunt?'

It transpired that Franny had discovered a very strong beer brewed by Courage especially for the armed forces, CSB (Celebrated Sparkling Bitter). Three pints made a normal person legless; Franny had downed nine. The chances of him being able to play anything in the second show were getting slimmer by the second and I rushed off to find the officer in charge.

'We've got to start the show now – the drummer's shit-faced!' I said.

'We can't start yet,' he answered. 'The first ship's arrived but the second is still on its way.'

'Well you'd better radio that ship and tell it to hurry up,' I said. 'If we wait much longer we're not going to have a bloody show!'

So he radioed the ship to get a move on and it arrived

doing Warp 9. It came in so quickly it hit our side. The brakes went on, caused a tidal bow-wave and the fenders smacked loudly into ours.

Goodbye bollocks! I thought, expecting the ammunition to go up in the crash. And all because of Franny!

Next day we flew to Kelly's Garden to do another show and Franny was still pissed. The troops were in their seats ages before the start of the show and fell about when Franny went out to set up his drum-kit.

He spent forever trying meticulously to get the tiny hole of the cymbal over the rod of the stand – or, in his case, the two holes of the cymbals over the two rods of the stands. When he eventually finished, the whole audience burst into rapturous applause. Franny, being a showman, turned around to take a bow, fell arse over tit and demolished the lot!

On the last night we did three shows at Stanley Town Hall. The first went well and, for the second, Sir Rex Hunt turned up with his wife, Lady Mavis. The most moving concert was the last. By then all of us on the trip were completely wiped out and we knocked back a bottle of brandy between us backstage during the show, just to keep awake.

While Julie was on we couldn't resist playing a prank on her. She'd made the fatal mistake of leaving her camera lying around. We grabbed one of her dummies in the wings, a sweet little girl. Out came the dummy, out came our dicks and click! click! click! I'd love to have known what the woman in Boots thought when those pictures were developed.

Towards the end of the concert, Joe and Val sang a song which sent a prickle to the back of every neck in that hangar. And they introduced it perfectly. 'This might be from an American film about American pilots,' Joe said, 'but tonight this is for the guys who can do it for real. From *An Officer and a Gentleman*, "Up Where We Belong".'

Just before I went back on for the last time, Julie found me.

'Do you think someone would like to auction my suspender belt?' she asked.

'Yes,' I said. 'I'll auction it. Is it for charity?'

'No,' she said. 'It's for me.'

With that she whipped off a black Marks and Spencer suspender belt – worth all of about £3 – and handed it to me. She stood with her stockings at half-mast looking like Nora Batty.

I walked out on to the stage and held up the warm undergarment.

'Who wants a suspender belt?' I asked. I looked back into the wings, where Julie had £ signs ringing up in her greedy eyes.

'I'll have it,' shouted a little squaddie from the front row.

'Here you are, son,' I said, giving it to him for nothing.

When I came off Julie was furious. I kept out of her way and went for a few pints up at the island's famous sea-front hotel, the Upland Goose.

We all got dreadfully drunk. Eventually Julie turned up, wittering something about being distraught and having a nervous breakdown. One young officer, who had taken a shine to her, asked me: 'Do you think a bottle of champagne would do the trick, Jim?'

'A bottle of stout would do the trick,' I replied.

We flew back the next day to RAF Brize Norton, and when we landed we had another party. My parting words to Julie Craig were: 'I hope I never see you again as long as I live.'

Things weren't nearly so fine between me and my own Julie when I got back to Wentworth. I turned up drunk, tired and emotional and she ignored me. So I went to my local and got even more drunk all on my own. When I got back home again I was missing everyone I'd met in the Falklands so I decorated the front room with all my military souvenirs.

I thought, in the Falklands I met so many lads who were desperately missing their wives back in Britain, yet here I was in Britain and my wife couldn't give a toss.

'Do you think that not being interested in what I've done is right?' I asked Julie angrily.

'Do you think this is right?' she answered. 'Is this sanity? Do you think decorating your lounge in all this stuff is how real husbands behave?'

'No, not really,' I said. Without another word she went to bed and I sat there in tears, alone for hours amid my memorabilia.

I was soon back to work in the clubs and in Manchester I met Julie Craig again. That was all I needed. What was it with me and girls called Julie?

One day Humphry Berkeley rang me to say that Baroness Falkender had invited Julie and me to the House of Lords for lunch. Would we like to go? 'Of course!' I replied at once. I'd never been inside the Houses of Parliament. Julie and I turned up on our best behaviour and, to be topical, I was wearing my Falkland Islands tie.

First we were taken to meet the Speaker of the House of Commons, Bernard Weatherill, who threw a bit of a pre-lunch reception for us in Speaker's House.

Then we went for our lunch with Baroness Falkender in the House of Lords. Over coffee I was asked if I'd like to watch Prime Minister's Question Time live.

Julie and I turned up in the public gallery as distinguished strangers. My first thought, looking down into the chamber, was just how small it was. Then several Labour MPs spotted me and called up. 'OK Jimbo?' they shouted. 'Having fun?' The lot of them were right hooligans!

Seconds later Mrs Thatcher swept in and Prime Minister's Question Time was underway. I watched Enoch Powell, transfixed. He appeared to sleep through the whole thing. Thatcher, my idol, was in fine form. Someone from the Opposition benches asked her a really awkward question which went on for ages.

When the question ended she got up, looked at the questioner, said 'No!' and sat back down again. It brought the House down!

'Come this way,' Humphry said to me. 'There's someone who wants to meet you.'

Julie and I followed him along the plush-carpeted, wood-panelled corridors. He opened a door and I was stunned for a moment. We were in the Prime Minister's Chambers – and there was Mrs Thatcher and several of her staff.

The others left and she came and shook my hand. I introduced her to Julie. She could see we were both rather taken aback. Then she spotted my tie and took me into an adjoining room. In it was a big table, the table from which she'd planned the Falklands War.

Mrs Thatcher offered us a cup of tea, and was 'mother', pouring the tea and passing around biscuits. I took a mouthful of biscuit and couldn't swallow it – dry mouth had struck again!

We talked about the Falklands. I'd been very impressed by her strength during the war and, in the flesh, she seemed even more dynamic than I'd expected. Hardly another Ronald Reagan.

She thanked me for going to the Falklands and told me how important she thought the shows were. She then talked, with a twinkle in her eye, about morale amongst British troops serving in Beirut. She told me they were long overdue another visit from the CSE gang.

After about an hour she glanced at her watch and said: 'I've got to go now. I've got the Prime Minister of New Zealand waiting to see me.'

Although in front of Mrs Thatcher we were the picture of happiness, Julie and I were really falling out. At home, when she was shouting and screaming I'd walk away from her. There were few lengths to which I wouldn't go to avoid her whining – one was the bottom of our swimming pool!

To escape her nagging some nights I'd put on an aqualung and jump into the deep end of the swimming pool. I'd even take a spare tank with me sometimes.

I could sit on the bottom of the pool for hours, just looking around. The weightlessness and calmness of the water is one of the few ways I can instantly relax – breathe in and float to the surface, out and drop to the bottom. Once or twice when I was hiding from Julie I even fell asleep down there.

This time when I left for summer season, in Great Yarmouth, Julie wasn't in the least interested in coming with me. I knew she was firmly entrenched in the Wentworth set I loathed so much and was glad to be rid of her moans for a few months.

But I did miss Cameron. He was now two years old and getting into everything. So far from home, and my family, I got on and did the shows. I was bored, lonely and after a while slipped into a season of heavy drinking.

At Christmas 1983 I was starring in an ill-fated show in Coventry, handy for Julie's parents but little else. The show, it has to be said, wasn't one of Laurie Mansfield's best ideas, and I loathed it.

To me, 'Jim Davidson's Magical Christmas', conjured up a show for kiddies full of magic effects and people popping up all over the place. It didn't sound like a show with three stand-up comics, me, Roy Walker and Bobby Davro. Laurie knew I was against the idea and couldn't see the point of Davro being on the show. *Copycats* was the right TV show for him. I like Bobby as a person but as an act he's never himself!

On the opening night we faced an audience of 1,400, mostly children. It was a disaster. The first night wasn't magical, it was awful.

The only thing which went down well was a sketch at the end of the show when, during the final number, the two puppets Zippy and George, from the children's TV show *Rainbow*, popped up in the middle of the band. They were operated by my two roadies, and I did their funny voices. It went down a bomb.

Laurie tried convincing me the show would improve over the next few nights. It didn't. If anything it got worse.

I was staying in a hotel opposite the theatre and we were all off for Christmas until New Year's Day. Julie's parents were nearby, in Hinckley, and that was where the two of us arranged to spend the holiday.

On Christmas Eve I went with Julie to visit her grandparents in Coventry Hospital and met some of the others stuck there for the Christmas break. Then we went back to her parents' house.

Before turning in for the night, I decided I'd better move my car, which was parked out in the road, into the driveway. Loads of Julie's family were coming to see us for Christmas drinks next day and I knew we wouldn't be able to move for cars then. But before I could pull the car into the driveway, I needed to clear several paving slabs to the side.

I fumbled hopelessly to pick up the first concrete slab.

'Look at the bloody state of you,' Julie jeered.

She had a point. As I lifted it I knew at once it was too heavy. It cut into my fingers and hurt so much I threw it forward out of my hands, but forgot to take my foot out of the way. I collapsed in agony. Julie, by my side, completely ignored me. Her dad, Colin, came running out and helped me into the house, where I lay down on the floor.

I unzipped my Chelsea boot, took it off and slowly poured out about a cupful of blood. I felt my big toe and it was all squashy. Then I eased off my sock and my big toe was two inches long, totally crushed, and bleeding badly.

Julie yelped and ran off to faint somewhere. Colin telephoned for an ambulance and while we waited for it to arrive he poured me several stiff whiskies.

'Don't let them cut my toe off!' I pleaded with him. 'Whatever happens, please don't let them do that.'

'Don't worry,' he said, pouring me another large whisky.

When the ambulance arrived I was rushed to Coventry Hospital, the very place I'd been visiting ten hours earlier! A doctor came to examine me and started prodding and poking.

I must have reeked of whisky and, by then, I was definitely drunk. I know it was wrong, but I was in such pain I quickly lost my temper with him. 'I'm not having this!' I snarled. 'Get me into a fucking private ward! Get me a surgeon! Get me a plane! Get me to Harley Street!'

He just ignored me and got on with cleaning me up. The

bone had snapped completely and my big toe was hanging on to the foot by a thread.

'I'm going to take the nail off,' said the doctor, injecting the toe with local anaesthetic.

'Surely you can knock me out?' I pleaded, petrified of more pain. He still ignored me, whipped off the nail, patiently sewed the toe back on and set the whole thing in a plaster.

I woke up on Christmas morning as white as a sheet, in agony and embarrassed. I had a hangover and nine and a half toes.

I knocked back the powerful pain-killers the hospital had given me, but they had little effect. For the next few days I hobbled about the house and lost my appetite completely.

I had to go back to work on New Year's Day and was still in a terrible state. I hobbled about and felt dreadful. After the show I telephoned Laurie in tears and he came up to see me at once. 'The pain's just too much, Laurie,' I said. 'I've got to have two weeks off, at least.'

I was invalided out of the show and taken to see a specialist in Harley Street. When I met the specialist I could have kicked him, if I'd had a decent foot spare. The best money could buy wouldn't even give me a local anaesthetic when he took the plaster off and the pain was unbearable.

But at once, without the plaster, the foot did feel less painful. The specialist inspected it carefully and dressed it. I hobbled back to Coventry to finish the run and then returned to Wentworth to put my foot up.

I was still hobbling around the house when Eamonn Andrews nobbled me with the 'Big Red Book' on January 17, 1984.

I'd been stuck in Wentworth for ages. The day before, fed up, I told Julie I was going down to the pub.

'Oh, don't go down the Red Lion,' said Julie.

'Why not?' I replied. 'I'm going for a drink.'

When I got home, not drunk, I told Julie the foot was hurting so I was going to bed with a sleeping tablet.

'Don't take a sleeping tablet,' she said.

'Why do you keep telling me what to do tonight?' I asked. 'I'm in agony. You don't understand.'

The next day two friends from Thames came to see me. They had a drink and I hobbled them around the house. I started proudly showing off my hefty hi-fi system to them unaware that, at that very moment, a battalion of the Royal Irish Rangers, whom I'd met in the Falklands, were marching up my drive with Eamonn Andrews. They were playing their bagpipes and drums but because my hi-fi was blaring I couldn't hear a thing!

'I can hear something bleeding through on your speakers,' said one of them. 'Turn it down a bit.'

'There's nothing bleeding through,' I said.

'Yes, I can hear bagpipes,' he replied.

'You won't now!' I said, turning it up to the full monty.

'I think that was a knock at the door,' he continued. I turned the music down and looked out of the window before opening the door, as I always do. There were the Rangers and I just knew Eamonn had to be with them.

As I opened the door I heard those immortal words: 'Jim Davidson, This is your Life!' He'd got me!

When they nab you for the show you're off immediately; they don't hang about. Eamonn had a bottle of champagne waiting for me in the car as we drove back together to the Royalty Theatre in London. I'd worked with him a few times before, he liked me and I loved him. As we drove through Staines I went quiet and looked out of the window.

'What's the matter?' he asked.

'You see that pub there?' I said, pointing to a place called the Crooked Billet. Then I filled up and couldn't speak.

'What's up?' he asked again.

'My cat got killed there,' I said. No, only joking!

What I really said was: 'I painted that pub years ago. Little did I know then I'd be driving past it one day going to what feels like the highest accolade a British entertainer can have.'

When we got to the theatre, I was shown to a little dressing-room to await my fate. 'God!' I thought. 'My dad will be on. And my sister's bound to come from America. I wonder who else?'

When Dad did come on it was one of the greatest moments in my life. I choked up a bit there. Mum and Dad both looked equally proud. The other guests included Bob Todd and the team from *What's On Next?*, Windsor Davies, Danny La Rue and Omar Sha-fucking-rif. When Omar came on he whispered in my ear 'Your dog won 3–1!' then hugged me.

At the very end, a little girl called Michelle Walters came on. She was very pretty and in a wheelchair because she suffered, I think, from spina bifida. I'd met Michelle's father, Derek, out fishing. He lived in Faversham and told me his council had refused him a grant to build a necessary extension to his home for Michelle.

I did a show to raise the money for Michelle's room and kept in touch.

I did Derek a terrible disservice one day out fishing. We went to the Faversham school pool and he caught a 38½lb carp – quite a famous fish. I took loads of pictures of him with his handsome catch for the family album.

When I got home I couldn't get the camera open to get the film so I asked Julie to take it to the chemist's. 'Tell them to get the film out even if they have to break the camera,' I told her. At the chemist's they forced the camera open and, horror, there wasn't even a film in it. It was the one that got away. Sorry, Del!

10

Standby Tibby Tibbs

Despite the nice smiles for *This is Your Life* at the start of 1984, Julie and I were mostly at each other's throats the whole time. She stuck to her Wentworth lifestyle and I made myself scarce as much as possible.

I had a perfect excuse to get out of her hair two weeks later. After meeting Mrs Thatcher I'd received a request from the very highest level to tour Beirut.

The CSE had asked me to line up some showbiz pals, but the only mate prepared to join me for the three-day visit was minder Terry! Still, the CSE found two dancers and a novelty trumpeter, so between us we could keep the lads happy.

To keep the press off the scent we made out that we were going to Germany. In reality we were going first to Cyprus and then on to do a concert on a ship just off Beirut. If we got back in one piece that's when we'd tell the papers what we'd really been up to.

We met at 9.00 pm at RAF Lyneham for our seven-hour flight to Cyprus. It was a terrible night, raining, windy and cold. I met the dancers and knew there'd be no mischief there – one was married to Jane Beaumont's brother Andy, and the other was her bosom pal!

A few hours later we were cleared to leave and boarded the Hercules C130 with a few servicemen also heading out to Cyprus.

Terry was bored at the prospect of a long, uncomfortable journey and downed a couple of sleeping pills. Then he made himself a makeshift mattress out of our luggage and promptly fell asleep. I went upstairs and sat in the flight deck on a little bench seat. Next to me was an expensive-looking officer called Colonel Fawshaw.

As the colonel and I waited we started chatting. He was based in Cyprus and asked me where I was headed with the CSE party. 'Beirut,' I said nervously.

'Oh, you're going over to that nasty bit, then?,' he asked.

'Yes,' I said, even more nervously.

'Well, I hope you'll be all right,' he replied. 'It seems to be all calm and collected out there at the moment. They seem to like the old British. They don't like the French very much, though, and they don't like the Yanks. A lot of them have just been killed, blown up by a suicide bomber. But I'm sure you'll be all right. How many shows are you doing?'

'I really don't know,' I said.

Outside it was still hissing down horribly. We'd waited ages to take off, and then the Hercules thundered down the runway, got no more than fifty yards and abruptly aborted take-off. Hydraulics failure. The plane turned around and taxied us back to the pad. By now it was about midnight and we all had to disembark and wait in the darkened terminal building.

I roused Terry from his deep sleep. He dragged himself on to his feet, peered out of the window and said:

'Cyprus is just like Lyneham, isn't it?' He actually thought he'd slept through the seven-hour flight and we'd arrived!

I persuaded my new friend, the colonel, to get the bar in the officers' mess opened for us. Terry went back to sleep on a sofa but the rest of us sat around drinking until the plane was repaired four hours later.

By now we were all so tired that within minutes of take-off we were sound asleep. I woke up a few hours later, in mid-flight, and fell asleep again. The next time I woke up we were landing in late-afternoon Cyprus.

Everyone in the party was exhausted. The first show was at 6.00 pm in a little cinema and we went on shattered and hungry. The concert was a hit, though!

After the show we were meant to get a decent night's sleep before flying out to Beirut next morning at 5.30 am.

I had no chance of that. I bumped into all the Scots Guards I'd last met in The Falklands and got chatting and drinking with them.

In the morning I put on my flak jacket before boarding ET, the twin-rotor Chinook helicopter flying us to the Beirut ship. I sat down and looked around. Opposite me was a box with '0.50 Browning' printed on it – a stack of live bullets!

We waited for a few minutes before the helicopter started up. We got about four feet off the ground, then crashed back down again with a deafening jolt. Another hydraulics failure!

We flew off in ET's sister Chinook, EZ, and landed on RFA *Reliant* – and a Chinook is a bloody big helicopter to land on a RFA – refuelled, then took off again.

Along the coast of Beirut we reeled down low over the beach, just like *Apocalypse Now* (or, as dear Stukie would call it, *Acropolis Now*). We flew over the surf then up through a wadi, a dry river gully. It was surreal; we were flying below buildings. I'd heard stories that HMS *Glamorgan*'s Lynx helicopter had gone through a wadi a few days before us and been damaged after the baddies had stretched cables across its path.

At the back of the helicopter a man was ready to release flares and chaff, small pieces of silver paper to deflect radar-homing missiles.

At last we landed. I ran to a waiting Land Rover and got in. We looked back to see our two girl dancers sauntering over as if they were on holiday. They weren't a bit fazed by the war-torn surroundings of Beirut and ambled across, even stopping to pet a little rabid-looking dog on the way.

Our surroundings were bombed out and derelict. We drove up to a place called Hadath, home to one company of the 16/5th Lancers. We met them all, had a quick bite to eat then got ready for our two shows, for seventy-five men at a time. This was Beirut. The press and news crews were everywhere. The CSE people introduced me to the reporters, which meant the cat was out of the bag about our secret trip.

I had a pint of beer, my first drink for ages, and it went straight to my head. I boldly suggested that the MoD invite some of the American Marines, also stationed out there, to our two shows. In the end about twenty Americans came to each performance.

At the start of the first show the warm-up, the trumpet player, walked out. His act was a real oddity. He'd play tunes by blowing into kettles and other equally unlikely instruments. What the audience didn't know was that the poor chap suffered terribly with piles. At one point in the act he looked at me in the wings with a pained expression on his face. He walked over to me and whispered something wonderful off-mike.

'It's fucking murder, Jim,' he said. 'Every time I hit a top F another one pops out!'

Next on were the girls, greeted by the traditional sea of loud, hungry wolf-whistles. Dancers always go down well with soldiers. When the two girls came off, I walked out and spotted some American Marines in the front. They were mostly black – and big black blokes at that! Not that it made any difference to me what colour they were. It did make a difference to the 16/5th Lancers. They might be a cavalry regiment, but far from being a well-bred, posh bunch they were all from Birmingham.

I was greeted with whoops and Brummie cries of 'Go on, Jimmy!' and 'All right, Jimmy!' The Americans clapped politely even though they couldn't have had the foggiest idea who I was.

The opening line from the first Brummie heckler caused sharp intakes of breath all around. 'Go on, Jimmy,' he said. 'Take the piss out of them fucking niggers!'

I went whiter than any white man can go. Then the heckler got a roar of approval from the Marines and we were off! It's funny to think I was frightened to death of these tough-looking Yanks, but this little Brummie squaddie couldn't give a damn.

I explained to the Marines who Chalkie was and went into the routine.

Between shows I met some of those Marines. They reminded me of the American Marines in Vietnam in a way; young kids, not a bit aggressive. These Americans were mild-mannered and polite in stark contrast to our aggressive lads. One Marine showed me a picture of himself with the American actress Brooke Shields, who had just supported Bob Hope in a concert on one of the big warship shows out there. The visit hadn't gone down too well with the Americans. It had been far too formal and it was even alleged that Bob might have been paid to be there.

I have no idea about the behind-the-scenes politics but I do know the show was carefully rehearsed and filmed, and that none of the men had got to meet the stars properly afterwards. All in all, the sort of forces' show I hate!

Our second show went well and, relaxing with a drink at the end of the evening, I met a smashing American sergeant. He looked like a young Count Basie and laughed so much tears were dropping off his face. 'Man,' he said. 'You're just like Bob Hope without the cue cards!'

Then a major came and found us. 'Come on then, you lot,' he said to the group. 'Off we go.'

'Off we go where?' I asked.

'To your hotel,' he said. 'You're not staying here. You're at a hotel in town.'

'I'm not!' I said. 'Are you mad? I'm pissed!'

'Let him stay here sir,' piped up a squaddie. 'They'll be all right.'

'No, I have my orders,' he said. I couldn't believe it. One minute, having just given our all, we were drinking with the men and larking around happily. The next we were in a jeep dodging between dirty great tanks and burned-out buildings on our way to the Mayflower Hotel in the middle of Beirut.

We checked in then quickly turned in. I went to my room but stayed wide awake. I could hear small-arms fire going off in the distance and it kept me on the edge of my bed all night.

Next morning the major knocked on my door. I knew I'd given him a bad time a few hours earlier and stood to attention, then smacked myself on the wrist. 'Don't fucking leave me here again, sir! Please?' I said to him.

Beirut was a bomb-site and quite scary. I got myself a regulation machine-gun and felt happier knowing where it was in case I needed it. We took a drive around the rubble and ruins of the battered city. We even saw the devastation caused by the suicide bomber the colonel had told me about. Where there had been a whole building there was now barely half a building, just a massive hole.

As we drove around citizens and soldiers waved and cheered approvingly. But the next minute the shit, to use the correct military jargon, hit the fan and the atmosphere changed abruptly.

Some deal had been struck which meant the British and Yanks were pulling out at once. Now guns were being cocked at every corner and we turned around and sped back to the landing zone to await an RAF airlift. Three cheers for the RAF!

While we waited, some US Marines arrived. We talked and posed for a couple of pictures until their helicopter arrived and then waved them goodbye. Five miles away in the mountains a gun started puffing. We had no idea where the shells were going. We couldn't hear them, we could only see small puffs of smoke going up. They might even have been shells landing, we just didn't know. We did know by then that the RAF shuttle was running slightly later than advertised.

'There is a slight problem,' an officer told me. 'The RAF are not going to pick you up until the landing zone is secure.'

'Oh,' I said. 'What happens then?'

Silence. Further anxiously awaited orders arrived saying HMS *Glamorgan* was sending its Lynx helicopter to pick us up. The Lynx was small, so it would need to make several trips to ferry us all to safety, but it was better than nothing.

Then the orders were amended. 'As the Navy are going to do it,' explained the officer, 'the RAF have said they'll do it.'

A minute later a dot appeared on the horizon. It got bigger and bigger until it was right above us. ET! She'd been repaired and looked wonderful. I got into the jump seat between the pilot, Flight Lieutenant Molloy, and the navigator and we set off straight into a wadi. It was the fastest I'd ever been in a helicopter and we flew out across the sea.

I looked to my left at a radar screen the size of a beermat, known as the IFF (Indicator Friend or Foe). It identified whatever radar was locked on to us and if we were being tracked by goodies or baddies.

It became clear that we were lost and I pointed at the radar a few times, winding up Molloy. An hour later we still hadn't completed the forty-minute journey!

'What's up?' I asked Molloy.

'Well,' he said, 'I'm having trouble finding RFA *Reliant* because there are too many things jamming the airwaves with all the activity out here. I keep punching in the details the *Reliant* is sending but my navigation computer rejects it.

Oh shit! I thought.

Then Molloy had a brainwave. He asked: 'Do we have any magnets on board?'

'Yes,' I said. 'We've got loads of speakers for the PA equipment.'

'Have they got magnets in them?'

'Of course!' I said.

'I'm going to have to jettison them,' he replied coldly. 'They're jamming up my nav. computer so they'll have to go.'

I ducked my head, wincing at the cost of trashing all our equipment. Then, through the glass below Molloy's foot, I saw RFA *Reliant*. We were right above it!

'Excuse me?' I said.

'Not now!' he replied.

'Excuse me,' I repeated, pointing towards his foot. 'Is that the ship there?'

'Yes,' he said. 'Quite right. Well done!'

Poor Molloy thought he'd heard the last of that but he hadn't . . .

Back in Britain, Julie was still frosty towards me so I found warmth outside the marital home in the curvy shape of Suzanne Dando. We'd first met three years earlier on the Children's Royal Variety Show at the London Palladium and I was smitten from the start. I'd ensured Suzanne had been invited to guest on *The Jim Davidson Show*, so I could see her again. Just after I got back from Beirut, we managed a few nights out together away from the vigilant press, but it wasn't easy.

The papers had already got wind of the fact Julie and I weren't on good terms. When I got my publicity agent, Clifford Elson, to release a statement to them that my marriage was fine they were even hungrier for a story.

I was swarmed by photographers and reporters everywhere I turned. They stopped at nothing. I was convinced they had bugged my telephone at Wentworth.

A few weeks later, I went out on a tour with Jethro, the great Cornish comic, and a very raunchy singer called Sissy Stone. Also on tour with me was minder Terry, with his unreliable 40ft WiniBego motorcaravan, nicknamed 'The Flying Flat', because it was so big.

Early in the tour I had a brief fling with sexy Sissy in the flat. I must have been the worst fuck in the world because, although I thought I was doing well, next morning she began an affair with the drummer instead!

When we got to the Pavilion in Brighton for a week a reporter from the *People*, Bill Dorran, turned up. Unlike the press pack, who ran around like headless chickens, Bill worked quietly on his own.

He hung around the stage door, not getting in anyone's way, and waited quietly for Jethro to appear alone.

'Hello Jethro,' said Bill.

'Hello Bill,' he replied.

'Jethro,' he said. 'Do you think there's any truth in Jim and Suzanne Dando?'

'No, Bill,' said Jethro, sucking slowly on his pipe. 'I don't think there's any truth in that rumour.'

'Ah, I didn't really think so, Jethro,' continued Bill. 'What makes you think that?'

'Well,' said Jethro, puffing on his pipe once more. 'He's been fucking that girl singer all week.'

A few days later, when we got to Worthing, Jethro did a wonderful thing. He was different from the rest of us in the business, who stayed up all night and slept all day. He'd been a builder so he woke up every morning, regular as clockwork, at 7.30 am.

This particular early morning Jethro got up and, at a loose end, took a long stroll around Worthing. He was so bored that by 9.00 am he'd had his hair cut twice – unusual for him, because he's still got white fivers! Anyway, he walked around and in one road spotted a man building a porch in his garden. Jethro stood and watched for a minute as the man sawed lengths of wood. Then Jethro went over to the edge of the garden. 'Excuse me,' he said. 'That saw of yours isn't too sharp, is it? If you've got a file, I'll sharpen it for you.'

'Oh, thanks very much, mate,' came the reply. Jethro walked up the path, took the saw and file and got to work. The man found another saw and got back to his porch.

After twenty minutes Jethro had finished sharpening the saw. 'Try that!' he said, proudly passing the newly sharpened saw across.

'Very nice,' said the man. 'Thanks very much.'

'Give me the other one, I'll do that too while I'm here,' said Jethro, starting on the other saw. Another twenty minutes later he'd finished that one. Then he offered to hold up a bit of wood to help.

After two hours Jethro had taken over the job completely. He got the man working as his assistant, fetching and carrying tools and lengths of wood. Even the man's wife came out from time to time, with yet another cup of tea. By 4.00 pm the new porch was finished.

'There. Not a bad job,' said Jethro, standing back and admiring his work. 'Be seeing you!'

With that, he strolled off back to the theatre. Just before I went on to introduce him that night he told me what he'd been doing all day. I thought he'd flipped. Then I walked out on-stage to introduce him. 'Please welcome, a great friend of mine,' I said. 'Jethro.'

As Jethro walked out a man started yelling excitedly from the back of the auditorium. 'That's him!' he said. 'That's the one who built our porch. It's him!'

It was as if Jethro was an unidentified traveller in *Star Trek* who appeared, helped people with their jobs then vanished into thin air!

While on tour I got a desperate urge to see Suzanne again, dangerous though it was: Bill Dorran's story with Jethro's quotes had only made the press keener still to catch me out.

I arranged to meet Suzanne after a show at her home near Gatwick. The press were at the theatre in force that night and I had to do something to put them off my scent. Jethro took my place, running with a blanket over his head past the photographers at the front of the theatre to a waiting car and away. The press boys jumped into their cars and followed.

Meanwhile, I ran out of the back of the theatre, also with a blanket over my head, to another waiting car which took me to Terry in his WiniBego a few miles down the road. Terry drove me to Suzanne's house in a little cul-de-sac. I jumped out and ran into her home, looked back and saw that the WiniBego, bigger than the entire cul-de-sac, had broken down!

After the tour I went back to Wentworth and a difficult Julie. Like the press, she was convinced I was up to something with Suzanne and was dying to catch me out. So to spend another night with Suzanne, away from prying eyes, I felt I had to go to extraordinary lengths. My only mistake was telling a mate in the Red Lion what I was up to.

I left Wentworth one morning then drove around the corner to Fairoaks, where I took a helicopter to Gatwick. There I met Suzanne and we flew off in a little private plane to Paris. I'd booked a wonderful suite at the George V Hotel.

We had a great time together and shared plenty of

emotions. She was sensitive to my feelings for everyone in the Falklands, where a friend of her brother had served on HMS *Coventry*, which had taken a direct hit in the war.

For some unknown reason, the day Suzanne and I flew to France Julie called in at the Red Lion. Of course, by then, all the regulars knew what I was up to and couldn't resist putting their oars in. Before Julie had even opened her mouth she was greeted by phoney French accents asking: 'Ello, 'ave you seen Jimmy today?'

She tumbled it and stormed home in a rage. Suzanne and I were in bed in our plush hotel suite when the telephone rang. 'Having fun, are you?' Julie screamed at me.

'Yes, thank you!' I said. 'Don't 'phone me here.'

I hung up. When I got back to Wentworth the next day I had to face Julie and she called me everything under the sun. What a surprise.

Not long after that, while I was recording *Up the Elephant*, I went out to the races one day with Clive Brandy. I bumped into a friend, an entertainer, who told me he was imminently getting married. I offered to throw him a stag party.

'Leave it to me!' said Clive, delivering his invariably costly battle-cry.

We decided we would paint the town red and two days later Clive 'phoned me. 'Well, I've booked the place,' he said. 'It's the most magnificent suite in a fantastic hotel in Mayfair.'

'How much?' I asked.

'Don't ask!' he said.

On the day of the stag party I met Clive in the afternoon. 'Now Clive, what's happening?' I said.

'About what?' he asked.

'Tonight's entertainment,' I said. 'I mean, hadn't we better get some escorts in, or something to sort our guests out?'

'I can't get involved,' said Clive. 'I'm a married man!'

'So am I!' I replied.

'In that case we'd better get two spares just in case we forget!' he said, running off to book nine ladies from an agency.

That evening Clive and I met the guests as they arrived. We opened the champagne and toasted the bridegroom's good fortune. Just as we'd started to run out of polite conversation the 'phone rang. A frosty receptionist announced that nine 'strange' ladies had arrived in the hotel to see me.

'Leave it to me,' said Clive, heading for reception. 'Hello, my name's Mr Brandy,' he said to the receptionist. 'I'm in charge of the hockey team meeting Mr Davidson.'

He greeted the girls and asked them to follow him. They all had painted nails and curvy figures – not one looked like she'd ever seen a hockey stick!

We got the girls drinks and it seemed like the party might at last take off. It didn't. An hour later the whole thing became awkward and embarrassing for everyone.

'What can we do?' I asked Clive.

'Leave it to me!' he said and sloped off to the bedroom. When he reappeared moments later he was bollock naked, grasping a bottle of champagne in his left hand.

'Right!' he bellowed. 'Are we going to party or what?'

We collapsed in giggles, all relaxed and started to have a good time. The bridegroom's friends found themselves partners, as did I, and the drunken orgy was underway. Poor Clive was left on his own with the champagne and canapés, but to him they were probably better than sex, anyway!

Another hour later Clive announced to the heaving mass of bodies: 'We've got a problem.'

'What is it?' shouted one of the guests.

'We've got to send down for some vodka. One of the girls doesn't like champagne, she wants vodka,' he said.

'Well get her some vodka, Clive!' I shouted.

'I'm going to,' he said. 'But you're all going to have to get dressed again for room service.'

The last thing we wanted was for the hotel to see our girls' hockey team playing away so we reluctantly calmed down and got dressed. As soon as room service had gone we stripped off again and got back to business. I got through all of the girls in turn and was knackered.

One minute the joint was jumping, the next it was

deserted. By 2.30 am the party was me and the last of the call-girls, plus Clive.

'Do you want to try some of this?' she asked, producing a little packet of white powder. Cocaine. I'd steered wide of drugs for a long time but that night the temptation was just too great.

I had some, Clive had some and then the hooker left us. Clive had a brainwave.

'Get another three girls!' he said.

I 'phoned and ordered three more and disappeared back to the bedroom with them for more punishment. Before I collapsed, shattered, I'd clocked up the full dozen.

I woke up alone in the hotel and grabbed a cab to Teddington for rehearsals with Thames. I was dying to tell somebody what sort of night I'd just had but the only person I felt I could tell was John Bardon, who played my dad in the series. When I found him he was sitting on a sofa in his dressing-room. I went in, closed the door and sat next to him. 'John!' I said. 'You won't believe what I've just done!'

Then I promptly fell asleep in his arms before I could say another word! I woke up, £5,000 poorer, with one hell of a hangover.

In 1984 Thames Television also allowed me to branch out in a new direction for TV specials. For the end of the year we planned *Jim Davidson's Falklands Special*. It meant I had to make two trips to the Falklands that year, the first in July and the second in September, when we'd be filming it with a suitably festive flavour.

Unlike Julie, Suzanne Dando was very interested in the Falklands War, my trips and me. Just before I left she sent me a note with a little rose, which I hid from Julie, wishing me a good trip and ordering me to return safely because she wanted me back in one piece.

I flew off with my head full of thoughts of Suzanne. I 'phoned her a few times while I was out there, although I didn't ring Julie once, and wrote to her.

When I arrived at the islands and walked into the RAF officers' mess at Kelly's Garden, the first person

I bumped into was helicopter pilot Molloy from the Beirut trip!

'Oh, fuck!' he cried, remembering getting lost off Beirut.

'Your story's safe with me!' I said, but it wasn't, was it?!

Back home the housekeeper let slip one day that Julie was having an affair right under my nose with, of all people, Clive Brandy's son, Martin. 'Clive, I don't know how to tell you this,' I started, 'but your son is giving my wife a bit more attention than is normal.'

'How dare you!' Clive ranted. 'Don't ever come into my house again, you filthy wretch. How dare you? I've never been so insulted in my life!'

I left him alone and two days later got a call from a very apologetic Clive. 'You're fucking right!' he said. 'I've done you a complete injustice and don't know what to say.'

Clive had 'phoned Martin who had admitted, gingerly, that it was all true. On hearing this Clive decided to put the fear of God into him. He said I was such a jealous husband I'd vowed to blow Martin's bollocks off (news to me).

Both Clive and I felt hurt by Martin and Julie. My only regret over the incident was that Martin was a golf coach and I'd hoped to get golf lessons from him! I was never angry with Martin, but Clive was happy to let him believe otherwise.

Many weeks later I had supper with Clive in Wentworth and asked him where Martin was. 'He's up at the house,' he said, 'hiding from you!'

'There's no need,' I said. 'Give him a ring, tell him to come down and join us for a drink.'

'Believe me Jim, he won't come anywhere near you,' Clive replied. 'If you want him to join us for a drink you'll have to go and get him.'

So I jumped in my Ferrari Boxer and drove to Clive's house to fetch Martin. At first he was frightened but I told him to relax and he got into the car. 'No hard feelings,' I said, then, teasing him, I put my foot down and drove him back to the restaurant at 120 mph!

'He's mad. He's going to kill both of us!' he must have

thought. I did notice a few beads of sweat on his brow as we pulled up outside the bistro and found Clive.

Then I was on at the Night Out, Birmingham, and rang home after I'd been on to see how things were. Lesley, the housekeeper, answered and said Julie wasn't there. 'She is out for the night,' she said, adding that Julie was with a bloke called Steve. 'She's gone to Annabel's.'

She also mentioned a hotel near Heathrow where Julie and her bloke were spending the night. I rang off and quickly called the hotel. I tracked her down there, but there was no reply from the room.

I jumped in my car and drove through the night to arrive at the hotel at dawn, but Julie had already checked out. I went home but she wasn't there either. I was in a terrible mood and, in anger, I threw a brick through the window of Julie's white Mercedes parked in the drive. I wanted to rip her clothes to shreds. I couldn't believe she could be so horrible to me – and using my money to pay for it all!

Lesley tried to calm me down a bit. 'Julie's found your secret hiding-place,' she said. 'She's seen all your letters and the notes from Suzanne.'

'Oh,' I said.

'If you want to see the letters she's been hiding from you, look under Cameron's mattress,' she added.

I ran upstairs and looked under Cameron's bed. There I found letters and cards from loads of men, including Martin. I thundered downstairs in an even worse mood.

'She's round at Chip Hawkes' house,' Lesley said.

'Right, that's her lot!' I answered and stormed out of the house.

Chip Hawkes, one of The Tremeloes, lived nearby and Julie spent a lot of time with his wife, Carol. I went over to the Hawkes' house and rang the doorbell. Carol opened the door. She took one look at me and said: 'She doesn't want to speak to you.'

'What do you mean, she doesn't want to speak to me?' I snarled. 'Get her out here now!'

'No!' she replied, slamming the door in my face.

So I simply stood there with my finger on the bell

for about fifteen minutes. Behind the door I could hear everyone running around nervously.

Next loads of policemen turned up in flak jackets, like a TV hit squad or the SAS. 'Where's the gun, Jim?' asked one of the coppers.

'What fucking gun?' I said.

'You've come over here with a gun,' he shouted.

'I haven't got a bloody gun,' I said. I was carted off to my house, where I sat down with a policeman and explained everything. He seemed quite understanding in the end.

'Do you have any guns here?' he asked.

'No,' I answered. 'Only this replica thing with a bayonet hanging on the wall.'

He took it away, had it examined and it was later given the all-clear and returned to me.

When Julie eventually came back we had a terrible fight and in a temper I hit her. She went back to the Hawkes' and I went to bed, feeling terribly upset.

Then her dad turned up from Hinckley and burst into my bedroom, ranting hysterically. 'You've hit my daughter,' he said. 'Come and hit me.'

'Right,' I said. 'Just let me get my trousers on. I've never liked you.'

He was taken aback. I was only little, but he'd never seen me when I was really angry. I chased him down the stairs and confronted him. 'Now, do you want to have a drink or do you want to fight?' I asked. So we sat and had a drink. I told him what had happened and sorted it all out. He agreed to take Julie and Cameron with him to Hinckley.

When Julie left, the housekeeper, Lesley, stayed behind. No sooner had my wife and son gone than Lesley dragged me into bed and nigh-on raped me. So I asked her to stay on as housekeeper! Lesley kept getting me back into bed and I also started to take a few local girls home from the pub. In no time I was exhausted!

I was in season that summer at the Winter Gardens, Margate, and staying opposite the venue in theatrical digs, known to all in the business as Ted and Lil's. I was well into my stride, bedding anyone. After the show I would either get completely pissed or pick someone up. Sometimes I'd hit the jackpot and do both. Othertimes I just got drunk and started feeling terribly lonely. Once more, I missed someone special on my arm.

When the Red Devils took part in a local display I went along and bumped into a girl singer, Tricia Duskey. She was Irish and had a wonderful accent to go with her personality and lovely looks. She was quite petite with shortish hair and a mesmerising smile.

She came back with me to Ted and Lil's for a few drinks. Then we went for a very long, romantic walk along the front. We started kissing and cuddling, then she really took the bull by the horns. 'Let's fuck!' she said. So we went back to my digs and did just that.

Tricia had split up with an agent she'd been dating called Brian Shaw. I invited her to stay at Wentworth and over the next few days she did. One hot night I got home and she looked unhappy.

'What's up?' I asked.

'Brian's 'phoned me up,' she said. 'He's very upset and wants to see me.'

'I don't want you to go and see him,' I said, afraid I was about to lose her. 'You've finished with him. I want you to be with me now.'

'No,' she said. 'I can't.'

'Please,' I urged. 'Stay with me.'

'I can't do that, I've got to call him.'

She went off to ring him and soon she was crying down the 'phone. Lesley came in, wondering what the hell was happening. 'I've really taken to this girl, you know?' I told her. The next day Tricia told me her mind was made up. She was definitely going back to Brian. I begged her to reconsider.

Just as she was about to leave I gave up. I set off up the road towards the pub for a sorrow-drowning session. I couldn't hide my feelings, I was in tears and already had the Tibby Tibbs story at the ready in case anyone spotted me.

Then Tricia ran after me. 'I'm going to give you a chance!' she said. She went back to Brian to sort things out and, when she returned as promised, I was back in paradise.

Before all the good weather had gone I had a party at home for the Davidson clan. I made a punch using what I thought to be a bottle of vodka. It turned out to be very strong Irish potato whisky, called poteen, which had been poured into a vodka bottle. Everyone drank the lethal mixture and became legless.

Brothers Billy and John and I made straight for the swimming pool to lark about. We invented a game called 'Launching Dead Bodies', falling as stiff as boards on to the water-slide for mock burials at sea. Then we played 'dolphins', splashing in the water, mouths open, as the others poured rum into our mouths from the side of the pool.

Uncle Georgie stripped to his underpants and dived in, closely followed by just about everyone else. When I got out of the water Mum looked at me nodding her head as usual. 'It had to be you and Billy didn't it?' she said. 'It's always you two, isn't it Cameron? You and that Billy!'

When I was getting ready to return to the Falklands for the second time in 1984, in September, to record the TV special, I asked Tricia to go with me. When she agreed I quickly had to contact Thames and get them to agree, too.

First Tricia wanted me to meet her 'mummy', at a wedding in Birmingham. Mummy was a big, fearsome Irish woman with a couple of equally big and frightening sons. At that first meeting things went badly between me and Tricia's family. I ended up being pushed by one of her brothers and, in a drunken temper, crushed a glass in my hand and cut my thumb open.

'So!' her mum said abruptly. 'You're taking my daughter to entertain people who shoot Irishmen, are you?'

God! What do you say to a line like that?

'Well,' I said. 'It is the Falklands. They must be fucking good shots from there.'

She relaxed a bit, and when I mentioned that my mum's family were Irish, she began to take to me more. She realised I wasn't very political and gave the trip the green light.

So I set off to the Falklands to record the special with Tricia on my arm and, on her finger, a three-carat engagement ring! I came back from the trip with a souvenir, an Argentinian Colt .45 pistol. It was just a piece of rust when I found it, but back home I diligently cleaned it and mounted it in a display box on the wall.

The Falklands special was transmitted on Christmas Eve and I started a run back at the Circus Tavern, Purfleet, for the holiday. That Christmas all of Tricia's family came to stay, about eight people from various parts of Ireland and Wales, all eating me out of house and home.

Keith Emerson called in for a festive drink and was amazed by my tolerance. 'I feel really sorry for you,' he said. 'You're one against hundreds of them!'

In order to have Cameron near me again I rented a house for him and Julie round the corner from me in Virginia Water, Surrey.

11

Mrs Davidson Number 3

At the end of January 1985, I was back in the Thames Television studios making a new series of *Up the Elephant*. Before long Tricia and I started getting on each other's nerves and it all seemed to be doomed between us. When Tricia began to pick up her singing career we both knew our fling was coming to an end. She used to go to jobs all over the place, and came back to me for a few days at a time between shows.

Then, to add further grief, housekeeper Lesley left, saying Tricia had upset her.

I 'phoned Laurie Mansfield and told him how fed up I was with Tricia and how much I missed Cameron, and even Julie. As they lived nearby I could visit Cameron regularly, but it wasn't terribly satisfying and Julie was now energetically leading her own life.

Rumour had it that Julie was going steady with a record-plugger called Gary Farrow, who I believe now manages Jonathan Ross. Farrow had a reputation for being a right leery sod, a real Porsche-driving Jack the Lad. I could never work out why Julie picked such blokes. They were nothing like me – that's probably the answer!

Tricia's singing career started picking up nicely but mine took a real dive. I was skint and got a tax bill for £250,000. I decided I had to remortgage Wentworth. But I couldn't do that unless Julie signed over her claim to part of the property. Of course, dear reader, that wasn't why I eventually got back with her.

First there was a lot of grief to come. One weekend I was due to call on Julie and Cameron in the evening but earlier in the day I got completely smashed at home with Tony Barton, a comic. As we emptied our second bottle of whisky I told him about my lovingly restored Colt .45, my Falklands souvenir. I turned the house upside down looking for it.

'Where's my gun?' I asked Tricia. 'I'm going to kill Freddie Starr!'

She saw the joke. She knew Freddie because she'd worked with him on a tour and she knew I loved him. I found the gun and proudly passed it to Tony. I said it wasn't dangerous, it couldn't be fired.

'Let's take it down to the pub,' he said. 'We'll have a laugh with it there!'

I slipped the gun into my trousers and we got ready to leave. Then I remembered I had to visit Julie and Cameron and decided to call in on the way. 'Come on, Tony,' I said. 'I've got to call on Julie first, then we'll go to the pub.'

We jumped into the car and drove over to Julie's house. I knocked on the door and she opened it cautiously. 'You can't come in!' she said, clearly uncomfortable at my turning up.

'He's here, isn't he?' I replied. Tony and I went in and there was Gary Farrow. I walked up to him, arm outstretched. 'Hello mate,' I said, shaking his hand. 'Excuse us a minute.'

Then Julie and I went into the kitchen to talk privately. 'Get rid of that prick!' I said. 'You've got to come back with me.'

'What about Tricia?' she asked.

'Tricia doesn't like me any more. Tell him he's got to go and bring Cameron back home.'

We went back to the lounge and I said hello again to Gary. 'You're quite a nice bloke, aren't you, really?' I asked him.

'Yeah,' he said.

'To tell you the truth,' I went on, 'I've heard you're a right leery bastard and that you'll probably punch me in the mouth.'

He said to me, really condescending and cocksure, 'No, I wouldn't do that.'

'Oh good,' I said, pulling the gun out of my pocket. 'I won't need this then!'

I put it on the coffee table in front of me and Farrow shat himself!

'Don't worry,' I said. 'It's not a real one. I brought it back from the Falklands.'

Then I showed him how to strip it and put it back together. I slipped it back into my pocket, had a quick brandy, then left with Tony for the Red Lion.

I was soon so far gone that one of the locals got me to put my car keys on the bar, in case I tried to drive 'under the influence'. A few minutes later I put my hand in my pocket and found the gun.

'Oh look!' I said, pulling it out. Three blokes, who I think had also been having it off with Julie, hit the deck!

'You could fire that, you know,' said a man next to me.

'But it was all rusty,' I said. 'All the insides must be useless.'

Then I sobered up enough to realise how serious it would be for me to be caught with a gun and decided I had to get home fast. When no one was looking I grabbed my car keys from the bar, made a dash for the car and drove home.

As I turned the corner I could see four policemen waiting outside my front door. I hastily slung the gun on to the floor, parked the car and got out.

'I have reason to believe you've been drinking,' said one of the policemen.

'Surely not!' I said. 'You must be a detective.' Then I ran off into the bushes and, a few minutes later, was found giggling to myself, handcuffed and put into a police car. I tried getting out and, when I couldn't, pushed out the back window with my clenched fists. I was taken to the police station bound for the cells, pissed and thoroughly horrible.

'Before you lock me up,' I said. 'Where's my car?'

'We've just brought it in,' said the sergeant. 'We're about to search it.'

'Well,' I said. 'Before you do search it, can I tell you something? There is a Colt .45 gun under the back seat.'

'No there isn't!' he said.

'Yes there is!' They took me, still handcuffed, to the car and I showed them where the gun was.

They didn't know what to do with it. They called a cop who was an ex-guardsman. He arrived and inspected it, and concluded that it wasn't loaded and hadn't been fired. I was free to go – until the court case in May.

The day Tricia finally walked out was the day I made my second parachute jump. It was filmed for one of my one-hour specials and was just as nerve-racking as the first time, and even more exhilarating. On landing I quickly gathered up my parachute and raced off to ring Tricia to tell her I'd managed it.

'Have I got news for you!' I said. 'I've just made my second parachute jump.'

'And have I got news for you!' she replied. 'I'm off!'

When I got home, sure enough she'd gone. If anything, having her out of the frame made things easier for me to woo back Julie and our son. A few weeks later they were back with me. It was great having Cameron around all the time though he was only three and I think he was confused by what was going on.

May 1986 was a particularly ghastly month and I was barely out of the papers. I had to appear in court for my mad night running around with the Colt .45. I was charged with unlawful possession of a firearm and refusing to give a breath test, fined £700 and banned from driving for eighteen months. The fine could have been a lot higher, but I showed the court pictures of my other memorabilia and begged forgiveness.

The chairman asked if I had anything to say and I was tempted to ask for the gun back, on condition that I got the barrel filled in, of course. I decided not to chance my luck!

Then Gary Farrow gave the papers his story, though I doubt it was a free gift. 'Nick! Nick! went Click! Click! Click!'

The story was riddled with inaccuracies. Even the headline was wrong. The gun was a Colt .45 automatic. They don't go 'click! click! click!', they just go 'click!' Rick Price said that if there had been any justice in the world the gun would have gone 'click! click! Bang!'

Next it was Lesley's turn to stitch me up in the papers. She flogged her stories about my home and friends, claiming my house was full of blokes from the SAS and that I had guns just about everywhere. Rubbish from start to finish. Three weeks later Lesley had the cheek to ask me for a reference for a job. I wrote a glowing tribute, thinking she'd apologise for being so nasty to me. Of course, she did no such thing.

It wasn't much later that I agreed to take part in a stunt with the Marines at a big display. They were doing a freefall exercise from a helicopter at 10,000 feet, and, for a joke, I pretended to do it as well.

'Ladies and gentlemen, can I please have your attention?' asked the announcer. 'Please give a big welcome to plucky Jim Davidson, who's just agreed to join the Marines in their daredevil freefall display!'

With that I ran out with the lads to rapturous cheers from the crowd. I took a bow and, in all the gear, really looked the part. I clambered aboard the waiting Wessex and we took off. Already hidden inside the helicopter was an extra man, my double. We swapped clothes and when it was my turn to go he went instead.

'There's Jim Davidson now,' the commentator told the kids, running off the first of a string of gags. 'The one with the brown trail!'

After all the team landed, the helicopter dropped over the arena and hovered two feet from the ground. 'Who's this?' asked the announcer.

At that point I was meant to make the small jump out of the helicopter, revealing the joke, and take a bow. Instead I belly-flopped on to the ground. Still, it got a laugh!

As I walked back to join the real freefallers, I passed a little kid of about eight. 'Fucking coward!' he said, glaring at me.

My first reaction was to punch him in the mouth. Then I decided I wouldn't pull a prank like that again if it meant little kids would think I was a coward. Then I laughed to myself, because I knew he was right. I am a coward. There's no way I could have hurled myself out of that helicopter with the Marines, who are a fearless bunch.

I'm sure freefalling is a terrific sport, if you're certain your parachute will open at the right time. No matter how many times my 'chute was checked, I know I'd be thinking of nothing else.

My mate Nish is planning to snatch the world freefalling record, from 135,000 feet. He's doing it from a hot-air balloon somewhere in outer space. 'If I stand on my head as I fall I'll hit Mach 2!' he told me.

'And if you land in Saudi Arabia you'll hit Maktoum!' I joked.

In the summer of 1985 I wasn't in summer season but back in the studio, making the fourth series of *Up the Elephant*.

For the rest of the year Julie and I tried very hard to make things work but we really weren't making it a second time. At Christmas 1985 I was in pantomime in Oxford, in *Cinderella*. When the run finished at the beginning of February 1986 I went back to Wentworth, Julie and Cameron. We tried to make another go of things but knew after four years our marriage really had failed.

I eventually walked out after a particularly drunken row when I threw her about in jealousy and rage. I threw some clothes into a couple of bags and left.

'Goodbye!' she cried after me, knowing this time it would be for good. I went to stay at the Holiday Inn, Slough, for a few days and returned briefly, with two roadies, to pick up a few things.

I'd paid £180,000 for Wentworth and Julie eventually sold it for more than enough to pay off the mortgage. After me she married a millionaire, but he wasn't wealthy for long because she divorced him, too, after a while. I'm sure Julie was a lovely mum. It's just that we were bad for one another. I suppose I am bitter. I was hurt a lot more than I showed by the failure of our marriage.

Stuck in the Holiday Inn I felt really miserable. No family. No home. No one. I asked everyone to try to find me a flat and in the end Laurie got me one, costing £600 a week! It was Mary Quant's old apartment, just off the King's Road in Chelsea, and bang opposite a gay pub called the Queen's Arms.

When I moved into the flat with my few bits, helped by Rick and two other roadies, we went into the pub for the first time. 'Three pints of lager and a coke, please,' I said.

'Do you realise this is a gay pub?' asked the barman. So I asked again in a lower voice! The pub became my local and the barman a real pal. Like everyone else, I affectionately called him Doris.

Once I was installed in the flat I started to slide downhill fast. I'd 'phone up hookers for company and God knows what. I went on the piss all the time and got myself into a real state. I wasn't feeling too good and didn't feel up to working. The split-up with Julie had cracked me up. I became resigned to the fact that I'd never have a decent home, that from now on I'd always be living out of suitcases and in little rented flats.

To avoid being alone, I'd go out drinking. I started going to Tramp regularly, where Johnny Gold, the boss, looked on me as a boy who hadn't quite grown up yet – and still does, I think.

Bill Wyman was a regular there. He was charming and always had Mandy Smith with him, a very pretty girl who looked about nineteen or twenty. Bill started talking to me and I couldn't work out what was going on in his life. He kept mentioning the press on his tail and the problems he was having. 'I have to be careful because of Mandy, you know,' he said.

I nodded several times but still didn't understand what he meant. I thought Mandy was married to someone else or something like that. Later I found out she was barely sixteen!

I was sitting with Bill and Mandy the night a beautiful woman called Janine Andrews walked in. She looked terrific, all six-foot-four of her, wearing a big blue frock over her enormous knockers.

'I know her,' said Mandy.

'Really?' said I.

Janine was with a girl known as Geordie Jenny, and I'd met her before in Wentworth. I started chatting to Jenny and then spoke to Janine, who had a glorious, thick Brummie accent and was warm and slightly dizzy.

The next night I went back to Tramp and Janine turned up and joined me for something to eat. She told me she'd been in the James Bond film *Octopussy* and I could believe it. She'd also been a page three girl and had a perfect body, just sublime. She invited herself around to my flat to cook for me – and actually did!

She came over to cook several times and eventually one night we had a kiss and cuddle to clinch things. We started seeing each other regularly and I became completely besotted with her. I even bought shoes with highish heels to keep up with her.

Janine also loved going out for supper, so we'd dress up and go to restaurants night after night. She fancied herself as a bit of a singer and, just as I'd done with Tricia, I asked her if she wanted to come on my next forces trip – another TV Christmas special, this time in Germany. I threw a birthday party for her and gave her a portable CD. To me it all seemed very serious, but Janine had other ideas.

I flew off to America for ten days and had terrible jet-lag. I missed Janine badly. Every few minutes I tried to 'phone her, but she was never at home. I tried Tramp, but she wasn't there either. No one had seen her. I was convinced she'd left me and I started to drink heavily for the rest of the trip. I was a real mess. When I eventually got back to London I arranged to take Janine out for supper.

Something wasn't right, and to soften any bad news I got thoroughly drunk. Then we went back to the flat, but she toyed with me and my feelings for her. 'What are you doing to me?' I asked. 'What's happening between us?'

'Well,' she said bluntly. 'I'm with someone else and you're all right but you're nothing special.'

I started crying and in a temper threw a bottle of Remy Martin brandy through a double-glazed window. Janine stormed out into the pouring rain and I chased after her. She ran back to her own flat and slammed the door, leaving me standing there, knocking and crying.

'Go away,' she said, through the door. 'I don't want to speak to you. Go away.'

I walked off broken-hearted and cried until dawn. Next morning I had to be photographed for the cover of my joke book, *Too Risky*, and I felt like death. I managed a smile for the photographer, but he was the only one. I went home to be greeted by the Irish landlord.

'When you break a window you don't half fucking break one, don't you?' he said.

I sat down with a bottle of brandy and drank the lot. It transpired that Janine had a long-term boyfriend, who I nicknamed 'Bagpipe Billy', and that they had continued their relationship throughout the time I was with her. He was with the Bay City Rollers and lived up in Scotland, and he'd been out of the country for a time touring Japan. I also learned that Janine had gone off me the day I threw the birthday party for her. I'd bought her a portable CD player, but someone said she was expecting something much more expensive, like a sports car.

Anyway, Janine moved up to Scotland to Bagpipe Billy and I returned to the old routine of Tramp every night. I really was miserable, drinking so much I had to be carried out. One night Costa, a barman at Tramp, said: 'Jim, you've got to snap out of this depression. Look on the bright side – you won't hurt your neck looking up at her any more, will you?'

Despite the jokes I was shattered by Janine's behaviour. For about a fortnight I was in a drunken haze, not sleeping, just moping all the time. I found it difficult to work and developed what I thought was full-blown stage-fright. I was drinking myself into oblivion every night and couldn't recover from the hangovers any more.

In desperation I went to see a Harley Street psychiatrist. I don't think he liked me. He asked plenty of questions, and whatever I replied he'd tut to himself. He didn't seem the least bit interested in the cause of my problems, my disastrous personal life.

'Have you got a girlfriend?' he asked.

'Sort of.'

'Do you see her a lot?'

'No,' I said. 'Well, she doesn't want to know me. She's got this boyfriend in Scotland.'

'And what do you think about that?'

'What do you think I think about that?' I snapped. 'It's horrible.'

Basically, he told me I was mad. Then he ordered me to cut down on the drink and gave me some Valium to help me sleep. That took me back. I thought, I won't end up nicking another mini, will I? He also put me on a course of beta-blockers to overcome any panic attacks before an audience.

To add to my problems, I woke up yet again one Sunday morning to find I was headline news. This time Janine had done the dirty, painting me to be a horrible, scruffy drunk who had chained her to the kitchen sink, refused to spend a penny on her and, on top of it all, was a bad fuck!

That night I went to Tramp to drown my sorrows and in walked Janine, but, hardly surprisingly, she kept her distance. A little later in came my mate, stuntman Rocky Taylor. He'd read the papers and told me to ignore them completely. Rocky had arrived with the actress Leslie Ash. I told him I'd always wanted to meet her and he introduced us.

We hit it off at once. I told her I'd just been stitched up by Janine and I talked about giving her a piece of my mind.

'Don't even think about it,' said Leslie sweetly. 'Come with me.' She took my arm, and even though I'd only just met her we left together and went to Stringfellow's, much to the delight of all the press photographers camped outside. Leslie and I teased them, holding hands across the table then, as soon as they tried to snatch a picture, coyly letting go.

In the end we agreed to pose for the photographers, me presenting Leslie with a rose across the table. 'She's the one for me!' I told them. 'I'm in love – this time it's for real.'

Leslie offered me a lift back to my King's Road flat, then invited me to her place for coffee. I felt I'd hit the jackpot again. We had a coffee and a few drinks and chatted for hours. And just as I was about to leave, she made the night complete.

'I wouldn't mind a cuddle,' she said. That was the start of our romance. We saw each other a lot over the next three or four weeks but somehow it wasn't quite right. She obviously didn't want to settle down. And she didn't like the way I was desperate and lovelorn. She knew I'd have been happy with almost anybody to get away from my nomadic show-business life.

That summer I was in Great Yarmouth, trying out something new – an adults-only run at the height of the season. Even though this was 1986, such a short time ago, trying to break conventions was an uphill task.

All year I could tour clubs throughout the country giving my audiences what they wanted, a blue act. Come the summer season, though, everything had to change. Summer season shows all had to be family affairs, variety shows with glitzy dancers and conjurers. Not only that, but summer shows had to keep up with convention and not run late.

That year in Yarmouth, against tremendous local opposition, Laurie got me a booking at the Britannia Pier to try out an adults-only show.

Because of the protests, the show was scheduled to start at 9.00 pm at the theatre, following the nightly performance of the pier's clean family show, *The Secret Diary of Adrian Mole*. *Mole* struggled to win audiences but my run sold out. Despite the initial protests, the idea had worked.

When the season ended I was off to Germany to film the Christmas forces TV special. Arrangements for the trip hadn't gone smoothly. When the idea was in its infancy I wrote to Mrs Thatcher to ask if she thought it a good idea. She said, in effect, yes, make it happen.

The intention was to film the show in September, but with a suitably festive theme so that it could be transmitted at Christmas. On arrival we'd spend a few days among the 'tankies', our lads with the tank regiments, filming inserts of them on manoeuvres. The main show was to be staged in a boxing stadium for 4,000 troops, most of them Scottish.

With me were Richard Digance, singer Diane Solomon, several girl dancers, a huge band and, for an emotional finale, 400 angelic Brownies. The highlight for me was a trip in a Harrier Jump Jet.

Making it all happen seemed to be a nightmare. We needed to get artistes, TV and stage crews, lighting and sound technicians – as well as a mountain of equipment – to Germany but we couldn't afford to hire a plane. We asked the MoD to pull a few strings with the RAF to shuttle some of the stuff across but got the cold shoulder.

Frustrated, I went back to Mrs Thatcher. 'My dear Jim,' she said, 'there are aircraft going in and out of Berlin every moment of the day. I'll have a word with someone.'

I thought our troubles were over. But even the Prime Minister couldn't crack it. I think some MoD stick-in-the-mud fought back her wishes with an I-don't-care-who-she-is attitude. In the end we had to send all the equipment by road, which was very expensive and very slow.

In October we all met up at our hotel in Gutaslow ready for work. The director was Stuart Hall (not to be confused with the *It's a Knockout* Stuart), who'd also directed the Falklands special. Shadowing me all the time was my mate and minder Nish, the freefalling expert, nicknamed 'Big Nose'.

The first gig was that night for a load of tankies somewhere in the middle of Germany's nowhere. Coaches ferried the concert party and crew to the secret location and filming started as it got dark, with the massive tanks as backdrops.

Much to my embarrassment Hall had got all the poor squaddies sitting in a circle singing 'Silent Night'! They hated having to do it and it looked terribly contrived so

I got into a heated argument with Stuart. 'I'll never work with you again!' I shouted.

'Right,' he said. 'I'm wrapping. I've had enough of this. If you don't want to play, forget it.'

I stormed off to have a few beers with the tankies and a relieved company and crew set off in the coaches back to the hotel. Not me. A little later I was trundled off into the night with a three-man TV crew and Bob Louis, the producer. We were taken to a tiny country inn, where a big military exercise with more tanks was underway. The plan was to kip at the inn then, at first light, film with the squaddies over breakfast.

We were ready for a good night's sleep. But, probably because we were filming a Christmas special, when we arrived there was no room at the inn! There were just three spare beds, which were promptly nabbed by the crew. Bob looked around and found, of all things, the sauna and decided to sleep in there. But I had nowhere.

I went upstairs and found a double bed with a fully-clothed man in it, fast asleep. Thinking he was one of the crew, I took off my boots and got into the bed. I woke up at one point to see a pair of eyes belonging to my sleeping partner staring at me in disbelief. It was Stuart Hall! The poor man, who had probably been having a nightmare about me anyway, turned over and there I was.

Filming didn't go smoothly the next day because it rained heavily. Eventually, wet through, we finished and the coach picked us up to take us back to Gutaslow. Many of the others had been partying non-stop since the night before. Big Nose loved rubbing in just what a good time he'd had when I wasn't around. He'd even started flirting with Lynsey, one of the dancers I was rather keen on.

The equipment for the big show in the boxing stadium took forever to set up, and then we rehearsed over and over with the full company, including all the Brownies. The concert ran smoothly until I went out to sing a rousing, patriotic song called 'England' – to 4,000 jocks! Fortunately we also had some pipers, so that partially compensated for the gaffe.

In the finale all 400 Brownies crammed on to the stage. They were so overwhelmed by the size of the raucous audience that they were struck dumb. Back in Britain we had to stand around microphones doing Brownie impressions to dub on to the soundtrack!

After the show I had a few drinks, then Nish took me to a seedy bar in downtown Berlin. It was a grubby, smoke-filled club and, on-stage, a naked guy sat in a bath with a bird bouncing up and down on him.

Nish and I sat at the bar and had a drink. Suddenly two really beautiful oriental darlings walked in. One had long, blonde hair, the other short, dark hair. The blonde was the best-looking and I thought, being the star, I'd end up with her. Nope. She walked up to Big Nose and started cuddling him. I sat and had a few drinks with the other girl who, in an oriental way, reminded me of Val from the Old Kent Road.

A little later Nish disappeared with his pick-up and I staggered off drunkenly with mine for a tinker about. And, not to put too fine a point on it, got a blow job.

A few minutes later I took her back to the bar and bought her another drink as I waited for Nish. He turned up all smiles with his blonde, who said goodbye and left. Nish sat next to me and ordered a drink.

'There's something funny about this girl,' I said to him. 'There's something wrong with her.'

'What do you mean?' he asked.

'I don't know,' I said. 'She wouldn't let me do anything to her, she just wanted to give me a blow job. That did me, but it was all a bit odd.'

He thought for a moment. 'Here, she could be a *kitai*.'

'A what?'

'A *kitai*,' he replied. 'It's the word in Singapore for a bloke who's had the operation, had the dick off and a fanny made.'

I looked at him, unsure of what to say for a second. 'The hardest bit of the operation must be sewing in the anchovies!' I replied eventually. 'Are you really serious?'

'Yes,' he said. 'I'm king of the *kitais* – I've had seven of them!'

'What do you mean?' I asked. 'They haven't got dicks have they?'

'Oh no,' he said, 'they've had the proper sex change.'

'Well, how can you tell if she's a *kitai*?' I asked, intrigued.

'They're the better-looking ones! They don't go all horrible, they keep their looks and their figures.'

'How else can you tell?' I persisted.

'By their feet,' he said. 'She can't change the size of her plates. Take a look at her feet!'

I dropped something on the floor to inspect the girl's feet closely. But I couldn't see a thing. 'No good,' I slurred to Nish, getting back on my stool. 'It's too dark down there.'

'All right, well you can also tell if she's got an Adam's apple. If there's an apple, it's a bloke.'

The poor girl must have thought I was a strangler because then I started putting my arm around her neck, feeling for an Adam's apple. Still no joy.

'I still can't tell,' I told him. Then Nish had a brainwave.

'Look!' he said loudly, pointing up at the ceiling. The girl looked up, and there it was clear as day – her Adam's apple! Nish asked her directly, in her native tongue, if she was a *kitai*. She got really angry, slammed her drink down on the bar and stormed off, insisting unconvincingly, 'Me no lady-man!'

So, where does the accusing finger point? The best thing about sex with a man is that afterwards you can roll over and talk about football. Seriously, though, do you know I've not had a card, nor a letter, nor a 'phone call from my *kitai* since that night. Me and blokes are through!

The next morning I woke up with a hell of a hangover and vowed that if I was going to go with anything out there, I'd have to fuck it to be sure it was a female.

The next night we got to Fallingbostal to entertain the tankies and, very late at night, drunk again, Nish and I were taken to the local brothel. Behind the bar was a horrible bird with terrible teeth and a better-looking tart in mid-snog with a German. Nish decided, once again, he was interested in the quality and set about finding ways to get the other client out of the way.

When the stranger and his hooker retired to one of the bedrooms, Nish decided he'd have to throw a condom water-bomb at them to kill the passion. A little while later I saw him staggering along the corridor, naked and awkwardly carrying a Durex filled with three gallons of water. Just before he got to the bedroom door it burst all over him!

I took the bird from behind the bar into the jacuzzi and gave her one. No messing around this time. No dick. No Adam's apple. No problem.

Next day Nish and I dragged ourselves back to the hotel in Gutaslow to rejoin the others. All that remained for the TV special was my trip in the Harrier Jump Jet a few days later.

The next day it dawned on me that I'd got the most dreadful bout of gonorrhoea. I asked myself why I hadn't worn a condom. Mind you, it would have been difficult in the jacuzzi – it would have floated off!

Panic! What could I do about it? I knew I couldn't go to a military doctor because the news would spread around all 4,000 troops like wildfire. I told Nish and he turned up at the RAF base to try to pinch some medication. The dose didn't hurt but it was slightly uncomfortable and I decided that, as I would be back in Britain soon, I'd wait and put myself back in the safe hands of my Harley Street doctor, Dr Freddie Lim.

The day before the Harrier stunt I turned up with the TV crew at 4 Squadron. Wing Commander Pete Harris told me all about the trip and the jet, which he was going to be flying.

That night I didn't drink much and tried to get an early night, although I couldn't sleep well as I hadn't had much to drink! In the morning Pete Harris took me to the Harrier and, with the TV crew recording everything, explained all the controls.

He pointed under my seat at yellow and black markings, which meant 'Danger – explosives'.

'When we're in the air,' he told me, 'if I say "eject" you eject straight away, don't ask twice, just do it. And if I eject and you don't, you'll see "Follow Me" on the soles of my shoes.'

What happened next didn't make the Christmas special and, if you're reading this, Pete, here's why I threw my Danny La Rue-type tantrum!

I thanked the group captain for allowing me to make the flight in the jet.

'It wasn't me,' he replied. 'It was the big bosses! You're very lucky. Are you looking forward to the flight?' he asked.

'Yes, very much,' I answered.

'Come on then,' he said. 'I'll take you down for your medical.'

'Pardon?' I replied.

'I'll take you off for your medical,' he repeated. So off I went with him to the doctor. I thought he'd check my blood pressure and that would be about all. With luck, I thought, I might even be able to scrounge a few beta-blockers from him to calm me down.

Well, it wasn't just the blood pressure the doctor wanted to check. He looked into my ears and down my throat, then listened to my heart and chest. Any moment I expected a frigate search!

'Looking forward to the trip, Jim?' he asked.

'Yes I am, Doc,' I answered, thinking he'd finished.

'Good,' he said. 'Now, just give me a sample of your urine in that bottle over there.'

'Stick the fucking Harrier up your arse!' I snapped. I knew if I pissed in his bottle he'd soon know I'd caught something horrible – there would be bits of dick floating in it!

'I don't want this!' I said, acting angrily. 'How dare you! I'm supposed to come along and ride in a Harrier. You've all told me it's safe and given me the medical. Now I've got to piss in that bottle. I don't want to do it any more and I'm not going to. Fuck ya. I'm off!'

I started to leave and, having heard the rumpus, the group commander came in.

'I'm not having all this,' I told him. 'What's going on? A medical? You told me it was going to be safe, why do I need a medical? I've got a film to make, I can't be bothered with all this. I'm not getting in that Harrier now. Shove it! I'm just not going to piss into a bottle. It'll end up being sold around the camp, I know what armies are like!'

The group captain asked the doctor: 'Are Jim's ears, nose and blood pressure all right?'

'Yes,' he replied.

'All right, that'll be OK then, Jim,' he said.

Having bluffed my way out of the urine test I clambered into the Harrier for the trip.

Back in Britain I turned up at Dr Freddie's clinic after rather a boozy lunch. 'Hello, Freddie,' I slurred. 'It's me again!'

'Lie down then,' he said, preparing something in his cupboard. When I looked around, Freddie was standing behind me with a syringe and huge needle. I was instantly stone-cold sober. He stuck the needle in my bum and, in sheer fear, my muscles grabbed it so hard it wouldn't budge.

'It's the experience I had in Berlin,' I explained. 'I don't trust baring my arse to anybody any more!'

A few days after that I unexpectedly met someone I instinctively trusted with my life – Susan Sergeant. I was appearing in Northampton for a night and she turned up at the stage door with her sister. 'Do you remember me?' she asked.

I just said in a pained voice: 'I love you!'

I invited her back to my hotel with her sister for drinks. I thought once we got back Susan would leap into my arms, but she didn't. We had a few drinks and chatted over childhood memories. When she and her sister got up to leave, Susan kissed me on the cheek and said goodbye.

I walked up to my room slowly, feeling dejected. I sat next to the open window and flashed my light on and off slowly, hoping someone might flash back to me from the Northampton darkness. They didn't.

At Christmas 1986 I was booked to appear in *Cinderella* at the Bristol Hippodrome. I turned up to do some advance publicity and one of my interviewers was a local television reporter and newsreader with HTV, Alison Holloway. She was very pretty, with blonde hair, and slightly flirtatious.

After the interview she left with her crew and I was hooked. This'll do me, I thought, not for the first time in my life.

When I got back to London I wrote to Alison. I said nice things about her, flattering her on her mesmerising interview technique. And I mentioned that when I returned for the pantomime I would like to take her for supper. I later found out that she had pinned my letter on the office noticeboard, for all to laugh at!

I got a short note back from Alison. 'Thanks,' she said. 'But my boyfriend isn't as charming as the pantomime prince!' He was, as it turned out.

I next saw Alison on the opening night. She found me after the show, on her own, and I took her to the first-night party. She was lively and jovial. Perhaps she'd changed her opinion of me because she'd seen me on-stage. I didn't know what had become of her boyfriend, nor did I care.

The next day she was leaving for a New Year skiing holiday and rang me from the airport. She asked if she could see me again when she got back. As she took off, I was on Cloud Nine.

12

Mrs Davidson Number 4

When Alison Holloway returned from her holiday we again hit it off brilliantly. Getting together wasn't easy because we were both well-known faces to the people of Bristol. Checking into hotels was out of the question. The last thing either of us wanted was the press in on the act.

Instead, we would rendezvous for afternoons and evenings in the flat of a gay friend of Alison and his lover. When the boys were out, we got a chance to do some kissing and cuddling.

One afternoon when we'd all been drinking the gay guys suggested Alison and I got married. So we did. On Thursday February 19 1987, up came the family, down we all went to the register office, then it was back to a hotel for a good bevy. I got legless.

At the reception my mate Snapper came out with a great line. Alison, having known me all of two months, told him: 'I can't understand it. I've never seen him as drunk as this.'

Snapper replied: 'Stick around, baby – you ain't seen nothing yet!' And he turned out to be right.

My relationship with Alison lasted all of a month after we tied the knot before it hit problems. We rented a flat in Clifton, Bristol, and I moved up all I needed – my hi-fi and fishing gear.

At Thames Television in 1987 we were changing direction

again. We had made four series of *Up the Elephant* and gone about as far as we could with the characters. So, after several think-tanks, the idea for a new series, *Home James*, was born. In this, Jack London, from *Up the Elephant*, moves upmarket to become George Sewell's Rolls Royce-driving chauffeur. The fact that I was banned from driving at the time was regarded as a good joke. I would have to do all my driving scenes sitting in the car on the back of a truck!

As I was living in Bristol, the ban was making my real life hell when we filmed the first series. For eight weeks Rick Price drove up from London in the early hours to collect me and get me back to the Thames studios in Teddington by 10.00 am. I'd spend the whole day rehearsing then catch the last train back home to Bristol. Some nights I wished I hadn't bothered.

Alison and I fought most of the time we were together. I'd been nine stone all my adult life, but now, as a result of a combination of giving up smoking, being plain unhappy and going to the gym, I ballooned to twelve stone. I was determined to lose weight so I started weight training and bought equipment for home work-outs, but it made little difference. Far from feeling better, I ached and had a permanent hangover.

Marriage to Alison was all a bit too proper, too clinical and formal for me. When she came home from work she would be slightly too jolly for the mood I was in. 'Hello, darling,' she'd say. 'Shall we go out for dinner or go to see friends?'

A lot of my problem was that I had no friends of my own in Bristol. I was married again but, most of the time, I was just as lonely as I'd ever been.

Then Alison started to get regular telephone calls from an old flame. It dawned on me, sadly, that she must have gone for me purely for novelty value. Until me she'd been into rugby-player types. Where most people had love-bites, she had stud-marks.

Alison really could fight and she had an evil temper. The papers ran a story saying I'd given her two black eyes in a row one night. Well, here's what they didn't print.

I got home from a night out alone at the pub. Alison came

in late after a day at the HTV studio in a horrible mood and went mental. She pulled my hair and thumped me – she could punch in the mouth like a bloke.

I ran to the bedroom and barricaded myself in with my weight-training gear. She burst the door open like the Incredible Hulk, pushed the weights out of the way and came after me. I threw her back across the room, and as something came crashing near me I slung a dumbbell her way. She kept coming and, pushing her away from me, I caught her in the eye with my thumb, bruising her eye and dislocating my thumb. I ran off to hide, snapping my thumb back into place as I went.

Next day she went to work and I went to see her. She was covering her bruise with make-up and cursing me.

A few days later, she was at the flat and asked me to throw her the keys for the white Golf GTi I'd bought her. I flung them over and the bunch accidentally hit her in the other eye! She wasn't hurt badly but once again she had a bruise.

Just after that a reporter nobbled me. 'I believe you've given your wife a black eye,' he said.

'Two!' I replied. I should have learned by then not to joke with the press. Next morning there was the story: I'd confessed to giving my wife two black eyes. I took a darn sight more than I gave, I know that much!

Alison's parents ran a fancy dress shop in Wandsworth, London, and I think as a girl she'd suffered from the I've-got-to-be-famous-for-Mum syndrome. She had gone to one of those drama schools for precocious kids.

Just after our punch-ups had made the papers Alison's mum said something odd to me. 'You've got to remember, Alison's not a wife, she's a newsreader,' she said.

'Oh dear,' I replied.

Then Alison had to go into hospital, for 'women's problems'. I collected her from the hospital and we went to stay at her parents' home.

I was in the lounge, drinking and watching *Star Trek* on the telly. Alison's brother, a bit younger than me and a bit bigger, came in from the pub worse for wear. He blamed me for Alison's problems, which wasn't fair, and tried to take a swing at me. I'd also had plenty to drink and chased him out of the house, putting my fist through a big six-foot glass door.

'I'm off,' I said as I drove off, pissed. I got fifty yards down the road before I was stopped by the police.

'What's happened?' asked the officer, who must have heard the commotion at the house. He got me out of the car and drove me back.

'Get in there, Jim,' he said. 'Stop being foolish.'

He was kind. He could have done me for drink-driving.

After that Alison didn't often want to know me. But the Conservatives did. In the run-up to what was to be Mrs Thatcher's last general election, in 1987, I received an invitation from her press secretary, Bernard Ingham, to help the Conservatives' election campaign. He'd asked me to attend a big publicity rally being staged with lots of other celebrities.

I politely declined. As I was banned from driving at the time I suggested it would be tempting fate. I didn't want to give a lefty paper the chance of saying: 'Jim Davidson's banned from driving – now he'll steer the Tories off the road!'

So I bowed out and earned myself a letter from No.10, thanking me for keeping in the background. It was another time I did myself more good by not appearing, another job well done by not doing it!

Whatever I did do when Alison was around always seemed to be wrong. Things reached an all-time low in May. Deep in depression at the prospect of a third failed marriage, I got pissed, grabbed the flag presented to me by Captain Sam Salt and went into a deserted church in Clifton. I sat there alone, hugging my flag, with tears rolling down my face. If I prayed for anything it was an end to the nightly punch-ups with Alison. Then I fell into a pub for the rest of the night.

Next morning, after Alison had gone to work, I sat in bed staring at the ceiling and hating everything: Alison, Bristol, everything. Then the 'phone rang: it was the answer to my prayers.

'Hello Jim. You don't know me,' said a woman's voice. 'You've probably seen me driving around town. I've got a Ferrari.'

Thank God, I thought. Whoever you are, do you want to have lunch?

'Do you have any influence over your wife?' she continued.

'Not much nowadays,' I said. 'Why?'

'Can you stop her from seeing Bill?'

'Who's Bill?' I said.

'Her ex-boyfriend.'

'Thank God!' I said. 'How long's all this been happening?'

'Well, she came round last Sunday,' the woman explained. 'He collects butterfly ornaments and she pushed a porcelain butterfly through the door. She still wants to see him.'

'Brilliant!' I thought, thanking the woman and hanging up. Without a second's hesitation I went to Torquay to wait for the summer season.

I popped back to Bristol a week later for a meeting and talked to a solicitor. 'You don't do divorces, do you?' I asked her. 'My wife's been seeing someone else.'

'I know,' she said. 'It's the talk of Bristol.'

'Blimey,' I said. 'Is it?'

'Yes.'

'Bill, the bloke who plays rugby,' I confirmed, nodding my head.

'Oh no,' she said. 'Not him. She's been seeing a university lecturer.'

'Are you sure?'

'Yes,' she said. 'It's well-known.'

As I drove back to Torquay I didn't feel so bad about failing with Alison. The marriage was broken and it was she who had cracked it. I had worshipped the ground she walked on and she'd walked all over me. We'd met in the panto season and were history by the summer season; that has to be some kind of record, even in show-business. I was sorry it went wrong. I had loved her and been faithful. She was a bit too grown-up for me, I think. I must have really got on her tits.

When Britain was going to the polls, Alison and I were going to Barbados on holiday. We made out to the press we were reconciling our differences and getting back together. In reality, we'd paid for the holiday in advance so we weren't going to miss it!

I rented a house and my brother Billy came to stay. Alison and I still got on each other's nerves, but we tried to make the best of it. The *Sun* tracked us down and their photographer, Steve Lewis, took a picture of me baring my bum near Alison.

When we got back to Bristol she got a real bollocking from HTV. Their serious newsreader was splashed all over the Currant Bun laughing at Jim Davidson's dick! And I was back in hot water, too. Having just got my licence back I was stopped outside a Bristol chippie and did the usual trick, refused to give a breath test. Because I was pissed, of course.

That summer, riding the success of the previous year's Yarmouth season, I was putting on the blue show at the Princess Theatre, Torquay. Once again I hit a wall of protests, from hoteliers and councillors who thought I'd be bad for business in the town.

I had my boat *Dishby Doo* with me for the season. Once or twice Alison turned up and we went out for a spin. But things were soon rocky between us again and she turned into a woman possessed. She would 'phone me all the time, hurling obscenities down the line. Even when Kevin, who sounds like me, answered the 'phone, she'd rant away not knowing it wasn't me!

Soon the 'phone calls weren't enough. She started turning up suddenly in Torquay, having driven down from Bristol in a rage. Torquay's elders may have thought my act was too blue for them but in the wings some nights there was much filthier language being used! Alison would turn up unexpectedly and bully her way backstage to yell obscenities at me from the wings. Kevin and the crew had to restrain her, otherwise she'd have walked out on stage, kicking and punching. She was a nightmare. The poor girl really did know how to get upset.

By August we were no more, although I did have to return to Bristol at the beginning of the month – to appear in court, where I promptly lost my licence again. Banned for three years.

In Torquay I started seeing a girl called Joanne Urch, a dancer who worked in Doodles, a Torquay nightclub. I thought she was about eighteen but she turned out to be sixteen and I was accused in the tabloids of having an affair with an underage girl – and they printed pictures of her looking about four.

Paul, an army pal, turned up one night. He asked Joanne to line him up a blind date with a stunningly beautiful seventeen-year-old.

The four of us went out on *Dishby Doo* after the show and moored up at Fisherman's Cove, six miles from the harbour. It was a beautiful, moonlit night. The four of us were up on deck. Paul was cuddling his friend and I caught his eye. He gave me the thumbs-up and looked up to the stars as if to say he was in absolute heaven. He is now, I hope. He died a few years later from a heart attack.

At the end of the summer I sold *Dishby Doo*. She hadn't been looked after properly in winter and I thought it best to get rid of her. In the final days of the season, in September, I flew up from Torquay to the Boat Show in Southampton with my mate Dave Franks. We were having a few whiskies at the bar when he stopped in his tracks.

'Oh God!' he said, staring across at a beautiful promotions girl at the Guinness stand. 'Look at that!'

I glanced over and there she was. A girl who turned out to be called Tracy Hilton. She was fabulous. I walked straight up to her and, apparently, my opening line was: 'You're going to be my fourth wife, you are!'

She hated me on sight. I tried chatting her up but got nowhere. After the show I flew back to Torquay to do the show and see little Joanne. For the next three days I kept flying back to the Boat Show in the daytime, to try to flirt with Tracy, then back to Torquay at night for the show and Joanne.

On the last day of the Boat Show I persuaded Tracy to

come with me to take a look at a £250,000 showcase 55ft Princess cruiser. It was beautiful, big enough to sleep eight. To impress Tracy I bought one, and signed the cheque for the £10,000 deposit under her pretty little nose. She wasn't a bit impressed – she put boating on a par with caravanning – yet still I adored her.

Before leaving I gave her my telephone number, though she didn't give me hers. When the Boat Show ended, so did my chances of seeing her. I went back to London to live with Mum at Holburne Road until I sorted myself out.

One night I went to Tramp and was introduced briefly to an attractive Indian girl, Pamella Bordes, a former Miss India. I said hello and then strolled off to order a hamburger. A few minutes later she followed me and began talking to me, but I wasn't in a receptive mood, I was thinking of nothing but Tracy.

'Do you mind!' I said, moving to the bar with my burger. She followed me.

'Why don't you like me?' she asked.

'It's not that,' I said. 'I just don't want to speak to anybody at the moment.'

She tried chatting me up again, then gave up and went off to join her friends.

I returned to Tramp the following night. Pamella did too, and she came straight up to me. This time I was a bit more relaxed and bought her a drink. I invited her out, to the musical *Time* at The Dominion Theatre, and we started seeing each other quite regularly, although I remained sold on Tracy, and was preoccupied with ways to track her down and see her again.

Soon I went off to entertain the troops in Hong Kong and, while I was away, Pamella found me a tiny, one-bedroomed flat to rent near Holland Park in Kensington. I turned up at Holburne Road to collect my few bits and pieces. My sister Eileen was there and watched me as I filled just three bags. 'Not bad,' I said to her. 'For someone who won *New Faces* in 1976 when he was only twenty-two.'

Eileen burst into tears and it was all I could do not to join her. It was pathetic. I'd been selling out shows around the country for over a decade, yet here I was, back to square one with nothing to show for it, broke again. When I moved into the flat Pamella had found I was in a dreadful state. My life really was an unmitigated disaster.

A few days later, at Tramp with Pamella, I bumped into one of the girls who'd worked with Tracy in Southampton. When Pamella wasn't around I quickly pumped the friend about Tracy.

'She's got a boyfriend,' she said. 'But I don't know how happy she is.' I tried getting Tracy's 'phone number but got nowhere. 'I think she's coming down to work on the Motor Show in November,' said the girl. When Pamella saw us chatting she pushed the girl out of the way in jealousy, spilling a drink over her.

I continued to date Pamella for the next few weeks and took her to my brother's pub in Belvedere, not far from Kidbrooke, one night. Afterwards we tried to go to an Indian restaurant. The waiters said we were too late, they were closed. Pamella spoke to them in their own language, asking them to reopen the kitchen, but they wouldn't.

The following night Billy went back to the restaurant. 'Do you realise who you wouldn't serve last night?' he asked them. 'Miss India!'

The little Indian manager just stared blankly at him. 'Oh fuck!' he replied eventually.

Pamella was a nice girl, good fun but a bit of a snob. She was also a bit like clingfilm, hanging on the arm too much. Every so often I'd ask her to back off a bit.

'Why do you tell me to fuck off?' she would ask.

'Because you get on my tits!' I'd reply.

'I love you,' she'd respond. 'I love you, Jimmy. Why don't you marry me?'

I think she liked me so much because, perversely, at times I seemed to hate her so much. At that time the only person I dreamed of marrying was Tracy, if she'd have me.

In November I met Mrs Thatcher again when she came to open a photographic exhibition for the Sharon Allen Leukaemia Trust at the Barbican. The photographs were from a book called *Faces of the Eighties* by Gemma Levine.

Many of the people in the book turned up for the VIP opening, including David Frost, Sir Robin Day, Jeremy Isaacs, Peter Bowles and Tessa Sanderson. The Prime Minister, who was also featured in the book, had agreed to attend. At the last minute Mrs Thatcher's whereabouts were leaked to the press and security was doubled up.

I was told that the Prime Minister wanted me to do all the introductions, so I ran around quickly learning all the names. Mrs Thatcher walked in and I did my job, with the occasional prompt. Then, as Gemma Levine started making a speech, Mrs Thatcher leaned over to me.

'What happens now?' she asked.

'Well,' I explained, 'After Gemma Levine has finished, Humphry Berkeley wants to say a few words. Then I'll get up to invite you to do the same and formally open the exhibition.'

'OK,' she said and shut her eyes. I'm sure, like Enoch Powell in the Commons, she then went to sleep. About fifteen minutes later, when it was time to introduce her, I gave a slight cough and she opened her eyes, stood up and made her speech.

For the next few minutes she spoke only of me! She mentioned the forces' trips I'd been making and ended her unexpected, embarrassing tribute by pointing straight at me. 'And the only reason I'm here is because of him,' she said. She didn't mention Gemma Levine once. As soon as the Prime Minister left I dashed off to work in a club. Talk about one extreme to another!

Towards the end of the month I was in Tramp when Tracy Hilton walked in. She looked like a million dollars. She was wearing a bright pink jump-suit and her hair was all over the place. She was out with some idiots from Ferrari who'd been at the opening of the Motor Show.

Nervously, I went up to her and tried to make her laugh. I gave her a lift back to her hotel, and promised to visit her at the show the next day.

At the Motor Show we had a couple of quick drinks and then I had to leave to go and work for the rest of the week in Newmarket. When I got there I sent Tracy roses and telephoned her every evening, but still I really didn't think she wanted to know.

Pamella came up to see me in Newmarket and stayed for a night. When she left it was the last time I saw her. We knew we were swimming in different directions and left it at that.

On Tracy's last day at the Motor Show I made a mad dash back to London in time to find her but missed her by an hour. She'd gone again, and I still didn't have a 'phone number for her.

At the beginning of December I was appearing at the Lakeside Country Club for a fortnight and kept thinking about Tracy. Several different girls turned up while I was there, but no one could compare with Tracy. I was drinking heavily again, wasting myself. I felt so low I decided I'd take myself off to America for a few days over Christmas, after a five-day trip I was due to make to Germany with Humphry Berkeley for our charity.

The final night at Lakeside was the night before my birthday on December 13. I got home having finished the run and felt rotten. I got up on the morning of my birthday and at 9.00 am sharp the 'phone rang.

'Jim?' said the voice. 'It's Tracy. I've left my boyfriend.' This time the blast of the Hallelujah Chorus was louder and clearer than it had ever been.

'Where are you?' I asked.

'Wolverhampton.'

'Right, meet me at the Albany Hotel in Birmingham this evening at 7.30 pm.'

I hung up and felt elated. I went to San Lorenzo's for a spot of lunch then caught the train up to Birmingham. I got a cab to the Albany Hotel and waited for her in the bar.

Tracy turned up, we had a few drinks and she stayed the night. We talked into the early hours and I didn't once try anything rude. I daren't!

Next morning I had to leave really early to catch a flight from Luton to Germany with Humphry. I hadn't slept a wink – that was impossible lying next to the woman of my dreams. As I left, Tracy told me she'd be waiting for me.

I took a minicab all the way to Luton and flew out. For the next five days in Germany I couldn't eat and I didn't sleep: they were the longest nights of my life. I yearned for Tracy so badly I ached.

When we landed, Tracy was there at the airport to meet me. She drove me home and stayed the night. Once again, we weren't the slightest bit rude. Next morning she returned to Wolverhampton for a few days to sort a few things out with her ex-boyfriend, who wasn't making life easy for her. He was quite well-to-do, for a hairdresser, and a typical flash BMW chap – a sort of Wentworth Husband. When Tracy had left him he'd put her four cats into a cardboard box and dumped them on her mother.

While Tracy was back home sorting out the cats' accommodation, I 'phoned her dad and got his blessing. He seemed genuinely happy for both of us.

I took her to Paris for Christmas and we flew out the day before Christmas Eve. I couldn't get a room at the wonderful George V so we checked in to another hotel nearby, but we went straight to the George V bar to drink. Everyone there remembered me, which I hoped might impress Tracy. I bought her a Cartier watch for Christmas and we walked around Paris romantically entwined. The only thing I didn't grant her was climbing the Eiffel Tower, because of my fear of heights.

For me this, after a lifetime of searching, was real love. I was so infatuated with her, in fact, that I didn't dare risk making rude noises in the en-suite bathroom. In the morning I'd get up and dash down to the toilet in the foyer on the ground floor, pretending to Tracy I was off to get a newspaper. I expect she was doing the same thing while I was out of the room, making a bee-line for the bathroom before I got back.

One night we finally consummated our engagement and flew back to England in time for a club appearance. Tracy moved in with me and we got on extremely well. I was desperate to make this a really lasting relationship and even threw her contraceptive pills out of the window in the hope she'd get pregnant and have to stay with me.

A few weeks later, with our relationship still going well, we decided to go on holiday to Gran Canaria. Laurie had told me we'd love it, but we didn't. We hated it and came home a few days early. The welcome-home reception awaiting us was stories about us splashed all over the papers. Her ex-boyfriend had told tales, suggesting she was a lesbian into bondage. I'm still waiting for it to happen.

The first part of the year was totally devoted to work with Thames Television. First I recorded another series of *Home James*, and immediately afterwards I hosted a variety series, *Wednesday at Eight*, from the Victoria Palace, where I'd auditioned for *New Faces*.

Tracy and I talked about moving out of the flat and settling down in our own home. My thoughts went straight to Wentworth, but I knew I couldn't afford anything like that again. We looked through *Country Life* and spotted two properties we liked in the Guildford area. On the way to see them we saw another house in Ewhurst, a five-bedroomed cottage, the oldest part of which was 400 years old. It was set in a two-acre garden and the whole thing had plenty of possibilities. Tracy fell in love with it there and then. 'Can we have it?' she asked me.

'Yes,' I said. And that was that, even though I didn't have a penny. I went down to Torquay for the summer season and, while I was there, arranged a £400,000 mortgage for the house.

When the sale went through we didn't have a stick of furniture. Tracy and her mum were the first to spend a night there, and had to sleep on the floor in sleeping-bags. But nothing succeeds like success. After a rocky reception for the blue summer season in Torquay in 1988, in 1989 I was booked to appear there again and was now welcomed with open arms by the town's elders.

Just in time for the summer season in Torquay I took possession of my wonderful new Princess boat. I called her *Afghan Plains*, after Rudyard Kipling's poem to a young British soldier, the last few lines of which read:

'When you're wounded and left on Afghanistan's Plains

And the women come out to cut up what remains
Roll to your rifle and blow out your brains
And go to your god like a soldier.'

I also like to think my boat gets a mention in one of my favourite films, delivered by one of my all-time favourite actors: *The Man Who Would Be King* and Sean Connery. The film is based on the life of Rudyard Kipling (played by Christopher Plummer) and the sub-plot's really about freemasonry.

In the story, Plummer warns Connery against an impossibly long and dangerous journey. Then up comes the magic line: 'Tell me, brother Kipling, what if we do get across the Afghan Plains?'

Afghan Plains is a great name, it sounds so good. The only trouble is, because of its suggested connotations, it's always taken for a drug-smuggler's boat!

When *Afghan Plains* was ready for collection from Plymouth, I turned up with Kevin and Paul, an army mate. She looked stunning. Fanbloodytastic. A vision in white; elegant and sleek without even a radar fitted to spoil her lines. The three of us set off for Torquay with nothing more sophisticated to chart our route than a small ship-to-shore radio, compass and charts.

It took a little while to appreciate how powerful she was. She sliced through the water smoothly and, like a Bentley, had the satisfying, resonating purr of outstanding quality.

When we pulled into Torquay Harbour, Tracy was there to meet us. Kevin's wife Elaine also came aboard and we decided to celebrate on the boat with a Chinese takeaway with all the trimmings. Kevin went to collect the food and almost fainted when they showed him the bill, £600. When Kevin returned we were all still excitedly, opening cupboards and walking around on deck. Then, just as we were about to help ourselves to the food, catastrophe struck! The whole lot fell on the floor. There was Who Flung Wot absolutely everywhere.

We all got down on our hands and knees to pick it up. It was a dreadful end to a perfect day. We were all still hungry as hell and now my beautiful new boat stank of sweet and sour!

Tracy and I decided to have a few weeks' rest on the boat but it never really suited her. Now that *Afghan Plains* had arrived, Tracy didn't like her a bit. But she gave us privacy from punters, as they are not allowed on to the harbour walkways. We'd spend a great deal of time relaxing on the boat and, in the afternoons, I would potter around on little exploratory excursions. The most ambitious trip was about a week later, and I ended up in the original shit creek!

I had a bit of a hangover and decided, with Kevin and Elaine on board, to take a trip up to the River Hamble to moor alongside some friends for the night. I still hadn't had a radar fitted but I thought I knew my way around the waters well enough. I'd done the Torquay to Cowes trip a few times; out of Torquay heading east, picking up Portland, jiggling about a bit and then finding the Isle of Wight and so on.

We set off happily enough. When we got halfway across Lime Bay, with twenty miles in either direction to Torquay or Portland, a heavy mist descended. As it got thicker I realised we had a horrible journey ahead of us. I thought it best to turn back, following the route we'd already taken. Just as I turned *Afghan Plains* around a full 180 degrees, pointing her homeward, Kevin persuaded me to carry on instead.

So I slowly swept *Afghan Plains* around another 180 degrees. Now, in theory, we had turned full circle. But we hadn't. We'd turned 175 degrees the first time and then 189 degrees. So we were three degrees off-course, and heading into no man's land. I knew something was wrong and started to feel increasingly nervous. Then I had a full-blown panic attack. I dashed downstairs to the smallest room on the boat, a great relief.

Some things on a boat you mustn't take for granted, like the loo. Boats have a shredding mechanism to slice up body waste and move it into a holding tank or, if you're in the mid-ocean and outside the territorial limit, directly into the sea.

One of the most embarrassing things about having guests on board, in fact, is telling them they mustn't put tampons or cotton wool make-up balls down the loo. Tracy, however, didn't know all this and had been throwing everything in sight down the pan.

After my relaxing constitutional, I pulled up my swimming shorts and pushed the foot pedal to start the shredding process. The loo made a few gurgling noises, and as I stood up I was covered from head to toe in shit and cotton wool buds!

Minutes earlier I had been so nervous I'd felt myself losing my confidence. Now worse still had followed – I was all excretered up and looked like Sabu the Elephant Boy.

One step to my left was the shower so I got in to wash the mess off my body. I turned the tap and a solitary drip came out of the shower head – no water! We'd forgotten to fill up our water tank before setting off.

I couldn't believe my luck. Water, water everywhere but not a drop to wipe the shit away. So I did the next best thing and slipped out of the bathroom to the galley to grab an ice-cold bottle of Perrier from the fridge.

I nipped back to the toilet and poured the chilly mineral water all over to wash myself clean. Now I was all frothed up and reckoned I was about to die of hypothermia. To finish off the job properly I needed a second bottle of Perrier. For a moment I thought I'd heat it up a bit in the microwave to take the chill off it. But I couldn't risk starting up the generator and alerting the others so I had to make do with another fizzing, icy shower.

When I got back upstairs I didn't say a word. We were still very lost and, in the end, I managed to flag down a cruiser for help. I called them up on the radio and asked them if they knew where the Isle of Wight was.

'Have you got a compass?' the man asked.

'Yes, thank you!' I answered cheekily. He then gave me a course to steer and, eventually, we made it to the Hamble and safety.

During the summer season Tracy told me some wonderful news – she was pregnant with our first baby. We were both thrilled to bits.

13

Hello Knobby

Just before the end of the run in Torquay in 1988 I took Tracy, very pregnant, for another trip on *Afghan Plains*. I'd had proper navigational equipment fitted by then, including a plotter, and I wanted to go to Guernsey for a night out. Rick Price was with us as well as a skipper from Guernsey, who we didn't realise was a complete idiot.

It was a choppy journey and poor Tracy got terrible sea-sickness. By the time we arrived, she had turned green. Once back on dry land she made a speedy recovery and we had a wonderful night out. But next day the weather was terrible, particularly for sailing. Tracy was against facing a return journey by sea, and so was I, for that matter. So, with Rick, the two of us flew back to Exeter.

A few days later I returned to Guernsey with Kevin. The sea was still so rough we could see the waves from the plane and when we touched down we had half a mind to catch the next flight back to Exeter again. But I wanted to get *Afghan Plains* to the mainland and got a dreadful dose of get-home-itis with her, a terribly dangerous thing to have. I found the skipper I'd taken back to Guernsey days earlier and he showed me the course on the chart.

Kevin and I set off. We pulled out of Guernsey and turned left like the man had told us to do, following a course to steer us clear of rocks.

In the distance ahead I thought there was some kind of

regatta going on. I could see boats with big white sails. When we got to them I realised my mistake. They were huge waves, known as 'snarlers', fifteen feet high, which were heading straight for us.

Afghan Plains is seventeen feet high and we were standing six feet on top of that. Each wave shoved us skyward then sent us crashing down again. The only way to cope with them was by trying to accelerate over them, even though it meant plunging her 30ft nose – over half her length – underwater each time.

One wave nearly got the better of us. It crashed into us head-on and knocked Kevin to the deck. No matter how hard I tried I couldn't seem to steer her out of the waves and I was convinced we were going to sink. As the next wave headed for us I trimmed the nose right down to slice through it. We pushed through, then I accelerated up to the full 28 knots and climbed the wave again. At the top I threw the boat around to slide down the other side of it. Then I accelerated up the next wave and did the same again and again.

We made about thirty feet per wave, heading back into each new wave the same way. If we hadn't we would have turned over for sure.

Kevin and I drank as much whisky as we could, without getting drunk, to help us flatten the waves and deaden our nerves. We had a beam-sea hitting us, which means it was coming at us side-on, and we were rolling about forty degrees all the way back. But we did make an impressive 18 knots and soon had little more to worry about than how badly we both smelled.

We made it to the mid-Channel lightship, where there was an eight-foot swell, then changed course bound for Torquay. In my mind I begged *Afghan Plains* to help and get us home safely. Come on girl, you can get us back to Torquay, I prayed. Do that and I'll give all the profits from my last night of the season to the Royal National Lifeboat Institute.

As we pulled into Torquay I rushed on to dry land and kissed the ground like the Pope! I'd been frightened to death by the journey we'd just survived, but even if I do say it myself, I carried off a great piece of seamanship. *Afghan Plains* hadn't let me down and, as I'd promised, I gave all the profits from the last show to the RNLI with a letter asking that the gift wasn't publicised.

A few months later I was walking around the Boat Show in Southampton. When I got near the RNLI stand one of the jolly men in uniform pounced on me. 'Jim,' he said. 'It's fantastic what you've done for us. Your donation got a mention in our house magazine but don't worry, the press haven't been told. You're not even a member of the RNLI are you?'

'No,' I replied.

Then the man grabbed a colleague. 'This is Jim Davidson, two and a half grand he sent us. Wonderful! He's not even a member of the RNLI. Well, we'll soon change all that. How big's your boat, Jim?'

'Fifty-five feet,' I replied.

'This is the size you need for a boat that size,' he said, giving me an RNLI pendant. 'And have you got a car?' he went on.

'Every few years I have, yes,' I replied. 'My licence has been in the DVLC in Gwent so many times it's got a Welsh accent!'

He laughed and handed me a sticker. Then he put a form in front of me, handed me a pen and said: 'Sign this.'

I signed on the dotted line.

'You're now a member of the RNLI. God bless you,' he said, quickly adding, 'Fifty-five quid, please!'

At Christmas, in order to be near pregnant Tracy as much as I could, I was in *Cinderella* close to home, at the Dominion in London. It was one of the happiest Christmas holidays I'd ever had.

When the pantomime ended in January 1989, I was straight back at Ewhurst with Tracy, painting and decorating most of the time. Her love inspired me and I went back to work with a vengeance, first touring the clubs for six weeks and then returning to record the next series of *Home James* at Thames Television. When Tracy was about to give birth at Mount Alvernia's, a Catholic hospital in Guildford, I was filming in London.

Minutes after Charlie was born on April 16 1989, Tracy rang me and said: 'I've had the baby!'

Great! I thought. I've missed the pleasure of watching her give birth! That's not to say that I wouldn't have done anything for Tracy and Charlie, but I'm just not very good at watching babies being born.

I left the studios and drove straight over to be with her, armed with plenty of flowers. We kissed and cuddled and little Charlie bawled his head off. Bliss!

The staff at that hospital didn't like me much. In fact, a fierce Irish woman who worked there bit my head off whenever I turned up.

'Can I see my wife?' I asked her on one visit.

'She's not your wife, you're not married!' she growled.

The 1989 summer season was back up in Great Yarmouth. That year I found the oddest and nicest bunch of men you could ever meet, the Caister-on-Sea lifeboat crew. They run their own independent crew there, in defiance of the RNLI, who'd decided to close down in the area. But not only were these chaps an independent bunch, they were also pretty unlikely lifeboatmen. None of them could swim!

They were all great characters. Percy, the bowman, had just one tooth in the middle of his mouth, like a cat-flap, and sang shanties in the local pub when he was off duty. The skipper was about 150 years old if he was a day and Benny, the coxswain, was a typical salty type, happy and perfectly straightforward.

I got on with them all and went out with them several times on their tour of duty. 'Percy, is it true you can't swim?' I asked on the first trip.

'Yes,' he replied.

'If the boat sank in the middle of the North Sea, what would you do?' I said. 'You can't swim and you don't even wear a lifejacket!'

'Well,' he answered slowly. 'Where am I going to swim to from the middle of the North Sea? As for a lifejacket, what's the point of hanging about and freezing to death. Get yourself underwater and drown, that's my advice!'

Towards the end of the run Dad died. He'd been ill for ten years and had become a frail old man of seventy-nine. We knew towards the end how ill he was because if we gave him a bottle of scotch it would stay in his room, untouched.

I went down to see him at Holburne Road with Tracy. He looked weak and I got really scared at the thought of him dying. Tracy and I drove back to Ewhurst in silence.

I returned to Great Yarmouth and a few days later got a call early one morning from my brother Billy. 'Dad's dead,' he said. I could hear the women in the background, saying: 'It's always you, isn't it Billy? You couldn't break it to him gently.'

Billy drove up at once to see me and that night I went on to do the act as usual, upset as I was. I asked the audience if they wanted to ask any questions and the first was from an old man. 'How's your dad?' he shouted out.

'He died this morning at 8.00 am,' I said, and it got half a laugh.

'You're joking,' he shouted back. 'Don't be wicked.'

Before I could say a word, Billy interrupted. 'He's not fucking joking!' he called out. I met the man afterwards and it turned out he'd known Dad and was genuinely concerned.

I went back to London for the funeral and during the service, as requested by Mum, the song 'My Way' was played. It certainly did sum up Dad. He only ever did anything his way. After the service we all had plenty to drink and, drunk as a sack, I stumbled, broke a window and cut my foot open badly. I needed twenty stitches, was bandaged up and limped back to Great Yarmouth for the last fortnight of the season.

For those two weeks I just drank to drown my sorrows. Dad had died at a good age, but it didn't make parting with him any easier. One night after the show I was in a heap in a bar and a flash Herbert came over, hoping to become a local celebrity by picking a fight – the man who shot Liberty Valance.

He tried nutting me and must have thought I was Irish.
'Mind my foot!' I hollered.

It's because of nutters like that man who try shooting
Liberty Valance that I end up surrounded by my own
people for a lot of the time. Kevin, my driver and roadie,
has been with me, on and off, since 1977. Sometimes the
people working for you make mistakes, but you stand by
them. Kevin's been banned from driving for the second
time, so now I have to drive him everywhere until he gets
his licence back! He's getting worse than me at keeping hold
of his licence.

To put the record straight, I've never lost my licence for
drink-driving. I lost it twice for driving with no insurance
and twice for refusing the breathalyser. There's a subtle
difference!

In October 1989 the musical *Buddy* opened at the Victoria
Palace in London, and launched me firmly on another
career: sound design. I've always had my own sound systems
of one sort or another locked up in garages around London.
As a favour I'd sometimes lend them out to mates but I didn't
really turn it into a big business.

But when *Buddy* was being planned I was approached and
asked if I could put a sound system together for the show.
Laurie was one of the show's co-producers and convinced
his colleagues it was a job I was well qualified to carry
out. So I formed a company called Alpha Audio and was
in business.

At the end of 1989 I was appearing in *Cinderella* in
Bradford. I hated being away from Tracy and Charlie but
this time I behaved myself. When the run finished I took
Tracy off to Barbados and we got married on February
2 1990.

Laurie Mansfield was best man. He said he was happy to
do the honours for the first time as it was the only marriage
of mine he'd had any faith in. A photographer from the *Daily
Star* snatched a picture from behind a wall – and all you could
see was Laurie's bald patch. One minute it was a claim to
fame, the next a claim to disaster.

There's an old joke: 'How do you stop your girlfriend

sucking your dick? Marry her!' My friend Chris, a loud and funny American, was at the ceremony which was conducted by a nice black vicar. At the end of the service the vicar said to Tracy and me: 'I now pronounce you man and wife.' Chris shouted out: 'There go the blow jobs!'

I saw Danny La Rue shortly after we got back from Barbados. 'Why did you get married, Jim?' he asked.

'Well,' I explained. 'I've just had a little boy and I thought it was the right thing to do.'

'I've had lots of little boys but I've never got married!' he said. That's Danny for you!

It was a little girl Tracy really wanted and we set about trying for another baby.

In March I recorded a new series for Thames Television, *Stand Up Jim Davidson*. The idea was simple, a man and a mike uncensored after the 9.00 pm watershed on ITV. I had a third series of *Home James* to make before the summer, but the sitcom was coming to the end of its life. The blue stand-up routine was unheard of for mainstream TV but, with a new hierarchy now running Thames, the time seemed right.

We were recording the six half-hour series at the Royalty Theatre and a lawyer was drafted in to make sure I didn't go too over the top. The series was a hit with audiences at once, clocking up 10 million a week. But the success gave my enemies in the press plenty of ammunition. There I was on screen, swearing and cursing, heading for trouble.

One night, as the series was underway, I went home and had a drunken row with Tracy. She wanted plastic surgery to straighten her nose. I couldn't understand why. I thought it was a lovely nose which didn't need touching. Anyway, I went to push Tracy, missed, accidentally caught Jackie, our nanny, and the police were called.

On top of the bad press for my swearing on television, I found myself plastered all over the papers, accused of hitting my nanny. The timing couldn't have been worse. Tracy went ahead and had her nose straightened. The first time we appeared together in public she had a whopping great plaster over her face.

When the reporters asked if I'd hit the nanny I joked: 'It's not my fault, the wife ducked.' I might have known from countless previous experiences never to joke with the press. They take your words and twist them to their own ends. This time they labelled me a nanny-killer and nose-breaker.

The reports went down badly at Thames. I think their attitude was, 'It's one thing to hit your wife, another to do it during a television series. How irresponsible can you get?'

I finished the series, each show delivering up great audiences, and went straight into recording what was to be the final series of *Home James*.

Just before summer season started in 1990, in Torquay, I took part in a battering dinghy race around Scotland. It was a very rough water course and, lasting four days, one of the most gruelling things I've ever been through. The whisky helped, though!

Three friends joined me, Vaughan Browne and Steve Carey in the dinghy and, as ground crew, a friend from my village called Roger Swallow. He'd recently undergone a heart by-pass operation – the stitches were still wet – but he insisted on joining us. As it turned out, I was the one invalided out for part of the course with claustrophobia and bronchitis.

We got ourselves a 21ft Flatacraft ribbed dinghy with two massive 75 horsepower engines rigged at the back. We had a top speed of 65 knots – if we didn't flip over! Instead of counter-rotating, the propellers both went in the same direction. The boat would soar ten feet into the air after hitting a wave, the propellers twisting our craft each time we left the water.

The course started and finished in Inverness. We turned up the night before, in a WiniBego motorcaravan. I had the makings of a serious cold and swamped myself in whisky to try to fend it off. The four of us went out on the piss with everyone else taking part, some of whom were soldiers who looked like they'd just stepped from the pages of *Soldier of Fortune* magazine.

The next morning my cold was worse but, despite hangovers, Vaughan, Steve and I pushed on. We turned up in our dinghy ready for the start, looking like Michelin men, buried under crash helmets, corsets (to keep our innards in as we were hurled along the course), waterproof suits, Kevla support backpacks, heavy racing lifejackets, gloves and goggles.

The first two days were bumpy, but nothing we couldn't handle. When the going did get rough we got out our hip-flasks and gulped down whisky, the perfect wave-flattener. But it's not easy trying to flip open a crash-helmet visor and drink from a hip-flask at sixty knots in a dinghy. By the time we took on the roughest part of the trip, where the waves were at their cruellest, Vaughan and Steve had bolted two large cyclists' water bottles to the front of the superstructure. A large tube was attached to the bottles, which were filled to the brim with whisky and water.

We tried out the ingenious drinking devices in the harbour that night and they worked a treat. With a good suck you could sling a large whisky and water down your throat in one swallow.

Next morning the waves did look nasty, but at least we had our life-saving whisky bottles bolted into place, ready to serve us when the time came. The waves threw us around badly. Each time we banged back down into the boat the pain was unbearable.

We passed the tube around freely to get through that dreadful part of the course, only to find worse waves ahead of us. 'More whisky?' I yelled, grabbing the tube and sucking hard. Nothing happened. 'Malfunction!' I shouted. 'It's dry, we can't have drunk an entire bottle of whisky already!'

We looked around and realised when we'd been dropping the tube between mouthfuls, the life-saving liquid had been siphoning into the boat. I was picking splinters out of my tongue for a week!

We went right around the top of Scotland, really beautiful country. I backed out of the last leg because I had bad bronchitis and was finding it difficult to breathe. Coupled with general fear, this had brought on terrible claustrophobia. I had to get back on dry land and Roger took my place – probably the first by-pass to by-pass Scotland by boat!

When we got back to Inverness, Vaughan and I took the dinghy out again for the speed trials. We came second overall and first in our class, which won us a holiday in Turkey. Roger's still out there trying to win a ticket back!

Laurie turned up unexpectedly at Ewhurst one day. The television franchises were coming up for renewal and Thames were anxious about their image. Benny Hill had unceremoniously been given the boot, after years of winning them audiences and making them millions. I was to be next in the firing line. My three-year contract had eighteen months to run, so Laurie negotiated a settlement and I walked away from Thames after fourteen years. I decided I'd had enough of television for a while.

I went into summer season in Torquay and had *Afghan Plains* moored there. One lunchtime I set off with Kevin bound for Portland and I must have pissed in Neptune's breakfast because as soon as we set off a heavy fog came in and visibility dropped to as little as twenty-five yards. At times I couldn't even see the end of the boat. My eyes were glued to the radar and I had Kevin up front looking out for submerged obstacles, like lobster pots.

We were crawling at about eight knots and at regular intervals I blasted the boat's horn. Then, approaching Weymouth, a blip came up on the screen and got bigger and bigger. We heard a thunderous hooter and then, out of a clearing in the fog, fifty yards away, a 5,000-ton ferry suddenly loomed. I quickly made radio contact and we steered away from each other at speed. It had been close.

We sailed on the rest of the way in total fog. I pointed at the chart and said to Kevin, 'We'll be here.'

Then, as if we had walked through a net curtain, the fog cleared and we were returned to crisp daylight. We were within ten metres of my guess, with Swanage ahead of us.

That prediction being spot-on made the trip for me. The biggest thrill I get from boating is getting from A to B successfully.

Tracy and I were still trying, without success, for another baby. She went along to see several doctors about her failure to become pregnant but they didn't seem able to help. Then Tracy's gynaecologist, Percy Coats, suggested a course of action.

'When you know it's time to conceive,' he told her, 'go and make love to your husband and come straight back here.'

I could think of nothing worse! Fortunately, a few days later, I bumped into my old mate Dr Freddie Lim. 'Hello Jim,' he said. 'I haven't seen you since Germany.'

'No,' I said. 'I'm married now!'

I mentioned the problems Tracy and I were having getting a sister or brother for Charlie. 'Tracy's had all the tests,' I explained. 'Everything has been checked but no one can work out what's wrong.'

'When your first son was born, did he have sticky eyes?' he asked.

'Pardon me?' I said.

'Sticky eyes. Did Charlie have them?' he said.

'I think so,' I guessed. 'They've all got sticky eyes when they're born, haven't they? I tell you what, Fred, I'll get Tracy to give you a ring.'

'Better than that,' he replied, 'bring her over to see me.'

Tracy mentioned to her doctor that I was taking her to see Dr Freddie. 'I hope Jim hasn't given you anything nasty,' he said anxiously!

So Tracy and I turned up at Dr Freddie's. He examined her and carried out a few little tests. As before, everything appeared to be fine. Then, just as we were leaving, he gave her a small bottle of very mild antibiotics.

Back home Tracy rang her doctor and told him about the antibiotics. 'That's ridiculous,' he said. 'We wouldn't consider giving anyone such a low dose of antibiotics, it wouldn't be worth it.'

Tracy told me and I spoke again to Dr Freddie. 'You leave it to me,' he said. 'These hospitals might know a lot, but I know bugs – and if there's a little bug in there it could be stopping Tracy having another baby.'

Within two weeks Tracy was pregnant! We were both overjoyed and Tracy was keeping her fingers crossed that it would be a girl. If, despite her prayers, she had another boy, I suggested a name for him. 'Let's call him Freddie after Dr Freddie.'

Shortly after that I bumped into Roger de Courcey and realised that in all my years I still hadn't got the chance to get one up on him. Wherever I turned up in a Rolls-Royce, he'd always have a Bentley. By then I had five cars, including a Bentley and a Morgan, but the time had gone, and we were slightly past showing off to each other. Damn!

Danny La Rue is the crowned king of topping everyone. Whatever you tell him you've done, he's done it first. He had a little stage manager who'd been with him a lifetime. One day he went excitedly running into Danny's dressing-room. 'Danny, Danny,' he said. 'I've had a postcard from Shirley MacLaine!'

Danny looked at him, raised an eyebrow and said: 'I've had a letter.'

The day I took Tracy to have an ultrascan of her womb, to look at our tiny baby on the monitor, I had a terrible hangover. The doctor spread some kind of jollop over Tracy's belly, and up popped the tiny baby on the monitor.

'Oh, look at his little legs moving,' said Tracy, thrilled.

To me the baby looked like Alien in there. I was expecting it to jump out of Tracy any second!

'Can you see its dick?' I asked the doctor bluntly.

'Yes, it's there,' she replied, pointing at the screen.

'So it's a boy?' I answered.

'Oh yes,' she said. 'It's a boy.'

Afterwards Tracy and I went outside and she had a few tears in her eyes. I knew she had her heart set on a girl, but it was not to be. After the scan the baby's nickname became 'Knobby', because I'd seen his little knob on the screen!

One day I had a meeting with Laurie and he asked me to take a look at an idea for a television series for the BBC, *Big Break*. The quiz show had been piloted with Mike Reid, from *Eastenders*, rather formally, with a sober snooker commentary.

They wanted me to give the show a go but I wasn't so sure. I didn't feel I really needed the exposure any more. Until I parted company with Thames Television I'd been on British screens since Nineteen Hundred and Frozen to Death.

I didn't know the first thing about snooker but Laurie said it didn't matter. The producer was looking for someone who could make it all a bit lighter, something not just for snooker fans. I could see the show had potential and I agreed to make a pilot. But instead of a formal snooker referee offering commentary, the droll John Virgo would be brought in. We made a pilot for the show and waited to hear back from the BBC top brass.

Then I went out on a gruelling nationwide tour with Richard Digance and Chas 'n' Dave, a fairly boozy affair. Chas Hodges does like a drink and can come out with great lines, like the time he got into a row with the American singer Jack Jones.

Richard Digance was appearing on *The Des O'Connor Show* for the first time, along with Chas 'n' Dave, and I promised to turn up at the television studio to give him a bit of moral support.

I was standing in the corridor outside the dressing-rooms telling Dave a joke when Jack Jones' head appeared from behind his door. 'Hey, would you mind the language!' he hollered angrily. 'There's ladies in here!'

'Sorry,' I said. Later Dave told Chas about Jack Jones shouting at us. After the show Chas got very pissed in the Green Room and staggered up to Jack in full view of all the VIP guests. 'If you don't like the fucking way Londoners talk,' he growled, 'don't come to fucking London! Right, Yank?'

That was Chas Hodges for you. He always tells me off as well. If ever we've worked together and I've tried to lark about he's bollocked me firmly. He's forgetting I got him and Dave their second television show. That's fucking gratitude for you. Only kidding, Chas 'n' Dave.

When I got home from the tour with Richard and Chas 'n' Dave Laurie had some great news for me to round off the year. The BBC wanted to sign me to record a series of *Big Break* in the New Year.

14

And Tracy Asks Why I
Grind My Teeth!

In February 1991 I recorded my first series of *Big Break* at
the BBC Television Centre. John Virgo was back with me
and we really hit it off. I'd always do what I could during
rehearsals to put him off. The show was scripted and in the
afternoon we'd rehearse some of the questions I'd be asking
him in the evening, so he knew what to expect. But when
we were recording I'd usually throw in a different question,
just to watch his face drain of any expression and his eyes
go dull.

By February Tracy looked like she was about to pop
any moment. The night she had to go into hospital to
have Knobby I was up in London, not at the BBC but
working on a job Alpha Audio was undertaking. We were
installing and operating the sound for Sheila Ferguson,
who used to be one of The Three Degrees – a Degree,
in fact.

Sheila's shows were always spectacular. After the rehearsals in the afternoon I knew she was going to give a terrific
performance and I was looking forward to a great night. Just
as the concert was about to begin, I got a call from Tracy on
my mobile 'phone.

'You'd better come quick,' she said. 'I've got to go into
hospital to be induced.'

'Why?' I asked.

'Well, I've got high blood pressure and the hospital doesn't like that,' she said.

'OK, I'll come and pick you up,' I replied.

I drove back to Ewhurst, picked up Tracy and took her to the Royal Surrey Hospital in Guildford. She was shown to her private room and settled herself in. Then her obstetrician, Mr Coats, turned up to examine her. 'Right, Jim,' he said a few minutes later. 'Tracy does have high blood pressure, but now that we've got her here we won't actually induce her tonight.'

'Oh,' I said, wondering how the hell someone is 'induced' anyway.

'No,' he continued. 'I won't induce her tonight because lots of other people have since come in to have their babies.'

'Cheek!' I said. 'I'm private, not NHS. I'm all BUPA'd up, luv, can't the others wait?'

'No,' he laughed. 'They can't wait if they're actually having them! Don't worry, Tracy's in no danger.'

Mr Coats left and I sat with Tracy for what seemed like a lifetime. Women can be wicked cows when they want to be. Only at 10.50 pm, when she knew it was far too late for me to get to any pub anywhere, did Tracy dismiss me.

'You go home now,' she said. I kissed her and left, quickly putting Plan B into operation. I booked into the Post House Hotel across the road and went straight to the bar for late drinks. I told everyone I was about to become a dad again and it seemed everyone in the hotel bought me a drink that night. In the early hours I fell into bed, completely drunk.

Next morning, February 20, I was woken by the telephone ringing. I had the mother of all hangovers and was so badly dehydrated there wasn't a drop of water in my body. My tongue was stuck to the roof of my mouth.

'Hello?' I groaned.

'Jim, it's me,' came the reply. 'You'd better come over, I'm going to have our baby in a minute.'

'All right, I'm on my way,' I said, adding, 'Who's speaking, please?'

I staggered into the bathroom and looked in the mirror.

My face was exactly the same shape as the pillow it had been squashed into all night. And it stayed like that for the rest of the day. As I walked into the hospital I felt terrible. When I reached Tracy she already had a drip in her arm to help her on her way. Then, just as she started smarting with pain, she whispered, 'You don't have to come in to watch.'

'OK, I'm off!' I replied, leaping to the door. 'I'll go and get you some fruit.'

As I was leaving, Tracy started the contractions. I walked to the supermarket up the road and by the time I'd found the fruit I'd already had four cans of Carlsberg lager to make me feel better. I strolled back to the hospital with four more cans – of Guinness this time. I walked as slowly as I could, in the hope that Tracy would have had the baby by the time I got back. No such luck!

I still looked terrible, but I felt much better when I walked back past the nurses at reception. Tracy was in terrible pain. The epidural man arrived and gave her an injection in the spine to numb the old Jack and Danny. She went into the bathroom and when she came back the pain-killer had started to take effect and she was walking like Douglas Bader.

She couldn't feel a thing. The baby could have walked out with a top hat on and Tracy wouldn't have minded! When it was time for her to go off to the operating theatre, I held her hand and wished her luck.

'Well done, love,' I said. 'It'll all be fine.'

'Will you be all right?' she asked me, sweetly.

'Of course,' I said. 'Don't worry about a thing. I'll be right here when you get back.'

Sitting alone in the room I thought this was one birth I was going to enjoy. I put my feet up and put the television on for the football. Perfect. I took my first can of Guinness and just as I opened it to take a mouthful, in walked Mr Coats, all dressed up like Dr Bob in *The Muppets*.

'Perce,' I said. 'How are you?'

'Fine,' he said. 'Come on Jim, come in to be with Tracy.'

'No,' I said, 'I don't have to. I've been excused. I've got a pass-out from Tracy. She's let me off.'

'Come on, be a man!' he said.

'That's why I'm in here!' I answered. Then I relented. 'OK. I'm right behind you.' I started to follow him with my Guinness can in my hand.

'You can't bring your Guinness!' he said. 'Leave that in here for later.'

So I took a quick sip of Guinness and got froth all around my mouth. I walked past the receptionists foaming at the mouth.

I stood by Tracy's side, holding her hand and waiting for the drama to start. We were surrounded by hundreds of monitors and machines all going ping and ding at regular intervals.

The waiting was amazingly casual. Mr Coats and everyone else in the delivery room chatted. Then one of the machines sprang into action, going 'Ding! Ding! Ding!'

'Here we go!' said Mr Coats. 'Tracy's just had another contraction and now she's fully dilated.'

'I'm almost that myself!' I slurred, fainting on my feet. I went all dizzy and had to go outside for some air. Then, from the corridor, I could hear a little baby cry and stuck my head around the door. Tracy, Perce and all the staff were laughing.

'Hello Knobby!' I shouted. And that was it. Tracy was dead pleased and Freddie has turned out a nice kid. When you're reading this when you get older, Freddie, you'll find out you're named after my old mate the doctor – hope you don't mind!

When *Big Break* was aired it shot up the ratings and was hailed by all as a great success. In Great Yarmouth for the 1991 summer season I put together my best ever live act. I had the band, a brilliant sound system and superb lighting, with lasers as well as computerised syncrolights.

I invited Mark Stuart to come up, the man who'd given me my first real taste of fame in *What's On Next?* and taught me so much. He'd never seen me work live, and I wanted him to be impressed and proud. I wanted to make a video of the show and, when Mark came backstage afterwards, I asked if he'd direct it.

'No,' he said. 'It's not my scene. It's not my style. It's too blue for me and too loud.'

When the words came out it was like being punched in the face. We were both disappointed that night.

While I was in Yarmouth I looked up my mates from the Caister-on-Sea lifeboat crew. Poor Benny, the coxswain, had died letting off a maroon to call the crew to an emergency. Something had gone tragically wrong and it blew him to bits. The whole community was shattered by Benny's death. On the last night of the season I got all the lifeboat crew on stage and, led by Percy, they sang a beautiful shanty in memory of Benny. There wasn't a dry eye in the theatre, and those of us on-stage were blubbing as much as the audience.

I helped raise money for their new inflatable inshore lifeboat, which they named after me (in 1992 alone the *Jim Davidson* saved 13 lives). I also helped raise the money for another, bigger boat, called the *Bernard Matthews*, whose namesake also supports them. Bootiful!

I heard from my ex-wife Julie, who wanted Cameron to go to boarding school and me to pay the fees. At first I fought her all the way on the idea. Then a funny thing happened on the way to Australia. Because of my fear of flying and the length of the journey, I took my laptop video player and half a dozen tapes of *Star Trek: The Next Generation*.

In one of the episodes Worf reveals to his son that he is his true father. When I landed in Australia I telephoned my solicitor and told him to ring Julie. I wanted her to go ahead with boarding school and give him a great start in life. I didn't care how much it cost. 'Tell her to thank The Klingons!' I said.

Today I try to find time to write to Cameron when I can, to keep in touch. It's not easy to see him or talk to him very much, but that might all change when he gets older.

That Christmas, 1991, I was back at the Dominion Theatre again, starring in a blue Christmas show, in order to be near Tracy and the children.

When the Conservatives started electioneering early in 1992 for the general election I had a clean licence again and nothing blotting my copybook. I was invited to one of the early planning receptions and briefly met John Major. Then I met Jeffrey Archer, who took up my offer to help the Tories.

Every morning Jeffrey 'phoned me with campaign details and instructions. He'd explain what was going on around the country and where he was sending me to wave the flag. 'Morning, Jimmy!' he'd snap efficiently. 'Today you must go to so-and-so and, when you get there, see so-and-so.'

One of the first jobs he gave me was to turn up representing the Conservatives on a radio show from Covent Garden, opposite Ben Elton, a Labour supporter, and a few others. I think they heard I was on the show because I was the only one who turned up! A few days later I met the Conservative candidate for Cheltenham, John Taylor. He'd just had a bad press because one of the local Tories in Cheltenham had caused a racial stink by calling him a 'nigger'. John asked if I'd go with him electioneering on the streets of Cheltenham for a day and I agreed.

We went walkabout in Cheltenham. We called on people in their homes and met them in the pubs. It was all a bit of fun, nothing too demanding.

Next I got a 'phone call asking me to make a similar walkabout with David Mellor in Putney. I can't remember where I was the night before but I knew I had to drive through the night, after a gig, to meet him on time in London. We walked along Putney High Street and a tannoy blared out: 'Come and meet David Mellor, your Conservative candidate.'

Standing next to him, for the first time I could really feel the anger of the people who don't like Conservatives. They had a go at David and then they started moaning at me.

'You turncoat for the working class!' one man shouted.

'I've been working class once,' I lobbied back. 'Sod that, I hated it! Getting up and going to work? No thanks!'

Over lunch Mellor and I swapped jokes. I found him extremely down to earth but totally switched on. He knew about show-business and exactly what he was on about. It was very unfortunate for us all when his affair with Antonia de Sancha blew up in the papers. He was the Minister of Fun: he was only having fun! The worst day's work he ever had to do was the day he resigned.

I was campaigning for the Conservatives because I didn't want Neil Kinnock running the country. He'd have put tax up just to get at me. I'm not a paid-up member of the Conservative Party, I just didn't want 'that lot' running the country. It's bad enough there being so many lefty comics without lefty MPs!

The Labour Party are such an ugly lot of bastards. You can't have ugly people running the country. Robin Cook should be on a toadstool with a fishing rod in his hand. Margaret Beckett looks as if she's had a bit too much air let out of her and needs a good pump up. Another job for David Mellor!

In June I was back in the studio recording my second series of *Big Break*. It didn't end there, either. The BBC came back again and again for more and so far I've done four series with many more in the pipeline.

I was back in Torquay for the 1992 season, with *Afghan Plains* and the occasional visit from Tracy and the family. When I returned from Torquay I heard, on October 21, that Bob Todd had just died, and I felt I ought to call Mark Stuart to tell him. 'Hello Mark,' I said. 'It's Jim. I'm afraid I have some bad news. Bob's died.'

'I had a feeling you'd say that,' said Mark. Neither of us really knew what to say. We knew we'd miss him and still do to this day.

The story I like to remember Bob Todd for best is a *pièce de resistance* of pranks. Bob liked, more than anything else, to scrounge a free drink. And he was so popular that there would always be someone who would do the honours.

He walked into a pub in Streatham early one afternoon and asked for the landlord.

'Are you Bob Todd?' asked the barman.

'Yes, Bob Todd,' said Bob.

'Can I buy you a drink?' he asked.

'That's very kind,' said the ever-thirsty Bob. May I have a large scotch?

'Of course,' he replied, serving Bob the drink before going off to fetch the landlord. Bob threw it back in one. The landlord appeared behind the bar with an equally warm greeting.

'Bob, I've always wanted to meet you,' he boomed. 'Can I get you a drink?'

'That's most kind,' replied Bob. 'A whisky, please.'

'Coming up.'

'Oh, could you make that a large one?' said Bob quickly.

'Of course, have a large one!' said the landlord.

'And a barley wine to go with it?' added Bob, realising he was on to a good thing.

'And a barley wine, why not?' said the landlord, serving Bob his two drinks. 'Now then, how can I help you?'

Bob pretended to go dizzy then blank out for a minute to milk the sympathy fully. 'Oh, I'm in terrible trouble!' he said.

'Trouble?' inquired the concerned landlord.

'Yes, trouble,' said Bob, handing back his empty whisky glass.

'You'd better have another drink,' said the landlord anxiously. Bob knocked it back and shook his head dramatically before revealing more.

'I've sold my house and it's all gone wrong!' he said. 'I don't know what I'm going to do. Do you think I could possibly have another drink?'

'Of course, of course!' By the time Bob had drunk this one he was turning red in the face and started spluttering and coughing.

'The problem is this,' continued Bob. 'My wife is waiting at our new house with a man who's waiting for me to turn up with a cheque for him.'

'And what's the problem?' asked the landlord.

'The problem is I can't find the cheque!' snapped Bob. 'I've looked everywhere and if I'm not there by 3.00 pm we're going to be gazzumped. I really don't feel very well – could I possibly have another drink?'

The landlord tried to take control of what he thought to be

a dire situation. He gave Bob another drink and then asked the address of the house he was buying.

Bob pulled a piece of paper out of his pocket and read out '33 Acacia Avenue'.

'Acacia Avenue? I don't know an Acacia Avenue,' said the landlord. Then he asked around the pub if anyone knew of an Acacia Avenue in the area but no one did.

'Oh God!' exclaimed Bob. 'What the hell am I going to do? I've been walking up and down Kilburn all afternoon before I came in here.'

'Kilburn?' said the landlord.

'Yes, Kilburn.'

'Bob, this isn't Kilburn. It's Streatham!' he said.

'Streatham?' said Bob, aghast. He wobbled about a bit more then he asked for another drink to get him over the shock!

He had his drink then said: 'Well, where's Kilburn then?'

'Miles away!' the landlord said.

'Oh my God. I'll never get there in time.'

'Have you got a car?' he was asked.

'Yes, but I've drunk too much to get behind the wheel.'

'Well, could you get a cab?' said the landlord.

'I'd like to get a cab but I haven't got any money on me,' replied Bob.

'I'll get you a cab, Bob!' vowed the landlord, and he booked one over the 'phone. When the cab arrived he gave Bob £25 from the till and wished him a happy end to his troubles.

Bob thanked him profusely, took the cab straight to the station, caught his train home to Tunbridge Wells and took his wife out for supper. The end of a perfect day out!

When *Grand Hotel*, an American musical, came to the Dominion Theatre, my company Alpha Audio was approached to take care of the sound. I was convinced the show would run forever and it was a big sound job to take on. So I agreed to borrow half a million to buy and install the necessary equipment. Three months later *Grand Hotel* came off – and I was saddled with keeping up, on top of everything else, the payments on the loan. Ouch!

It wasn't money wasted though. The equipment was added to Alpha's stock and has since been out on many other jobs instead. Today Alpha is worth about £3 million and, most daytimes when I'm free and at home, I drive over to the company's premises and keep an eye on how everything's going. The company is building up a good name for itself as a solid sound business and we've now done loads of prestigious contracts, including sound for tours by such names as Chuck Berry, Ray Charles and Don Williams. I've also formed a new lighting company as well, called Cellulite!

Just before Christmas 1992 I was back in the papers again when I got home to find Tracy drunk and about to drive her car. I confiscated her keys, which made a change. She got very angry and up came the police again. So I got them to breathalyse her!

Next day Ewhurst was swarming with reporters and photographers. We had about thirty of them standing in my garden and they looked at me hoping I'd bash one up, get drunk and abuse someone or take an axe and chop up the house.

One of them said: 'Is it true Tracy has an injunction against you? Have you been thrown out?'

To get rid of them I said: 'Yes, we're separating.'

They all ran off to file their stories and I went back into the house. The business about the injunction or even splitting up was totally untrue, but it did get rid of the bloody reporters and allow us to start our short Christmas!

On Boxing Day I flew out for a five-day trip to Bosnia and Croatia with my driver Kevin and Les Austin, the boss of the CSE. We flew to Split, in the former Yugoslavia, which was bathed in beautiful sunshine as we landed. It was so warm the orange trees even had fruit on them.

I met a few of the Croatian soldiers, a really tough-looking bunch – instant mates! Split was a noisy place to sleep. All night the sky was lit up with tracer bullets and filled with the sound of distant explosions.

Next day we were introduced to David Wood, the quarter-master with the 35 Regiment and our escort for a 650-kilometre round trip. We were heading up the mountainous supply route winding up to Vitez to put on a show for 400 lads, then going on to the secret base of the Cheshires Regiment.

The journey to Vitez took nine hours. Along the way we passed plenty of checkpoints and, at one, I saw a kid no older than ten armed with a machine gun. 'I hope he likes grown-ups!' I thought.

At Vitez our makeshift concert hall was a garage and I did over an hour for the boys. Next morning a four-inch blanket of snow covered the ground. We set off again in convoy, our Land Rovers now fitted with snow-chains, further up the narrow road leading high into the mountains. To one side was a sheer drop of 6,000 feet. The Land Rover behind mine lost a snow-chain, slid and turned over. Poor Les went through the windscreen, but miraculously survived, and another passenger broke some ribs.

We all crammed into the two Land Rovers and continued to Tomislavgrad, which felt like the highest place in the world, to meet the guys in the 35 Regiment.

Flying home two days later I realised I didn't have a clue who was fighting whom and what it was all about.

This year started with a gamble, the biggest of my life. I was convinced Britain was ready for *Sinderella*, my blue pantomime for adults. Since my very first late-night panto, in Birmingham back in 1976, I knew it was what I wanted to do. *Sinderella* was booked for a ten-week tour, starting in March when the true pantomime season was over.

I was very nervous backstage on the opening night in Ipswich. I'd sunk most of my money into the idea and if it didn't work I stood to lose nearly everything.

I needn't have worried. The audience didn't like it, they loved it. And they roared for three hours non-stop. In days the show was sold out for its entire run. We finished touring at Easter and I went straight into negotiations for the West End, where we open in March 1994.

When the tour got underway I finally turned the tables

with my brother Billy, and gave him some money to help him buy his pub in Belvedere. One night, very pissed, he looked at me affectionately and said: 'Thanks, Davidson, you saved my life!'

'I owe you one,' I said. 'For the Cortina. Actually I owe you two – I also put you down for a loan to buy my Honda bike but you never knew!'

While *Sinderella* went from strength to strength, the whole family was dealt a blow. Mum wasn't at all well. She'd developed a pain in her chest and, after tests, was diagnosed as having lung cancer. She didn't drink much all her years, but she had been a smoker. She had radium treatment, but it couldn't contain the tumour. She was prescribed steroids, which made her quite chubby, and was told that she had between a couple of weeks and a couple of years to live. I called her every day and made out that everything was going on as normal. She was fairly upbeat most of the time.

When *Sinderella* reached Wimbledon, I sent a car for her and she came along on the opening night. She came to the party after the show, met the cast and told me she'd loved the production. But her health started to deteriorate rapidly. She was put on morphine and, as I started rehearsals for my Blackpool summer season in June, I got a call from Billy. He said she now had two weeks to live, if that.

When I saw her she was upset and I tried to make her laugh. The night before she died I slept on the kitchen floor. In the morning, Saturday June 26, she was in a semi-coma and in the afternoon I kissed her as she slept and said goodbye. Tracy collected me and we got back to Ewhurst at 4.30 pm where, exhausted, I went straight off for a nap. An hour and a half later Tracy woke me. 'Your mum's dead,' she said softly. Then Billy 'phoned.

'We're orphans!' he said. It's always you, isn't it Billy?

Today I'm trying very hard to come to terms with how to be a good husband and father, but it's not easy. I've realised, even though I usually work late into the night and sleep very little, that I have to accept my children wake up at dawn and jump all over me. And

I do have to find time to get to school sports days if I can.

It's not easy, though. My daily routine isn't like that of people who work in the daytime and relax at night. When I'm performing at night I spend all day hanging around, waiting to get it over with so I can relax and get home. Most of the time I can't even get home. I'm stuck in yet another hotel or waking up in a strange, empty house. I get homesick all the time.

As I write, the summer season is underway at the North Pier in Blackpool. I haven't seen Tracy and the kids for several weeks and I hope they'll come up and see me soon. For the last twenty days I've been able to think of nothing else but rehearsals, run-throughs and getting the show exactly right. It really does become the most important thing in my life.

I don't think Tracy fully understands just how difficult and cut-throat show-business is, although I think she understands some of the pressures because of the hours I work week after week, year after year. I'm not happy about my life, but I don't think I ever have been. I always think it's going to get better any minute, but now I'm forty I'm just beginning to realise that it probably won't!

At heart I'm a coward who really just wants any easy life. I still get scared and can't work on auto-pilot, even after years doing the nightly act. I try to put as much as I can into the act, so that it is more than just a man and a mike.

When the plug was pulled on *Grand Hotel* last year and I was saddled with payments for the sound equipment loan, I joked to people that I was taking *Afghan Plains* off to the Canaries, à la Robert Maxwell! Ironically, there are so many insurance policies out on me all over the place that I'm now worth more dead than alive. And with so many ex-wives, I need to earn a fortune to stay afloat – and Tracy asks why I grind my teeth when I'm asleep!

As soon as this summer season ends – in November – I'm off on a whistle-stop tour of the country until Christmas. It's the biggest I've ever mounted, with a crew of thirty-six on the road with me, so do look in if you can. In the end, if you want to ensure the microphone works and the lights are right you have to have your own. Suddenly you're a multi-million pound industry.

My job's still the most difficult; I'm the one who has to make the audience laugh.

I let myself down because I drink too much, never sleep enough and don't eat properly. I use booze as a sort of medicine, to keep me going and calm my nerves. I need a brandy to get me on-stage, and another to unwind as soon as I get off. The first two weeks here in Blackpool I was working so hard, and was so worried about it all, I needed a brandy before I did anything.

Tracy gets worried about my drinking. When we moved to Ewhurst I stopped clubbing all the time and, preferring a bottle of vintage wine instead, tried settling down more. I had a party at home one weekend for my roadies and spotted our nanny serving up a bottle of claret I'd paid £150 for. I ran over and quickly threw back each glass as she poured them out!

I know I'm a dreadful fidget and I think that bugs Tracy. I've so much nervous energy I ricochet around the place all the time, and still a pub is one of the few places I can really unwind.

Tracy told me once she'd leave if I didn't stop drinking. 'Well, drop the house keys off at the pub,' I joked, though she didn't see the funny side of it. She once told me: 'You'll end up a lonely old man.' She was right. Here I am in Blackpool!

People ask me why I drink so much, and behave the way I do; why I do everything to excess. The answer is, I haven't got a clue!

We are settled in Ewhurst and have no plans to move. But I am selling *Afghan Plains*, which is sad for me, because Tracy's never liked her and I'm likely to be so busy in the next three or four years I'll never get out on her, which would be even sadder.

As this book goes to print Tracy's expecting our third child, codenamed 'Doris' because we know there's no knob this time. Tracy's chuffed to death, I think it will make her life pretty complete – if I behave myself.

It's difficult to know how to finish a book but I suppose Mum has provided me with the answer. When she died she took with her to the grave a secret which has always intrigued me. I think when Uncle Bill lived in Holburne Road he loved Mum a bit too much and so did the honourable thing and got out of the way. I tackled Mum on this a few times but she would never talk about what happened and laughed it all off.

But three little things tell me Uncle Bill could have been my father.

First, there was the mix-up when Dad registered my name soon after I was born. Could that perhaps have been intentional?

Secondly, when I walked into the church for Mum's funeral this year the music she'd chosen was playing: 'Clair de Lune', the same piece Uncle Bill had played while I was being born in Holburne Road, and which had prompted Mum to tears the day I played it to her.

Thirdly, across the corner of that watercolour Uncle Bill painted for my very first birthday were three little words: 'from his "A-bu"!'

One of the languages Uncle Bill spoke was Arabic. And in Arabic, 'A-bu' means 'father'. Still, dear reader, you can make up your own mind.

Epilogue

So now I've come to, if not the end of my story, then the end of my book. Looking back over its pages, I'm reflecting on my life.

I hope you might find coming to the end a bit like coming to the end of a novel you've really enjoyed: you're slightly sad knowing you'll miss the characters you've got to know.

I'm sad. I'm sad that some of the loved ones and friends have gone. But they haven't gone really, because I have them in my memory forever and I hope, wherever they are, they have their memories of me. I still miss 'em.

Stardate 41601.3

'Death is a state in which you live only
in the memory of others . . . so there is no end.'

Lt Natasia Yar
USS *Enterprise*